A World of Babies

Imagined Childcare Guides for Seven Societies

Are babies divine, or do they have the devil in them? Should parents talk to their infants, or is it a waste of time? Answers to questions about the nature and nurture of infants appear in this book as advice to parents in seven world societies.

Imagine what Dr. Spock might have written if he were a healer from Bali . . . or an Aboriginal grandmother from the Australian desert . . . or a diviner from a rural village in West Africa. As the seven childcare "manuals" in this book reveal, experts worldwide offer intriguingly different advice to new parents.

The creative format of this book brings alive a rich fund of ethnographic knowledge, vividly illustrating a simple but powerful truth: there exist many models of babyhood, each shaped by deeply held values and widely varying cultural contexts.

After reading this book, you will never again view child rearing as a matter of "common sense."

Judy DeLoache is Professor of Psychology at the University of Illinois, Urbana-Champaign. She is co-editor of *Current Readings in Child Development,* Third Edition (1998) and co-author of *Child Psychology* (forthcoming).

Alma Gottlieb is Professor of Anthropology at the University of Illinois, Urbana-Champaign. Her publications include *Parallel Worlds: An Anthropologist and a Writer Encounter Africa* (1993, with Philip Graham), *Under the Kapok Tree: Identity and Difference in Beng Thought* (1992), and *Blood Magic: The Anthropology of Menstruation* (1988, co-edited with Thomas Buckley).

D0144799

A World of Babies

Imagined Childcare Guides for Seven Societies

Judy S. DeLoache

Alma Gottlieb

CAMBRIDGE
UNIVERSITY PRESS

PUBLISHED BY THE PRESS SYNDICATE OF THE UNIVERSITY OF CAMBRIDGE
The Pitt Building, Trumpington Street, Cambridge, United Kingdom

CAMBRIDGE UNIVERSITY PRESS
The Edinburgh Building, Cambridge CB2 2RU, UK
40 West 20th Street, New York, NY 10011-4211, USA
10 Stamford Road, Oakleigh, VIC3166, Australia
Ruiz de Alarcón 13, 28014 Madrid, Spain
Dock House, The Waterfront, Cape Town 8001, South Africa

http://www.cambridge.org

© Judy S. DeLoache   Alma Gottlieb 2000

This book is in copyright. Subject to statutory exception
and to the provisions of relevant collective licensing agreements,
no reproduction of any part may take place without
the written permission of Cambridge University Press.

First published 2000
Reprinted 2000

Printed in the United States of America

Typeface Caslon 224 9.75/13.5, with Adobe Caslon   *System* Quark XPress™   [HT]

A catalog record for this book is available from the British Library

Library of Congress Cataloging-in-Publication Data

A world of babies: imagined childcare guides for seven societies / [edited by] Judy
S. DeLoache, Alma Gottlieb.
    p. cm
    ISBN 0 521 66264 8 (hardback) – ISBN 0 521 66475 6 (pbk.)
    1. Child rearing – Cross-cultural studies.   2. Socialization – Cross-cultural studies.
I. DeLoache, Judy S.   II. Gottlieb, Alma.
GN482.W67 2000
649¢.1 – dc21   99-045554

ISBN 0 521 66264 8 hardback
ISBN 0 521 66475 6 paperback

We dedicate this book to the babies of our world –
Ben, Nathaniel, and Hannah
and to our partners in parenting them –
Jerry and Philip

Contents

Contents

Foreword

by Jerome Bruner

There is nothing in the world to match child rearing for the depth and complexity of the challenges it poses both for those directly caught up in its daily intricacies and for the society to which child and caretakers belong. The truly extraordinary chapters of this book, so imaginatively written as "Manuals of Child Rearing" for seven different cultures literally all over the world, are testaments not only to the astonishing variety of ways in which those challenges are met but, as well, to the sheer ingenuity of our species in coping with the task of replacing itself.

To begin with, child rearing, given humans' cultural adaptation, is not straight-line evolutionary extrapolation of "biological species reproduction." Cultural adaptation, by any standard, is a big deal as well as a recent one, perhaps only a half million years old. Human immaturity seems shaped (if a bit haphazardly) to its requirements: not *only to growing up* per se (at best, rather a vapid idea) but to growing up Balinese or Ifaluk or Japanese. And it is not only prolonged helplessness that is special about human infancy, but its utter reliance on sustained and extended interaction with a committed and enculturated caregiver.

Foreword

The very act of "having a baby" brings the mother/caregiver into the culture in a new way. Bringing a baby into the world is fraught with cultural consequences. Your status changes, and even more to the point, the rights and responsibilities that go with your role in the culture also change. The child, by the same token, becomes a cultural being (or candidate). Becoming a mother/father/wet nurse is a cultural *fact* as well as a biological datum – a socially constituted one that provides a critical element of your identity. There may be something biological about the famously celebrated "full maternal feeling" for a young baby, but it carries no prescription with it as to whether the baby should be carried next to you in a sling, whether she should be thought capable of understanding what you or anybody else says, or whether she should be in her own crib or snuggled next to you in bed. There may indeed be "universals" in child rearing – like keeping a baby out of harm's way – but these universals are subject to such culturally local expression that one needs to look at them almost like art forms, religious beliefs, or mythic representations.

The young child goes through a similar process as a "candidate" member of the culture – and cultures vary in how they delineate that candidacy. If it is Original Sin that he carried into the world with him, then he is to be coerced from his stricken state. If he is of the Song of Innocence, another rule awaits. If he is a candidate for the organizational life, then perhaps Little League is the right acculturation instrument. No child is ever a *tabula rasa* in the eyes of the culture.

Judy DeLoache and Alma Gottlieb, in their wonderfully lucid introductory chapter to this volume, remind us that we in the "rational," technologically advanced West are no exception to this rule. They use the best-selling "child manuals" of Benjamin Spock, Berry Brazelton, and Penelope Leach to illustrate the idealized "fictions" that guide us in caring for the young. Should every young child (as with Virginia's Woolf's prescription for the "new woman" of her day) have a "room of her own"? Others, in other cultures, are shocked at the very idea that we hold to and practice such a belief. Indeed, as you will learn in the following pages, the range of beliefs about where a child should sleep is so varied that it merits a discussion of its own in the opening chapter.

Foreword

Perhaps even more than with most cultural matters, child-rearing practices and beliefs reflect local conceptions of how the world is and how the child should be readied for living in it. As the reader will soon rediscover, cultures differ, just as we in the West have differed in different eras. But I have always harbored the view that child rearing is a human activity fraught with so many emotional and social dilemmas, so many projective possibilities, and such grave physical consequences and strokes of fate (in many parts of the world, the infant mortality rate is still extremely high) that its practices and our beliefs about it are particularly liable not only to cultural shaping but also reshaping.

Even *legally* defined concepts such as "the best interest of the child," as specified in American state statutes or judicial precedent, alter with the changing cultural climate. Indeed, so local are child-rearing matters considered in American law that the words *children* and *family* are not to be found in the United States Constitution. And it is perhaps too easy to forget that in antebellum America, there was no legal protection provided for the black family in slavery. Such families often suffered separation if a good trading bargain were at hand for the slaveowner – though during that same period, "the family" was the undisputed icon in American fictions about child care. Yet, throughout this period, the superiority and "maternal qualities" of the black nanny were recognized and even honored in the very states where her family was ruthlessly scattered. It is difficult to resist the conclusion that child-rearing practices are somewhat less resistant to change than we sometimes think – though they are always a reflection of those cultural patterns discussed in this foreword.

Although the lore and culture of child rearing may vary widely from culture to culture, they also vary over extended periods of time. To borrow a conceit from the introductory chapter of this volume, had Berry Brazelton (my contemporary, friend, and longtime colleague) been Japanese and written a child manual just after his first residency in pediatrics at Kyoto, say, it would have been all about how to raise "wet" Japanese – that is, children who will consider themselves traditional, who are comfortable with ritual, who owe their first allegiance to their families. Had Brazelton written such a manual a mere quarter century later, it would surely be about

xi

bringing up children who dress in Western clothes, will be oriented to their peers rather than their families, and will endorse a degree of gender egalitarianism – that is, "dry" Japanese! Child rearing and its supporting systems of beliefs – perhaps like systems of law, as we learn from Clifford Geertz – change more swiftly than one might have predicted. Does it have to do with contested authority? There are many questions still to be addressed!

One last matter needs saying. This book is principally about societies that by Western standards are poor, badly nourished, technologically underdeveloped, and (as already mentioned) victims of unthinkable infant mortality rates. It is not about how changes in child rearing could, say, reduce the appallingly high rate of diarrhea among children in the developing world or protect them from infestation by bilharzia. It is about child rearing as it is. For those directly concerned with improving the care of the world's children, it has one big but quiet message. All child rearing is based on beliefs about what makes life manageable, safe, and fertile for the spirit. Even with the best, most rational, kindest advice from outside, child rearing will likely always be so. Changes, too, are subject to that proviso: They need to be absorbed into or be made congruent with the extant beliefs of those affected. In the first half of this century, the Australian government used to order Aboriginal children into the foster care of state-run orphanages to save them from a pagan upbringing. Fortunately, many of them were out of the government's reach in the outback!

Read these pages. This is a very moving book and a revealing one.

Editors' Acknowledgments

Giving birth to this book about babies and their parents has been a labor of love; through the gestation period, many friends, colleagues, and kin have served as expert and caring midwives.

We are very grateful to the other authors of the chapters for working tirelessly and with remarkably good cheer. It is a pleasure to acknowledge with deep gratitude the scholars listed below, each of whom is an expert (as a scholar or native consultant) in one of the seven societies discussed in the book. They contributed immeasurably to this project by offering extremely helpful comments and suggestions on earlier drafts (in some cases several drafts) of the chapters. We are in the debt of:

Michael Bakan

Maimouna Barro

Edward Bruner

John Demos

Marguerite Dupire

Françoise Dussart

Editors' Acknowledgments

Philip Greven
Bertin Kouadio
Catherine Lutz
John Pruett
Helena Wall
Margaret Wiener

We thank Philip Graham for the idea that led to the unique approach taken in this book. Jessica Kuper and Frank Smith, our editors at Cambridge University Press, provided enthusiasm and support that made it possible for this project to become a book. Harry Liebersohn was a frequent troubleshooter and source of helpful ideas. Diana Zion stopped everything to accommodate our emergency art request. Numerous colleagues and graduate students participating in a lively Friday Sociocultural Workshop held in the Department of Anthropology at the University of Illinois provided challenging comments on the project, leading us to sharpen our prose and clarify our claims. We are grateful to Lisa Johnson (of the Folger Shakespeare Library), Urs Ramseyer (of the Museum der Kulturen Volkerkundemuseum, Basel), and Lisa Singleton (of the Billy Graham Center Museum, Wheaton College) for expediting permissions and photo-quality prints for us to use in reprinting illustrations in their collections. We also thank Kathy Anderson, Andrew Behlmann, Betty Heggemeier, Steve Holland, Gavin Hyde, Barb McCall, Karin Pearl, Julie Pearson, and Jane Weber for their contributions to this project.

Judy DeLoache worked on the book while she was a fellow at the Center for Advanced Study in the Behavioral Sciences with support from the John D. and Catherine T. MacArthur Fund Grant 95-32005-0.

Finally, we thank our families for everything from inspiration and intellectual challenge to babysitting and cooking. Mostly, we thank them for their sustaining love.

Note to the Reader

Before you read any of the chapters in this book other than the first one, it is important to understand two things about them.

First, each chapter is written in the style of a childcare manual from one of seven societies around the world. The "author" described in each chapter's "About the Author" section is fictional; an assumed persona permits the creation of a manual in the style of famous authors of child-rearing books such as Benjamin Spock, Berry Brazelton, and Penelope Leach. We hope this format provides information about infant care practices in different societies in a lively and memorable way.

Second, the chapters are solidly based on research on the societies represented in them. You will learn what anthropologists, psychologists, and historians have written about what people in these cultures believe about babies and how they care for them.

The book is thus a mix of fact and fiction – fictional authors presenting factual information.

CHAPTER 1

If Dr. Spock Were Born in Bali

Raising a World of Babies

Judy S. DeLoache and Alma Gottlieb

* *Do babies have the devil in them, or are they divine?*
* *Should parents talk to their infants, or is it a waste of time?*
* *Do babies need a daily bath – or two or three daily baths?*

In this book, you will find answers to these and many other questions about infants and how to care for them. In fact, you'll find several different answers to each one. Most of these answers will be quite different from what the majority of contemporary middle-class North Americans or Europeans would say. Here are some examples of the contrasting views you will encounter in these pages.

To the Puritans in seventeenth-century America, infants were born in sin and in need of strict direction by their parents to help them resist the temptations of the devil. To the residents of Bali, however, babies are reincarnated ancestors and gods. Everyone, including their own parents, must treat infants with the respect and deference due a deity, which includes addressing them with honorific titles otherwise reserved for individuals of the highest rank.

Writers of Western childcare manuals stress the great importance of talking to infants to foster language development. The Beng of West

I

Africa also talk to their babies, but they do so because they believe young infants can understand all the languages of the world. In contrast, many other groups, including inhabitants of Ifaluk, a tiny Micronesian atoll, think that babies cannot understand anything that's said to them, so there's no point in speaking to them.

Most middle-class North Americans, who think of themselves as extremely fastidious about personal grooming, would assert that infants should receive a daily bath. This would be judged inadequate on Ifaluk, where young babies are bathed three times a day. Both groups differ dramatically from the residents of eighteenth-century England. According to physician William Cadogan, it was common practice to tightly swaddle babies (wrapping them mummy-like in long strands of cloth) and then leave them in the same swaddling cloths for days, or even weeks, at a time. This practice no doubt made life easier for parents, but it also reflected their belief that changing the swaddling cloths more frequently would rob an infant of "its nourishing juices."

As these few examples testify, people living in different parts of the world and at different historical times hold diverse beliefs about the nature and the nurturing of infants. This book celebrates that diversity. Each of its seven chapters is written as though it were an advice manual for new parents in a particular society. The seven societies we highlight (see World Map) include the Puritans of seventeenth-century Massachusetts and six contemporary societies: the Beng of Ivory Coast (West Africa), the Balinese of Indonesia, Muslim villagers in Turkey, the Warlpiri (an Australian Aborigine group), the Fulani of West and Central Africa, and the Ifaluk people of Micronesia. Although these seven by no means represent the range of societies worldwide, they are located on four different continents and differ substantially from one another in many ways. For example, three major world religions – the Judeo-Christian tradition, Islam, and Hinduism – as well as a variety of local religious traditions are represented. The residents of our societies earn their living in a variety of ways, from hunting and gathering to herding, fishing, and farming, to working in the tourist trade. Most importantly for our purposes, these seven societies represent a wide spectrum of beliefs and practices with respect to infants, and they all differ radically from industrialized Western societies.

Furthermore, childcare practices differ even within these societies, since subgroups exist within every one. Moreover, all of the

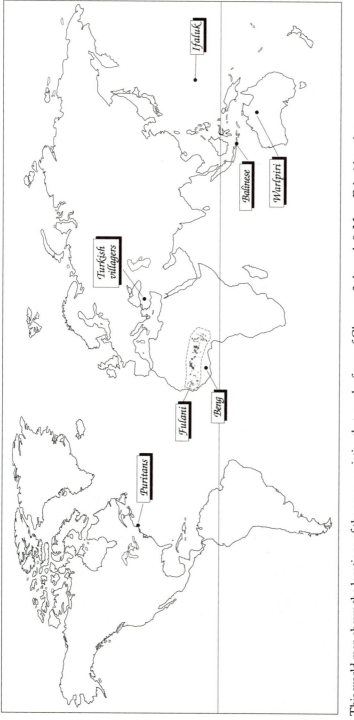

This world map shows the locations of the seven societies that are the focus of Chapters 2 through 8. Many Fulani have been nomadic or seminomadic; hence, their place on the map is represented by a range rather than a more specific location. For the Puritans, the depicted location is for 1630.

contemporary societies we include in this book have undergone significant social change in the course of this century, and, existing at
the intersection of many local and international forces, they continue to undergo such change. In the U.S. today, for example, many
Protestants share some child-rearing beliefs and practices with the
Puritans while they adamantly reject many more. Within other societies too, many of the "old ways" are no longer followed – a fact no
doubt approved by some of their members but deplored by others.

The world of babies is really many different worlds (Plate 1).

Plate 1. Although there is great diversity in infant care practices in the seven
societies discussed in this book, babies are considered precious in every one.
Photograph courtesy of Laura L. Betzig.

If Dr. Spock Were Born in Bali

UNDERSTANDING THE WORLDS OF BABIES

In the chapters that follow, you will be introduced to a few of these worlds. As you read our seven childcare "manuals," you will learn why it makes sense for a Beng mother to spend her hard-earned cash on a cowry shell bracelet for a colicky baby. You will find out why Fulani mothers place a small knife by a sleeping baby's head to keep the child safe. Knowing something about local religious beliefs will help you understand why Balinese people never let an infant's feet touch the ground, whereas a Fulani woman delivers her newborn directly onto the bare earth.

Although most people in the modern world are increasingly aware that behaviors and beliefs differ from one society to another, that awareness is not necessarily accompanied by comprehension, let alone acceptance. Understanding and appreciating the ways of other people presents a challenge precisely because our sense of how to do things we consider important – such as raising children – is so deeply ingrained. Every group thinks that its way of caring for infants is the obvious, correct, natural way – a simple matter of common sense. However, as the anthropologist Clifford Geertz has pointed out, what we easily call "common sense" is anything but common. Indeed, what people accept as common sense in one society may be considered odd, exotic, or even barbaric in another.

Oddity cuts both ways. Although our readers will no doubt be surprised by many of the beliefs and practices described in these pages, the parents who follow those practices would probably find our readers' values and behavior – *your* values and behavior – equally surprising. Every one of the seven infant-rearing "manuals" we present here is a "common sense book of baby and child care" (as Dr. Spock's original book was titled), but the advice our guides offer varies dramatically from one to another.

In assembling this book, our major goal is to illustrate how the child-rearing customs of any given society, however peculiar or unnatural they may at first appear to an outsider, make sense when understood within the context of that society. Along with this, we hope to dispel any assumption of an Everybaby or an Everyparent who somehow exists outside culture. Infant care practices vary so much across different societies and historical eras precisely because

5

they are firmly embedded in different physical, economic, and cultural frameworks.

Challenges of Caring for Children

The remarkable diversity of infant care practices is all the more remarkable when we consider that, to a substantial degree, these diverse practices largely represent strategies for dealing with similar challenges. Human infants are distinguished from other animals by, among other things, extreme helplessness at birth and a very long period of dependence on others simply to survive, let alone develop. Throughout the world, a crucial role undertaken by the vast majority of parents is ensuring the survival, health, and safety of their children. In addition, parents typically assume a major role in encouraging their children to form social relationships, acquire skills, develop certain personal characteristics, and adopt the values and beliefs that will enable them to participate fully in their society. In the following pages, we will focus first on the challenges involved in keeping infants alive and thriving. Then we will consider parental practices that promote cultural learning.

Helping Babies Survive and Thrive

The first challenge to rearing children is getting through pregnancy and childbirth successfully. As you will see in the chapters that follow, societies have important beliefs about conception and pregnancy, and the goal of many practices is to enhance the likelihood of a successful pregnancy and birth.

Infant Mortality. Promoting the survival of infants is very much tied to basic economic resources. In industrialized societies throughout the world today, the rate of infant mortality is very low (though it is significantly higher for families of low socioeconomic status than it is for middle-class and wealthy families), and most parents in these societies do not constantly worry about their children dying. Impoverished parents in many other areas of the world today are not so fortunate. Many "developing" or "Third World" countries have shockingly high death rates of infants and young children. Imagine holding your newborn baby in your arms knowing that he or she has a very good chance of not surviving childhood. In many settings, most parents have had this experience. For example, in one study conducted in Zimbabwe, three-quarters of a group of Shona women questioned had lost at least one child. In short, the routine survival of infants that is taken for granted in affluent nations may be a coveted goal in other nations.

Nutrition. Economic factors play a major role in affording infants a diet sufficient for survival and development. The seriousness of the challenge that parents face in feeding their babies is reflected by a recent estimate that 40 percent of the world's children under the age of five – approximately 190 million youngsters – suffer from undernutrition (not getting enough food to sustain optimal development) or malnutrition (more serious nutritional deficiencies). Inadequate diets are closely associated with poverty and myriad related factors.

Adequate maternal nutrition is necessary for prenatal development, and most societies encourage pregnant women to pay attention to their diets for the sake of the child they are carrying. In this book, you will encounter a variety of rules and recommendations for expectant mothers about foods they should eat to stay healthy, as well as many they should avoid. The reasons for forbidding certain foods range from ideas about nutrition to more symbolic notions about particular foods. For example, during pregnancy, Balinese women avoid eating too many foods considered "hot," including chili peppers, mangoes, and roasted pork; these would create an imbalance between hot and cold in their bodies, which could make them ill. In Australia, pregnant Warlpiri mothers were traditionally told not to eat the meat of anteaters or certain lizards that have spiked or sharp body parts. In Ivory Coast, a pregnant Beng woman avoids eating meat from animals that have undesirable characteristics that might be passed on to the baby in her womb, such as the patchy skin of the striped duiker or the snout of a long-nosed mongoose. In the contemporary United States, many pregnant women observe food taboos that, while originally based on scientific evidence, sometimes take on an aura of mystic compulsion. For instance, after research had suggested that drinking excessive amounts of coffee might have negative effects on prenatal development, some expectant mothers avoided not only all coffee but anything else containing even a tiny trace of caffeine, such as the occasional cup of black tea or dish of chocolate ice cream.

Throughout human history until the last few decades, breast-feeding was the only way to supply young infants with their primary form of sustenance. Most often, the biological mother has been a baby's primary source of breastmilk, although "wet nursing" – having an infant breastfed by someone other than his or her own mother – has been practiced in both Western and non-Western settings. In the ancient world, wet nurses fed other women's babies from Mesopotamia and Egypt to Greece and Rome. In western Europe, the practice began to be common in wealthy families in the eleventh and twelfth centuries and lasted through the eighteenth century. Infants of wealthy mothers were nursed by peasant women, who in turn handed their own babies over to others for wet nursing. This practice was so common that in 1780 in Paris it was estimated that of the 21,000 infants born in the city that year, only 700 were nursed by their own mothers. In some European countries, wet nursing did not cease entirely until World War I, when poor women could make more money working in factories than as wet nurses.

Elsewhere, infants who are breastfed primarily by their mothers may sometimes be nursed by other women. In many Muslim societies, infants who share the breastmilk of a woman become "milk kin." Having suckled at the same breast creates a bond between children as strong as that between biologically related siblings. In these societies, a marriage between "milk kin" would be considered incestuous.

Before the introduction of infant formula, a few rare attempts to substitute something for breastmilk as infants' main source of nourishment were disastrous. For example, in western Europe, foundling infants who were fed breads or cereals rather than breastmilk had an extremely high mortality rate – as high as 90 to 100 percent in one London parish.

Breastfeeding is still the primary food for young infants in all the societies featured in this book; indeed, in most nonindustrialized societies today, mothers continue to nurse their children for anywhere from two to four years. Yet the proven nutritional superiority and health benefits of breastmilk are now largely ignored in many places. In the U.S., for example, only 55 percent of infants are ever breastfed, and of those, 40 percent nurse for less than two months. This pattern is now being followed elsewhere. As early as twenty years ago, for instance, the majority of wealthy women in the Philippines and Guatemala who breastfed their infants weaned them by two months. Worldwide, the infant formula industry is convincing more mothers to try bottle-feeding via attractive promotional samples and advertisements. In a recent study, it was estimated that "[h]alf of the world's mothers use infant formula at some point in their child's first year."

In industrialized countries, infant formula can support satis-factory levels of growth and development, though with a somewhat higher rate of infections and other medical problems. In other coun-tries, however, formula-feeding presents far more serious health risks. Much of the world does not have safe water, so infant formula is often mixed with polluted water in unsanitary containers. Furthermore, poor parents often dilute the formula in an attempt to make the expensive powder last longer. Under such circumstances, parents' sincere efforts to promote the health and well-being of their babies can be tragically undermined.

The introduction of solid food – when, what, and how – differs greatly from one society to another. Balinese mothers advocate giving some solid foods to newborns, whereas Puritan mothers introduced them only after six months. Some societies make certain foods taboo to toddlers and young children for reasons that are complex both culturally and medically. For example, on the Melanesian island of Vanatinai, toddlers are forbidden to eat meat and fish. As a result, they become mildly undernourished, but, ironically, their undernour-ished state seems to give them some protection against the deadly malaria that is endemic to the region. No matter what mothers and local experts prescribe and proscribe as solid foods for young infants, virtually all people are convinced that their choices are the best pos-sible ones for their babies, based on their understanding of the biological needs of babies.

Illness. Whether an infant survives may also depend on the resources that are available for treating disease. Strategies for preventing, diagnosing, and curing illness vary dramatically around the globe. They are determined not only by whether medical clinics are available and affordable, but also by what parents believe are the underlying causes of given ailments. What you do for a case of diarrhea may depend on whether you think your baby has "caught a bug" or has been "caught by a spirit."

In many societies today, including some of those featured in this book, parents have exposure to both traditional healers and modern medicine. If they can afford it – a big *If* – many will use both. For example, a Beng mother might consult both a diviner and a doctor, and secure for her baby both a cowry shell bracelet and a tetanus shot.

However, in all too many non-Western nations, this seeming option is not available at all, as the bitter combination of poverty and lack of easy access to Western medicine often puts even routine biomedical preventions and cures out of reach of all but a small group of urban elites. Tragically, the global availability of effective medicines does not mean that in a given setting, such medicines are locally available.

Supervision. Babies also need protection from mishap and accidents. In part, strategies for preventing accidents are shaped by the nature of local risks: Cars whizzing by on a busy street, an open cooking fire in the middle of the family compound, or poisonous snakes in the forest require different approaches to keeping babies safe. Very different strategies are called for to protect against risks that are less visible but still perilous, such as the machinations of witches or malicious spirits who can harm or steal babies. For example, a Fulani mother may roll her otherwise beautiful baby in cow dung in order to trick witches or greedy spirits into thinking that her infant is not worth taking.

Other risks to babies' health and survival may depend on the work that their mothers perform to earn a living and how their infants are supervised. For example, in many societies in which all healthy adults work in the fields or tend livestock, babies are typically cared for during the day by older siblings, cousins, or other children. As long as the child babysitter can bring the baby along to the mother's workplace to be nursed, the infant can thrive (Plate 2).

This caretaking arrangement is less viable in other settings, where extreme poverty makes it very difficult for working mothers to care effectively for their infants. Such is the case in a shantytown

Plate 2. The Beng baby peeking out from behind his cousin is under her care during the day while his mother is working in the fields. Photograph by Alma Gottlieb.

in northeastern Brazil, where many mothers perform domestic work. Because their bosses see their house cleaners' children as dirty and contagious, the women's young infants are often left at home with an older child or even alone in a hammock. Deprived of their nursing mothers, these babies do not get adequate nourishment; some eat nothing all day. As a consequence, at least 11% of these babies die, and perhaps (because of underreporting) many more than that. Such disturbing scenarios may be multiplying rather than diminishing, as "structural adjustment" programs required by the International Monetary Fund impose new hardships on "Third World" peoples; urban populations, urban unemployment and urban poverty increase globally; and impoverished mothers of infants have fewer resources, both social and economic, on which to draw.

Helping Babies Become Good Balinese, Beng, ... , Warlpiri

The cultural foundations of many infant care practices lie deeply embedded in religious and spiritual beliefs, in folk theories about human nature and the nature of reality, and in basic moral values. Many childcare practices serve directly and indirectly to guide children toward becoming accepted members of their societies. Because of how they are treated by their parents and others in their lives, most children come to share those others' beliefs and behaviors.

Relationships. Emotional attachment is part of the human condition; virtually all infants form emotional relationships with other people. In many Western societies, it is generally assumed that infants will form a strong emotional attachment to their parents but that they will have a relatively small number of other relationships, possibly only with immediate family members. However, adults in many other societies place a premium on integrating infants into a larger group. In Beng villages, for example, this effort begins right away: A member of every household in the village is expected to call on a newborn baby within hours after the birth. In Bali, babies are held in a sling for most of the day. When the mother is tired of carrying her baby, or if she can't hold the child while working, she simply passes the little one to whoever happens to be around.

Elsewhere, the expectation that a child will be cared for by a group of people beyond the biological parents supports a variety of adoption practices. For example, on the Micronesian island of Ifaluk, the adoption of infants is very common. Because they retain close ties with their biological parents, the adoptees feel they are an integral part of *two* families. The caretaking arrangements of many rural African societies foster a different set of ties. When older siblings (who may be as young as six or seven) care for their infant and toddler sisters and brothers for much of the day while their mothers work, a strong bond between the siblings is created. In industrialized societies, infants and toddlers who attend formal day care programs often develop strong relationships with their day care teachers, as well as with a number of other children.

Beyond connections with family members and other living people around them, many societies also encourage ties with the departed. Those who view their infants as reincarnated ancestors may be concerned to maintain a relation between their flesh-and-blood child and the ancestor's spirit. In East Africa, the naming ceremony for a Baganda infant features someone calling out a series of names belonging to various deceased relatives of the baby. When the child smiles, it is taken as a sign that he or she is a reincarnation of the ancestor just mentioned and wants to be called by that name.

Elsewhere, connections with spiritual beings may continue actively throughout life. For instance, in Australia, pregnant Warlpiri women may dream that they conceived their child in a place associated with a certain spirit that has given life to the baby. Once born, the child has a lifelong tie to the land associated with that spirit and, as an adult, will always have a say in matters relating to that particular piece of land. In such ways, the nature of social ties differs dramatically from one social setting to another, according to local conceptions of land, life, and death.

Personal Characteristics

All societies value some personal attributes more highly than others, and in many – perhaps most – societies, parents actively attempt to direct their children to fit a cultural ideal. However, the extent of efforts to influence such aspects of children's development depends in part on assumptions about malleability – the degree to which parents assume that children's basic nature can be influenced. Not surprisingly, there is little agreement across societies about which characteristics can be changed by adult intervention and which cannot.

Both the personality traits that are encouraged and those that are discouraged in infants and young children often reflect deeply held values. One well-documented example concerns the contrast between individualistic and collectivist values and goals. Most Western, industrialized societies tend to emphasize individualistic over collectivist goals for a variety of historical and cultural reasons. Accordingly, traits of independence and assertiveness are generally valued in individuals and directly encouraged by parents in these societies. In contrast, many other societies maintain the opposite priority, promoting interdependence rather than independence and self-effacement rather than self-confidence in public settings. For example, Fulani youngsters are encouraged to become modest and reserved; and although Balinese children are supposed to "feel happiness in the heart" for an honor received at school, they should not show their positive emotion outwardly.

In one study, a comparison of Japanese and American mother-infant interactions revealed patterns consistent with the broad independence-interdependence dichotomy. The American mothers tended to stimulate their babies to increased levels of physical activity and encouraged exploration of the environment, whereas the Japanese mothers kept their infants in close bodily contact, soothing and quieting them. In other words, expectations about the sorts of children and, ultimately, the sorts of adults that parents want their sons and daughters to become shape the ways that parents interact with their children from infancy.

Life Skills. An important challenge for parents is to prepare their children for successful lives as adults. Children need opportunities to acquire life skills that will enable them to become fully functioning members of their society. In many settings, young children learn how to do work by serving, in effect, as apprentices to their parents (or other relatives). For example, little Mayan girls learn how to weave by spending long hours observing and helping their mothers at the loom. Children may also be instructed and encouraged more directly: Throughout much of rural Africa, farming parents regularly start showing their children as young as two years of age how to do simple tasks such as hoeing, cooking, and laundry (Plate 3). In Polynesia, Tongan parents begin teaching their toddlers about the world of work by sending them on nearby errands. In West and Central Africa, a Fulani father who keeps cattle presents his young son with a calf that forms the basis for the boy's first herd. At five or six, the boy will start learning from his father how to care for the herd, and by nine he should be well on his way to being a successful herder.

Nowadays, Western education is replacing many of the tasks that parents previously assumed in training their children for adult life. In appropriating a significant portion of this parent-child relationship, schools offer children the opportunity to gain new knowledge, develop

Plate 3. This West African toddler is helping her mother do the family laundry. Photograph by Alma Gottlieb.

new talents, and pursue new vocations beyond those of their parents. However, parents and children alike may pay a price for these opportunities. In "developing" nations, compulsory education may also cut short the sort of rural apprenticeship programs just described. In turn, this may make it difficult or impossible for young people to return to a rural livelihood, even if circumstances (such as urban unemployment, or rejection at the high school or university level) make a return to a more "traditional" lifestyle in their parents' community desirable or even necessary.

Values and Beliefs. It is of great importance to most parents that their children share their deeply held values and beliefs. In every

15

one of the "manuals" in this book, you will find numerous cases of advice to parents to look after the spiritual well-being of their children and teach them important rituals and practices. One dramatic example comes from colonial New England: Puritan parents were frequently enjoined by their ministers to begin on day one to raise a *Christian* child, and newborns were lulled to sleep with the "Cradle Hymn." Although less devout families in other societies may not use such direct means to teach spiritual values, most aim to impart to their children certain foundational beliefs and values, whether derived from organized religious traditions or not.

Let us consider now an extended example illustrating many of the points we have made about culture and child care.

Where Should the Baby Sleep?

Although sleeping is a necessity of life for all of us, never do we spend as much time asleep as when we are babies. People in all societies accommodate infants' need for sleep, but they do so in very different ways.

Throughout most of the world today, and throughout most of human history, infants have spent the night in the company of others. Sleeping has been a social, not a solitary, affair. The most common pattern is for an infant to sleep with his or her mother, although the father and/or older siblings might also sleep with the mother–infant pair. This arrangement is not motivated by lack of space: Even when families live in multiroom dwellings, parents in co-sleeping societies take their infants into bed with them. One of the pragmatic virtues of this arrangement is that the mother can easily breastfeed whenever the baby awakens, often without really waking up herself. Children continue to sleep with their mothers or other older relatives for varying lengths of time – one or two years for Mayan babies in Guatemala but, until recently, into the teen years in Japanese families.

A very different cultural practice characterizes the sleeping pattern of many North American households. In middle-class Euro-American families, the most common practice by far is for infants to sleep in their own beds, and often in their own rooms. In one study of such families, only 3 percent of infants under a year slept with their parents. Nowhere else do babies routinely sleep in such isolated circumstances, yet this practice is approved and recommended by the vast majority of American pediatricians, and it is standard advice in infant-care books and articles. Nevertheless, members of some groups in the U.S. (identified by ethnic identity and/or class) may prefer quite different sleeping arrangements. Research with African-American families, for instance, has revealed that slightly over half of infants and toddlers sleep nightly with a parent. In parts of Appalachian Kentucky, the practice may be even more prevalent; in one study of blue-collar families there, fully 71 percent of babies from two months to two years slept in the same bed or in the same room with their parents. Clearly, the popular North American image of the baby sleeping solo conceals many significant variations even within the U.S.

These wide variations in where infants sleep are associated with very different attitudes, beliefs, and values, as is shown in one study comparing attitudes of middle-class Euro-American mothers with those of Mayan mothers. The American mothers in this study tended to view co-sleeping as, at best, strange and impractical. At worst, they thought it suspicious or even immoral. In contrast, the Mayan mothers regarded physical closeness at night as part of normal caring for children. When told of the middle-class American practice of having infants sleep alone, the Mayan mothers were shocked and felt sorry for babies treated so badly. Indeed, the common nightly isolation of middle-class Euro-American infants is viewed by adults in many other societies as a form of child neglect or worse.

Why is there such a deep sense of disapproval of where other people choose to put their infants to sleep? One important reason is the fact that co-sleeping and solitary sleeping are believed to foster different traits, which are differentially valued. Both the Mayan and the American mothers in the aforementioned study saw co-sleeping as increasing the strength of ties between baby and mother – a benefit in the eyes of the Mayans but a source of concern for the Americans, who worried that it might make their infants overly dependent. Societal goals of interdependence are well served by parent–infant co-sleeping, whereas individualism and independence are not.

Decisions about where babies and young children should sleep are also shaped by local ideas concerning sexuality. In the U.S., many parents feel uncomfortable with the thought that their children (even as babies) might witness or hear their sexual activities while this may be less of a concern among other groups. In short, something so seemingly simple as where to put a baby to sleep for the night is saturated by multiple layers of cultural significance.

LEARNING TO CREATE THE WORLDS OF BABIES

The care and raising of infants are generally considered far too important to leave to personal preference. In every society, a set of practices has evolved that new generations of parents are expected to follow. How are these culturally approved caretaking practices learned?

Part of what every one of us knows about being a parent comes from our own early experiences. For better *and* for worse, we all acquire at least a good chunk of our model of how parents behave toward their children from how our own mother and father behaved toward us. Even those who deliberately reject aspects of their parents' child-rearing style in raising their own children nevertheless find themselves basing their behavior on their childhood experiences. After having children, many of us have had the sudden, sometimes disquieting insight, "Oh no, I sound just like my parents!"

In most societies until recently, children also learned about child rearing through observing adults other than their own parents. Living in close proximity to others – in extended family groups, small bands, or villages – children could observe firsthand how other adults treated their children. What they mostly saw, of course, was other people behaving pretty much like their own parents – that is, following common cultural norms. Such observations, repeated thousands of times, become part of children's knowledge base. Seeing mothers carrying their babies around in homemade cloth slings all the time, a child forms the idea that carrying is a natural part of mothering. Seeing mothers transport their infants in a succession of baby seats, strollers, and car seats, another child assumes the naturalness of manufactured baby carriers. When these children eventually become parents, they simply "know" how these things are done and do not reflect upon that knowledge.

Such opportunities to observe and learn about babies through direct observation and imitation have recently been diminishing, however. In many nonindustrialized nations throughout the world, cultural practices, including parenting practices, are changing. Some groups are gaining new access to economic resources and are experiencing upward mobility at the same time that other groups are becoming ever more victimized by global capitalism. In both cases, cultural practices are being transformed by new situations. In yet other places, long-term political strife and unrelenting poverty are causing tremendous upheaval amidst unthinkable suffering; the mushrooming refugee camps are creating new social forms whose cultural contours are just beginning to be charted. From the perspective of children, all these transformations share one consequence – young parents have fewer opportunities to learn stable traditions from those around them.

Industrialized societies are also marked by diminished opportunities for learning about parenting by directly observing other people and interacting with infants. Nowhere is this more evident than in the U.S. With occupational and geographical mobility, families are becoming increasingly isolated. Whether gay or straight, single or coupled, many young people just starting a family now live far from any relatives. There may be no mothers, grandmothers, or aunts close by to advise a pregnant woman about the birth process or to tell a new parent what to do when the baby cries, or when to expect the infant to begin walking and talking. Advice delivered on the telephone or, increasingly, via E-mail is useful, but a poor substitute for on-the-spot assistance. In addition, the high value placed on family privacy, combined with the modern pattern of newly married couples moving into their own homes, further diminishes the possibilities (for both children and parents) of directly observing how others care for their infants. Moreover, the smaller size of today's families necessarily means that a given child is likely to have less experience with babies than did children of previous generations. Some new parents may never have held a newborn before holding their own.

In this century, North Americans and western Europeans have made up for this decreased level of hands-on experience with children in a variety of ways. In a study of American parents in Massachusetts, parents most often sought advice about child behavior and development from pediatricians. The second most common source of information was books.

Over the course of this century, parents have turned increasingly to the childcare guides that have become a veritable growth industry. To be sure, advice manuals have existed in other times and places, from ancient and modern China to Renaissance Italy. However, the popularity of infant and childcare books skyrocketed in twentieth-century Europe and North America. The child-rearing guides of T. Berry Brazelton and Penelope Leach are perennial best-sellers. Over 50 million copies of the seven editions of Benjamin Spock's *Baby and Child Care* have been sold since 1946 – second in sales only to the Bible. The volume of these sales points to a transformation in how Western parents today learn to parent.

Advice for Parents

A massive amount of information is now available for Western parents to answer their questions and allay their concerns about children and child rearing. Bookstores in the U.S. and the U.K. typically boast shelf after shelf of books devoted to parenting advice, currently offering over 2,000 how-to-raise-a-child books. In addition to manuals covering child development in general, a wealth of books and magazines offer advice on specific topics and for specialized audiences. For pregnant women, there are books on the benefits of sound nutrition and yoga, as well as programs for teaching the baby while still in the womb. New parents can find whole books on how to encourage their babies to sleep through the night and how to accomplish toilet training in twenty-four hours. The fact that advice for parents is such big business suggests an eager readership.

These eager readers bring their own cultural and intellectual baggage to the books they buy and read. In the case of any popular literary genre, there must be a good fit between the basic cultural orientation of any author and reader – a shared set of assumptions about the nature of the world that allows them to communicate. Thus, childcare manuals are very much cultural products that reflect the dominant values and beliefs of their authors and intended audience. It could hardly be otherwise: No parent manual that flew in the face of beliefs and practices that are widely assumed to be right and good could possibly achieve such great success and influence.

At the same time, some of these best-selling parenting manuals have also been agents of change. Dr. Spock is credited, for example, with relaxing the emphasis on rigid scheduling that was so pervasive in American infant care when he began writing. In the next generation of pediatrician advice-givers, Berry Brazelton is acknowledged for drawing attention to the active role that infants play in their own development. And many parents appreciate Penelope Leach's sensitive efforts to see child rearing from the perspective of children, even infants. Mostly, however, parenting guides reflect existing values and practices rather than discuss or promote change.

How can these manuals at once de-emphasize change, reinforce common cultural practices, and (in some cases) transform these same practices? Some of the more influential books such as Spock's have been influential in subtle ways – first by appealing to what readers already know and then by playing down the revolutionary aspects of some of the advice they present. Indeed, as we mentioned earlier, the first edition of Dr. Spock's book was titled *A Common Sense Guide to Baby and Child Care.* The opening lines of that and subsequent editions have encouraged parents to rely on their own common sense: "Trust yourself. You know more than you think you do." Yet as we have suggested, many of the child-rearing practices that seem both so common and so sensible to Western readers might seem anything but that to parents elsewhere.

Imagine, if you will, a child-rearing manual from one of those other parts of the world. What if Benjamin Spock had been born on the Micronesian atoll of Ifaluk instead of in New England? Like his Puritan ancestors, Dr. Spock urged parents to dress their babies in "too little rather than too much," to accustom their young infants to a chilly house, and to take them outdoors even on cool days to acquire "pink cheeks and good appetites." If he had lived on Ifaluk, he would have recommended that parents wrap their newborns in several layers of cloth to induce sweating, carefully explaining how sweat helps young babies grow.

Similarly, rather than stressing how important it is for babies to form warm, close, and loving ties with their parents, a Berry Brazelton who had been born a Beng and became a diviner (rather than a pediatrician) would emphasize how critical it is for babies to form close and loving ties with their grandparents. Indeed, he would advise parents to teach their children how to dish out ribald insults to their grandparents to help the children feel free and familiar with their much older relatives.

Or suppose Penelope Leach were a Muslim villager from Turkey instead of a Cambridge University-educated psychologist. Would she still suggest that parents treat little girls and boys similarly? Or would she instead advise mothers that they should show their sons how greatly valued they are for being boys and encourage them to feel superior because of their possession of a penis?

And so we come to this book.

ABOUT THIS BOOK

The origin of this volume was a seminar on cross-cultural views of infancy that we co-taught a few years ago. Our interest in designing this course sprang from our fascination with the topic, coupled with our perception of the contrasting strengths and weaknesses of our two disciplines – psychology and anthropology. A revolution in psychological research on infants during the last two decades has produced a burst of new knowledge about development in the first years of life; however, the majority of this research has concerned North American and western European infants. Some psychologists have addressed cultural aspects of infancy, but most have ignored cultural and historical variability. For their part, cultural anthropologists are keenly aware of the enormous diversity in human behavior; however, most have paid relatively little attention to parenthood and even less to infancy.

To date, only a few full-length ethnographies have been published of infants in particular cultural settings, and there is no anthropological journal devoted even to childhood, let alone infancy. Despite excellent research and writing about infants and young children by anthropologists working in both the U.S. and Europe in recent years, the subject is still frustratingly marginalized within the discipline at large.

In teaching our seminar, our interest in cultural beliefs about infant care practices was intensified by an object lesson in just how deeply such beliefs are held and how resistant to change they can be. At the beginning of the semester, we asked our students their opinions about a set of standard caretaking issues, including where babies should sleep – with their parents, with siblings, or alone. We were not surprised that almost all of the Euro-American middle-class members of the class supported the standard cultural practice of infants sleeping in their own beds, whereas students from other cultural backgrounds were favorably inclined to co-sleeping. In explaining their varying positions, all the students offered an array of passionately stated reasons why babies should or should not sleep with their parents.

After a full semester of reading about and discussing the widely varying infant care practices of many different societies, our Euro-American students understood that the views of the vast majority of people around the world are quite different from their own. They had also learned some of the reasons that members of other societies see the issue differently, and they had gained a new appreciation for those different viewpoints. At this point, we again asked all the students for their opinions about where babies should sleep. In spite of their new knowledge and acceptance of other ways, there was almost no change in any of the students' personal beliefs and future plans. They remained convinced that it really is best for babies to sleep wherever they themselves had slept as infants, and they fully expected to follow the same practice when they became parents.

Another legacy of that class came from one of the reading assignments. Along with many readings in anthropology and psychology, we assigned an excerpt from one of the editions of Dr. Spock's *Baby and Child Care*, as well as a short anthropological article that playfully spoofed Spock's book by purporting to offer child-rearing advice for West African parents. Throughout the semester, as we discussed various world societies, the "Spock model" sparked many stimulating class discussions of the *What if?* variety – what would an infant-rearing manual from another society be like? What advice would parents be offered? The liveliness of these discussions led us to think that the familiar child-rearing manual format might be an effective way to discuss radically different infant care practices.

What we offer in this book, then, is a set of imagined infant care "manuals" that use fictional techniques to make nonfictional points. Significantly, the original idea for the anthropological spoof of Spock came from a fiction writer, Philip Graham. Occupying a border zone between fiction and social science, our "manuals" might be classified as "ethnographic fictions." On the one hand, the advice that is given in each of the "manuals" is nonfiction; that is, it draws on extensive ethnographic or historical research. Specifically, the basis for two of the chapters is the long-term fieldwork of their authors (Chapters 3 and 5). Four other chapters are based, either primarily or exclusively, on comprehensive library research into published accounts of fieldwork conducted by cultural anthropologists (Chapters 4, 6, 7, and 8). (See Note to Chapter 1 on page 221.) The remaining chapter, focusing on the Puritans, relies on archival research by historians (Chapter 2). For all seven societies, our authors have drawn upon a rich fund of reliable data to produce their imagined childcare guides.

On the other hand, the "manuals" are premised on a set of strategic fictions. The primary one is that each purports to have been written by a member of the society that is the focus of the chapter. Each fictive author is the sort of person who actually gives advice to parents in these societies – grandmothers, midwives, healers, diviners. In a few cases, the personas are modeled on real individuals known by the actual authors of the chapters. Three additional fictions are necessary to appreciate the "manuals." The reader must imagine that there is a child-rearing expert in the society who is literate enough to write such a manual – something that is more likely for some of the seven societies than for others. A related fiction is that the members of these seven societies would have any need or desire for an infant care manual, and that they could read one if they did. The third assumption is that the authors of our "manuals" would be aware of the cultural logic behind most of their societies' practices – something that is often not the case. (Think about why American mothers routinely dress their baby boys in blue and baby girls in pink, why plastic infant seats are preferred over a shawl for carrying babies in industrialized societies, and why European and American parents don't devote much effort to encouraging their young infants to sit upright. If you cannot immediately give the reasons for these preferences and practices, we've made our point.)

In short, from the series of fictions we have just identified, it should be clear that the seven imagined infant care guides presented here are in no way intended to advise members of these societies on how to raise their children. Rather, our "manuals" are directed to a Western audience interested in learning about childcare practices elsewhere. Our hope is that this format will communicate in a more compelling and immediate way than can a more conventional mode of social scientific writing.

In recent years, scholars have taken up a wide range of experimental writing incorporating a variety of fictional techniques. For example, the historian Jonathan Spence has written an engaging narrative of a Chinese peasant woman of the 17th century in which he cleverly interweaves passages from period fiction with historical documents to imagine more fully the woman's feelings and reactions. Other works by respected authors include a psychiatrist's "diary" of the imagined reflections of an infant; an ethnographically informed novel by an anthropologist about the lives of West African immigrants in New York; an ant's-eye view of the world by a science journalist; and an innovative book on the life cycle in Japan in which an anthropologist couples the lives of people he interviewed with the lives of literary characters from well-known Japanese works of fiction. Such bold writing experiments generally have two motives – to escape the bounds of standard academic writing, and to shed new light on a familiar subject by approaching it in a novel way.

The writer Eudora Welty has spoken eloquently on the usefulness of fiction for revealing truth:

[F]iction accomplishes its ends by using the oblique. Anything lighted up from the side . . . shows things in a relief that you can't get with a direct beam of the sun. And the imagination works all around the subject to light it up and reveal it in all its complications.

In this book, we use the conceit of the child-rearing manual as an oblique way to light up and reveal the complications of babyhood and the rearing of children.

We offer our imagined infant care manuals, then, as ethnographic/literary constructions that are written in the style of the very common genre of *How to* manuals in order to present some very uncommon *How to's*. In borrowing a familiar format to communicate a set of decidedly unfamiliar information, we hope to demonstrate a simple but powerful truth – that there are many models of babyhood, and that every such model is shaped intensely, albeit invisibly, by deeply held values and widely varying social contexts.

We have an additional motive for adopting – and adapting – the Spock-style genre. The authoritative tone of our "manuals," which directly address an imagined indigenous reader eager for advice, is also intended to poke fun – gently but seriously – at Western child-rearing manuals. Whatever their authors' intent, some of these books seem to suggest to many readers that the counsel they contain is best for *all* babies, regardless of significant differences both across and within societies. Indeed, these guides appear to imply that because babies present many biologically similar demands, the ways that parents respond to those demands are somehow outside the realm of culture.

The "manuals" we present here are not meant to be comprehensive ethnographic documents addressing all subcultural variations and historical changes – any more than a Western child-drearing manual is. In our book, the reader will find seven distinct "manuals," each made to sound (in keeping with the Spock model) as if its advice should be relevant anywhere. At the same time, you will find radically incompatible advice as you read across the other six chapters. Through this ironic juxtaposition – seven guides that dispense advice as if it were universally applicable – we invite the reader to step back and reconsider child-rearing advice as a cultural construction. Our critique of this popular genre may be of special interest to anthropologists interested in contemporary issues of voice, authority, and writing.

The constraints of the manual genre presented a major challenge for the authors of our chapters – how to deal with the fact that all of the six contemporary societies we include have undergone, and continue to experience, significant social change. In a few of these societies, some childcare practices recorded in earlier published ethnographic work are no longer relevant or are barely recognizable. And some members of these contemporary societies are endeavoring to challenge the ways of their grandparents and ancestors, embracing new practices that they deem "modern." At the same time, other members of these societies resist the temptations of modernity and prefer to raise their children following the ways of their grandparents and ancestors (even if those ways themselves have changed over the years).

In this book, we have chosen to emphasize "traditional" practices in order to highlight the major point we want to make in the volume as a whole: that despite current trends toward globalization, child-rearing practices still differ radically all over the globe, for multiple reasons relating to culture, economy, power, and history. We emphasize this point from our conviction that in a world of increasing communications across continents, it is all the more important to recognize and respect the continuing existence of cultural difference. International capital now flows across gaps once deemed unbridgeable, but culture still matters. And it matters, especially, to parents as they make decisions minute-by-minute that shape the sorts of people their children will one day become.

Organization of the Book

Seven chapters follow this introduction. Each begins with some background information on the society to help you understand the childcare practices you will read about. We include very brief discussions of geography, major historical events, and general economic and political factors, as well as particularly relevant aspects of the culture.

Each "manual" starts with a brief biography of its fictive author, followed by advice to prospective and new parents on a wide range of topics. Many of the topics are common to all the chapters, but others are not; the variability arises from differences in what is known about child care in these societies.

We invite you now to discover seven worlds of babies.

CHAPTER 2

A Parenting Manual, with Words of Advice for Puritan Mothers

Debbie Reese

THE PURITANS OF NEW ENGLAND

In the contemporary United States, stereotypes abound regarding the Puritans of colonial New England. Adherence to a strong work ethic, emphasis on moral character, suspicion of outsiders, and religious intolerance are among the characteristics commonly attributed to the Puritans. Historians, however, have characterized the Puritans in several contradictory ways: Some emphasize their responsibility for the founding of democracy in America, whereas others describe their creation of a grim and joyless theocracy based on rigid obedience of God's commands. Still other historians credit the Puritans with forging a complex intellectual and humanistic society whose faith served as a stimulus to strive for a better world for themselves and their children. Revisionist history is partially responsible for these differing views, although each model accurately reflects some aspect of New England Puritan society.

Puritan roots extend to seventeenth-century England, during the time of the reforms by the Protestant Church of England as it broke away from Roman Catholicism. Those who felt the Church of England was not doing enough to purge the theological influence of

Catholicism became known as Puritans because of their desire to further "purify" the church by ridding it of elements such as vestments, ceremony, and sacraments. Puritan leaders and parents believed that a move to the New World could protect their children from the "Common corrupcions of this euill world" – what they perceived as the corruption and profanity of seventeenth-century English society.

In 1630, under the leadership of John Winthrop aboard the flagship *Arabella,* nearly 1,000 colonists sailed to America on seventeen ships. They sought to build a "Citty upon a Hill," where, as a united body, they could "doe more seruice to the Lord," freely practice their beliefs, and serve as an example to all man. They established the first Puritan colony in Massachusetts Bay. From soon after they arrived, the Puritans began to spread into small villages in Rhode Island, Connecticut, New Hampshire, and eventually throughout New England. The immigrants were English men and women; scholars concur that most of their ideas, manners, beliefs, and prejudices were those of seventeenth-century Britons.

In Massachusetts Bay, the Puritans' early homes were hastily constructed, one-room structures of wattle and daub. To accommodate temperatures that ranged from −15°F to 98°F, the Puritans built frame homes, approximately 15 × 20 ft, constructed of heavy beams and plank walls, with small windows and a large fireplace. The main room was commonly referred to as the "hall," with a smaller, boarded-off section serving as a storage area or bedroom. However, the function of any room was not fixed; rather, each room could be used in several ways depending on the needs of the growing family. Nuclear families were common; it was rare to find a home that included family members spanning three generations.

The Puritan population in New England flourished, partly because of continued immigration, but primarily as a result of high birth rates and relatively low infant and maternal mortality rates. Women married in their late teens or early twenties. They could expect to bear children every two years until their early forties and to rear a large family. Anne Bradstreet, an acclaimed Puritan poet, birthed eight children, and Captain Roger Clap and his wife Johanna had fourteen children. From 1630 to 1640, a decade referred to as the Great Migration, the population of New England grew to about 20,000.

A Parenting Manual with Words of Advice for Puritan Mothers

In the New World, the Puritans relied on the Bible as they developed their society. Both church and state laws were formulated according to biblical injunction. For example, Matthew 18:15-17 states:

> Moreouer, if thy brother trefpace againft thee, go, and tell him his faute betwene thee & him alone: if he heare thee, thou haft wonne thy brother. But if he heare thee not, take yet with thee one or two, that by mouth of two or thre witneffes euerie worde may be cofirmed.
>
> And if he wil not vouchefaue to heare thee, tel it vnto the Church: & if he refufe to heare the Church alfo, let him be vnto thee as an heathen man, and a Publicane. (5, Matthew XVIII)

The Puritans interpreted this passage as an order from God for "brotherly correction" (Matthew: XVIII.15), instructing them to be vigilant not only of their own behavior but of the behavior of their fellow Puritans as well. Thus, the Puritans believed they had a duty to confront fellow community members with their failings, and if the accused did not make amends or change behavior, he or she would be brought before the church elders. Further resistance on the part of the accused could end in excommunication. Puritan church and state documents contain frequent reference to specific biblical passages such as that quoted above, supporting the laws written by Puritan leaders.

The Puritans built meeting houses to serve as their places of worship. Like the service itself, the structure was purposely kept plain to avoid anything suggestive of the Church of England "idolatry" that the Puritans were determined to eschew. The congregation met for worship twice on Sunday (morning and afternoon), with services lasting between one and two hours. The service consisted of prayers, a sermon, and the singing of Psalms. *The Bay Psalm Book,* published in 1640, was the first book published in the colonies. The congregation was expected to take notes during the sermon, for use and reflection during family worship within the home.

It was into this world that Puritan children arrived. The Puritans believed that infants were born damned and in need not only of baptism, but also of constant biblical teaching by parents. Determined that their society continue through the rising generation and those to come, the Puritans wrote laws such as the Law of 1642:

Law Requiring Education, which required that children be taught to read at an early age so that they could read and study the Bible themselves. Parents who neglected to teach their children to read could be fined and even have their children removed from their homes.

Contemporary scholars speculate that Puritan writers generally considered matters of child rearing too mundane to attend to in their published writings. It is true that in a discussion of women's activities, Ulrich (1977) states, "A virtuous woman wrote. A quill as well as a distaff was proper to a lady's hand." However, women's writings were largely in the form of letters and diaries. Rarely would women have published their writing for the public eye. Indeed, Puritan authors, both men and women, considered anonymity a virtue. They often did not attach their names even to their public writings.

If individuals' efforts were often buried in the sands of anonymity, the same is not true for the community as a whole. The intellectual and moral foundations of the Puritan community in New England continued to influence American society into the nineteenth and twentieth centuries; in particular, some scholars have argued that the Puritans strongly shaped important aspects of the modern capitalist system. Moreover, some of the Puritans' child-rearing strategies were strictly followed by many Euro-Americans into the early twentieth century. Ironically, it was a descendant of a Puritan – Benjamin Spock – who most effectively challenged some of those practices, such as strict scheduling of infant feeding times. He did, however, approve of other Puritan practices, such as having older infants sleep separately from their parents – a practice that is still followed by many Euro-American parents today.

For the "manual" that follows, I have invented an anonymous, mature, Puritan mother as the guide's author. Her purported anonymity is in keeping with the Puritans' value of modesty.

A PARENTING MANUAL

With Words of Advice for Puritan Mothers

A World of Babies

About the Author

The following pages present advice to parents on raising children to be good Christians and to serve God. The author of this guide was a woman who followed the Puritan convention of anonymity, so her descendants are unsure of her exact identity. Her words would not have been published in colonial America, when this guide was written. But a yellowed, hand-written manuscript was recently discovered in a trunk of old family documents. The trunk had been long forgotten in a dark attic corner of a house that has been in the same Bostonian family since the late 17th century – a family that traces its origins to the original Puritans. There are clues in the manuscript, as well as other items found with it, indicating that its author was a devout Puritan gentle-woman. She was a mother whose children were grown at the time she wrote this child-rearing guide, and she had attended the births of many of her neighbors' infants and had even nursed some of those babies.

Why did this seventeenth-century gentlewoman write a guide to raising infants, knowing it would not actually be published? Perhaps, as a devout and wise member of the church, as well as a mother, she was often called upon for advice by other parents wanting to save their children from the devil and desiring to teach them to glorify God's name. Since she could read and write, she may have been drawn to put on paper her thoughts about raising children. If so, she shared this impulse with one of her descendants: It appears that this anonymous gentlewoman may have been a distant ancestor of Benjamin Spock, whose famous baby and child care manual shows traces of his Puritan ancestry.

A PARENTING MANUAL

With words of advice for Puritan mothers in New England

Wherein is contained a discourse and description of

Pregnancy

and

Practical & Spiritual

Concerns of

Parenting

"By a Gentlewoman in those parts."

BLESSED WITH A CHILD

God's blessing on you and your family. You are giving thought to beginning your family or perhaps are already with child. Children are a blessing! Another shall be added to our glorious colony! With all that a child means to you and our community of God's people, this little book is written to help you bring this child up according to God's will.

Throughout this guide, I have endeavored to incorporate the words of God, as given us through our ministers. Faithfully, I have recorded their words during the sermon on the Sabbath, as the faithful should always do, for later study and reflection at home. I have also read the words of esteemed ministers whose sermons I have not had the opportunity to attend.

Always bear in mind the words given us in Thomas Leadbeater's sermon on the order in which we use the things of this world. Partaking of good meat and drink shall serve God by strengthening your body, that you may serve God with greater vigor. A good bed shall refresh the Spirit as well as strengthen the body. And if you feel the need for recreation, innocent play is not forbidden, as it too shall refresh your Spirit. Honor the Lord by observing these words not only for yourself, but also for your children. In all you do, do so to serve the Lord. Should anything you do become its own end – eating for the pleasure of eating, sleeping for the pleasure of sleeping – then you fail to serve the Lord, choosing instead to pursue the lust of the flesh.

A word of caution: living in this new land, we see the heathen Indians around us. Their ways are not our ways. You may hear of the Indian women giving birth and returning to their everyday duties within a few days. You may hear of the ways they indulge their children – not just in the first year of life but always. They even breastfeed for three years! They believe their children learn best simply by their parents' activities and by occasional suggestions to do this task or that one. Such a childhood eventually leads to an adulthood with many hours of each day spent idle. This life may be appealing to your children, but it is not our way, for our children must take up a calling early in life. You must tell your children that idleness is sinful. This is an important lesson that some of our women and children forget when they are carried off by these heathens. Some do not even want to return to our villages. Such is the power of Satan.

Remember your dual responsibilities of providing for both the physical and the spiritual needs of your children. If it is observed by one of the community that you are neglectful of either of these important duties, the Selectmen may order the removal of your children from your home, or they may order periodic visits to be certain you are living up to your responsibilities.

Above all, you must always pray for your children, this being the first and last duty of a parent, according to Scripture. As Reverend Mather has written: "Yea, When thou dost cast thine Eyes upon the Little Folks, often in a day dart up an Ejaculatory Prayer to Heaven for them; Lord Let this Child be thy Servant for ever!" So go forth. Raise the child up to glorify God's name!

PREGNANCY AND CHILDBIRTH

Conception

First and foremost, as a good Puritan, pray to God for conception to occur. Pray that it will please God to give you the blessing of children. Childbearing is your divinely ordained mission in life!

It is God's will that you engage in the "act of generation" by which you will become pregnant and deliver a child. You may hear from those outside our prayerful community that the child is not in need of prayer until after the birth. Do not heed their heinous words! Doing so will start you on a path on which you do not pray for your child, but continually fix the need for prayer at some unspecified, future date. Some mothers ask the midwife to pray for their child, and then, when the child is older, they place the responsibility for prayer on the child, and so it continues. Such women do not truly love their children and, worse, have little faith in God. So, pray, and pray, and pray without ceasing.

Another word of caution: There are those in our midst who would purposely work to abort a child in their womb − a child who has been formed by God! Such women have listened to Satan's counsel and are guilty of murder. God will avenge a child who dies by the willful and sinful act of abortion, perhaps causing woe and misfortune on you, your family, or even our entire village.

We have observed more babies born between February and April, when the extreme cold is gone, and long before the extreme heat arrives in midsummer. You can expect your children to be born approximately two years apart. You may wonder why this is so. While you are nursing an infant, usually for the first year of the baby's life, you have a natural protection against becoming pregnant again.

As is true for most mothers, you can expect to rear a large family. You have observed, no doubt, that Puritan women birth many children. On average, the number is eight, so that is likely to be the case for you as well. Your ability to bring forth a child is God's will, and your fruitfulness should be regarded as the highest form of good fortune.

Prenatal Care

Pray to God when you feel the child move in your womb. It is your responsibility to take proper care of yourself during the pregnancy, thereby taking proper care of the growing child within. Whatever you eat and drink will be passed on to the child. As written in the Bible (Judges 13:7), you should not partake of wine, strong drink, and unclean things: "Behold, thou fhalt conceiue, and beare a fonne, and now thou fhalt drinke no wine, nor strong drinke, nether eat anie vncleane thing..." (Judges 13:7).

The violence of passion, either due to grief or anger, or through the violent motion of the body through dancing, running, or galloping on horseback, may bring about a miscarriage. Be ever mindful!

Just as your husband has a duty to see to your well-being by providing you with the fruits of the Earth as provided by God, so he must see to the well-being of his unborn child. Should he deny your needs, he shall be guilty also of denying the child, thus guilty of sin and liable to God's judgment. Such a loss of the child shall be not only on your conscience, but on your husband's as well. The loss signifies a failure to care for a child formed by God.

Childbirth

Remember the words of Cotton Mather, our esteemed and learned minister. He said that, although some view the experience of child-bearing as a curse, it is actually a blessing from God that helps create a more tender and pious disposition in women.

When the time comes for the knot that has made you one with this child to be untied you will feel small pains. At this point, your husband should summon a midwife whose reputation has not been tarnished by accusations that she is a witch. Neighboring women will also be summoned. Among them will be one who can nurse your infant if you are taken ill and unable to do so yourself. These women will gather in your house, tending you in the inner room, which becomes the "borning room". They will drape the bed with heavy curtains of serge or harrateen and make certain that all windows are closed off, preventing air or light from entering the room. In the coming days, they will help you with cooking and other household chores until you are ready to resume them yourself. During your labour, your husband will be nearby, engaged in prayer, but he will not witness the birth.

You may experience an "exceedingly hard & Dangerous Travail," which can be eased with medicinal and culinary herbs. It may be very long, or perhaps the labor will be shorter with very sharp pains. Pray to the Lord to spare you of dangerous circumstances. When the child is born, he or she will be welcomed with great joy from all present, and your husband will rejoice in this blessing.

Take time to record the minute, hour, day, month, and year of the baby's birth in your family Bible. We know how significantly the planets influence many aspects of our daily life. Knowing the positions of the planets at the time of birth will help you to understand your child's nature. In addition to recording the birthdate, the newborn should be carried upstairs after silver and gold are placed in his or her hand. We believe this tradition will help your child rise up in the world and bring him or her wealth.

Perhaps during your labour, but certainly in the days to come, your attendants will serve the traditional groaning beer and groaning cake that was prepared in the weeks before the expected birth time. You will have many visitors, and it is proper that they are offered this special drink and cake during their visit.

After the birth you should expect to be in bed for two weeks. You must remain inside your home after the birth, and only after four weeks have passed can you go forth in the community.

In the weeks to come, you must also make certain a feast is planned for the midwife, nurses, and all the neighbor women who offered advice or help with household duties. The menu can include boiled pork, fowls, roast beef, turkey, pies, and tarts. A good, dry wine such as sack or perhaps a good claret can also be served. Before the guests arrive, change the heavy bed drapes to calico curtains and valences.

Your visitors may present you with gifts – especially our traditional gift of a pincushion, which may be decorated with pins placed so as to form words of welcome for the baby. Or perhaps the child's name will be embroidered permanently on the pincushion with silver beads.

A fact we must acknowledge before going on is that travail is not without peril for both you and the child. In my years, I have seen many women die giving birth. Infants also suffer death during birth, particularly if the child is not positioned correctly. If your infant dies within your body, the dead child must be removed by a skilled doctor in order to prevent your own death. Remember – children are pledges from God, and he can reclaim them at any time.

PARENTING: PRACTICAL CONCERNS

Breastfeeding Your Newborn

Holy women in the Bible breastfed their infants. Although mothers in England frequently send their infants out to a wet nurse, we follow the examples set for us in the Bible. Think of Sarah and Hannah, biblical women who nursed their young. It is right and proper that you follow their practice. The newborn infant should be put to your breast immediately and should have no supplementary or artificial feeding. Indeed, Reverend Gouge tells us:

> God has given to women two breasts fit to contain and hold milk: and nipples unto them fit to have milk drawn from them. Why are these thus given? To lay them forth for ostentation? There is no warrant for that in all

God's word. They are directly given for the child's food that comes out of the womb, for till the child be born, there is no milk in the breasts; anon after it is born, milk ordinarily flows into the breasts.

Mothers who breastfeed are more tender towards their babies: they cannot hear infants cry without quickly lifting and comforting them. During the first year, this care and attention are necessary to give babies a greater chance of surviving our harsh weather and the many illnesses that may befall them.

It will be obvious to you that nursing is God's will. Your infant is born knowing how to suck. Do not hesitate. During the first year of the child's life, offer your breast whenever the infant desires it. It is important to indulge the child in this way to ensure his or her very survival.

Take care with your diet. According to Scripture, a nursing mother should refrain from things that may be harmful to the milk the child receives. You should avoid wine or strong drink. The meat and foods you eat are turned into milk, so you should eat only health-giving foods, ever mindful that what you eat is passed on to the child through breastmilk.

You must nurse the child frequently enough to prevent the milk from backing up, and you should make sure the baby nurses equally on both breasts. If the milk backs up, the breast will tighten and cause the skin to distend, which can be painful. During the early days of nursing, a little soreness of the nipples is to be expected. You may even see a little blood running from your nipples. Rest assured, this is only a temporary condition. However, failing to properly position the infant at your breast may result in nipple soreness, cracking, abscesses, and inflammation. To prevent cracked nipples, mix wax with a little bit of rosin, and apply the mixture to your nipples periodically. If your nipples are inverted or flattened, seek the advice of a physician. There are medical treatments for this condition, which often results from wearing tight corsets.

Using a Wet Nurse

Only if you become seriously ill, with fever or a physical injury preventing you from nursing the child, may you consider sending the child to a wet nurse or bringing her to your home. In this case, the child should be with the wet nurse no more than two or three days. Going more than that without nursing the child will cause your milk to dry up.

In selecting a wet nurse, you must carefully consider the character traits of the woman, as they can be transferred to your infant. Ill-tempered and red-headed women are not suitable, because they may transmit vice, a treacherous mind, or a disagreeable temper. Before engaging her services, you must consider the behavior, health, age, breasts and nipples, complexion, color of hair, body size, facial features, speech, and the general appearance of the wet nurse. She can influence the infant not only through the milk she provides, but also from the child observing her behavior.

Introducing Solid Foods

You must continue to breastfeed until at least the baby's first birthday, but your infant will be ready for solid foods after the sixth month. At this time you may give the child an ordinary, moderate diet of milk, bread, and cheese. Later on, the gravy we call pottage and the gelatinous flummery flavored with spices and dried fruit that you prepare for the rest of the family are also acceptable for the child. In addition, you may feed the infant berries, ripe pears, and apples. You may prepare baked beans, Indian corn, cornbread, succotash, cornmeal mush, hominy, and other Indian foods cooked in their ways, and add them to your child's diet. With this diet, the child will grow healthy and gratefully accept whatever is given to him. Take care that your child is not daintily fed in the early years. This would lead to a sickly, squeamish child who demands only the choicest meats. Indulging a lust for flesh wrongly encourages the child to give more importance to food than to God.

Sleeping

Your newborn infant can be placed in a wicker or wooden cradle, if you have one. A deep hood over it will prevent drafts from reaching the baby. Quilts, blankets, and coverlets will also help keep the infant warm. If a cradle is not available, the infant may sleep with you at first, but by six months, the child should be moved to his/her own bed or to a sibling's bed. Many parents use a side bed for the young child, placing it next to their own. The child's mattress should be hard, made with quilts rather than feathers. You may lull your child to sleep by singing the "Cradle Hymn".

Bathing

The proper hour for bathing is either the early part of the day or the middle of the afternoon, just before the customary nap times. The child is likely to be tired and in need of sleep after the bath, so schedule the bath to precede his normal napping time. Bathe and dress your infant in the glow and warmth of the open fireplace. Give your infant a warm bath, which can be as short as three minutes, or as long as twenty. After removing the child from the water, make sure that all moisture is removed from the skin to prevent chafing.

Although it is a common practice in New England to give our young cold baths in order to harden them to the harsh conditions of winter, you should refrain from this practice in the early months. An infant is not yet strong, and the powerful shock of being plunged into a cold bath can be quite dangerous, even fatal. If it is your desire to harden your infant by the use of cold baths, you must do so gradually and cautiously over a long period of time. Do not begin this process until the child is at least six months old.

Weaning

The infant should be weaned from your breast some time after the first year. This is best accomplished by physically separating you and the child. You may send the child away to grandparents or other relatives, or you may go alone to visit a friend or relative for a short while. If you leave, your husband, the child's grandmother, or older siblings will care for the infant during your absence. A separation is best, because a mother's heart cannot deny the cries of her child seeking the breast.

Clothing

Our ancestors in England traditionally swaddled infants in a square of material around which long strips of cloth were tightly wrapped. This was believed to keep the infants' limbs straight and prevented the child from going about on all fours like an animal. It also helped ward off rickets. Some of our physicians here, however, recommend against the practice of swaddling. They point out that it is time consuming and may prevent the interaction between mother and child necessary for raising a child with the love and comfort needed in the first year of life. One exception is the use of a single band placed snugly, but not too tightly, around the abdomen of a feeble child. This band will prevent the rupture of the umbilicus by crying, coughing, or sneezing.

Depending on your wealth, you may have very few or plenty of clouts, or diapers. An ideal number to have is between four and six dozen. Wet and soiled clouts should be changed frequently to prevent skin inflammation. Before reuse, they should be properly washed and dried. The best and most absorbent fabrics for clouts are those imported from Germany or Great Britain. Local newspapers carry advertisements for clouting fabrics when they arrive. If these are not available or you cannot afford them, you can make clouts from household linens that have become softer with use. You may also wish to use a pilch, or thick square of flannel, to cover the diaper. This will prevent wetness from soaking through the clout to the bedding and can save you many hours of laundering blankets and coverlets.

No doubt you have been working diligently making embroidered clothing for your son or daughter. The shirts you make for the first six months should have an opening up the back. At six months, the baby will need a larger version of the same shirt. Your infant will be able to wear this type of shirt for about a year and a half. These shirts are commonly worn over a petticoat or a sleeveless gown with a very long skirt that extends many inches beyond the infant's feet. With the excess folded up over the baby's legs, the shirt serves as a warm covering. When the child is able to walk and run about, the garment may be shortened to allow for greater freedom of movement and prevent falls. Boys and girls alike wear these gowns,

44

because they are simpler to alter than breeches. You will want to save them for use with your next child. Put a warmly padded cap on the infant's head for additional protection from the cold.

As your infant grows, he or she should wear reasonable clothing with only a minimal amount of decoration and lace. Excess finery in clothing leads to corrupt young children, foolishly dressed, full of vanity that can flame up and scorch you. Such attention to clothing is only prideful and does not serve God.

Although it was common in England to dress children as young as 2 $\frac{1}{2}$ years in corsets and tightly laced clothing, some physicians here in New England have warned us that tightly laced corsets prevent natural movement and pose a danger to the development of the ribcage and lungs. Your boy or girl should be dressed in a loose-fitting gown until the age of five or six. This gown will give the child warmth and comfort. At that time, the child will begin to wear clothing that more resembles that worn by adults.

Walking, Physical Activity, and Play

Your baby will probably begin to walk as early as nine months or as late as a year and a half. Do not be alarmed, however, if your child does not walk until even later – many children do not walk until they are two years old. You may choose to use a go-cart or standing-stool to help the child learn to walk.

Your growing child may play about, running, exercising his limbs. His body is not yet strong enough for physical labor, and he will not be required to engage in work until the age of six. Until that time, play is fine, but at every opportunity infuse the play with Scripture.

Health Care

In all health matters, consult with your parents, relatives, and other members of the community. Our nostrums are well known for their effectiveness. For any illness your child may have, someone will know what to administer and when to call in a learned surgeon. For your part, learn all you can about the nearby plants and wildlife.

These are gifts from God, and everything He has given us can be used! Study nature carefully, and keep this in mind: Like cures like. For example, St. John's wort, whose leaves appear to be full of holes, can be rubbed on skin abrasions and wounds.

The most common illnesses among our newborns and children are worms, rickets, and fits. You may prepare nostrums for these illnesses yourself. The recipe for snail water, which can be administered for any illness as a lotion or tonic, follows:

Wash a peck of garden snails well in beer. Put them in an oven till they stop making their noise. Remove them from the oven, wipe the green froth away, and crush them, shells and all, in a stone mortar. Take a quart of earthworms, scour them with salt, slit them, and wash well with water. Beat them into pieces in a stone mortar. In a distilled pot, place two handfulls of Angelica, followed by two handfuls of Celandine. On this, add two quarts of Rosemary flowers, bearsfoot, agrimony, red dock roots, and bark of barberries. Add two handfuls of betony wood sorrel, and one handful of rue. Lay the snails and worms on top of the herbs and flowers. Cover with three gallons of strong ale. Let stand all night. In the morning, add three ounces of cloves, sixpennyworth of beaten saffron, and then six ounces of shaved harshorne. Put on the limbeck lid with paste, and extract the water. It should produce 9 pints.

From time to time, you may find it necessary to treat swelling or localized infection by the letting of blood. This treatment has been used well for many years in England and is very effective. However, it must be done carefully, according to the age of the child and the phase of the moon (which guides many of our activities, such as planting). The procedure can be done on an infant as young as three months.

Here are a few treatments for specific illnesses that may trouble your child:

Ague produces fever and chills. If you can find them, spider web pills are effective in curing ague. If they are not available, try the following homemade remedy: put a spider in a nutshell, wrap it with silk and hang it around the child's neck.

Colic can be treated by giving the child a broth made of the boiled entrails and skin of a wolf.

For stomach ache, prepare this nostrum: mix rattlesnake gall with chalk and shape into snake balls.

A stye is simply treated by sending the afflicted child to watch the blacksmith. Children stand close to the heat and steam as they watch the blacksmith at his work. Each time the blacksmith brings down his hammer, the child instinctively blinks hard. The combination of the heat, steam and blinking motion will, after thirty minutes or so, cause the stye to burst.

To ease the pain when the infant's teeth begin to come, purchase an anodyne necklace, as advertised in the newspapers. These necklaces will help the gums to open and allow the teeth to gently ease forth. Other necklaces known to be effective are those made with the teeth of a fawn or the fangs of a wolf. You can also rub the gums with a medication prepared from the brains of a hare mixed with honey and butter. Another treatment is to scratch the gums with an osprey bone.

PARENTING: SPIRITUAL CONCERNS

Your responsibilities for the welfare of your child do not end when you meet his or her physical needs. Providing for these basic needs assures your child of happiness in this life. Yet, there is a life of eternity that awaits us all upon our death. To ensure happiness in that life, you must tend to the child's spiritual well-being. This is not only God's will, but insofar as it applies to teaching your child to read, it is a law in our state, based on Scripture. Failure to teach the catechism can result in a weighty fine of twenty shillings!

Your child is born in sin, depraved, and prone to sin. Only through constant teaching of the Scripture within the home, from morning to night, may you help your child gain salvation and enter the kingdom of heaven. When your infant wakes in the morning, as you bathe, dress, and feed the child, at bedtime, and all those moments in between, repeat the word of God so that drop by drop, your child will be filled with the Glory of God's word. Evil nature can be trained into good habits that will bring your child nearer to God, but only if the training is started early. The younger the child, the more flexible and easily formed, so ensure success by beginning this training at birth. Infuse your child with good things and God's holy truths.

A good Puritan family worships the Lord together, within the home, each day. Worship of our Lord within the home should occur immediately upon rising in the morning and just before bed at night. A good Puritan father leads his family in prayers such as The Lord's Prayer. He may also read from the Scriptures and lead in the singing of psalms.

Baptism

Conceived in sin, your infant should be baptized as soon as possible after birth. Do not delay, even if it means the child will be baptized in a meeting house so cold that the baptismal water is frozen over with a thin layer of ice! No more than eight days should pass before you take your infant to the meeting house to be baptized (Plate 4). Wrap the baby in a baize bearing cloth, which is a christening blanket embroidered with a passage of Scripture. The

Plate 4. These Puritans, dressed in their plain clothes, are on their way to the meeting house. The infant may be going for baptism, which takes place at the meeting house, even when it is so cold that a layer of ice over the water in the baptismal font must be broken first. "New England Puritans Going to Church," by George Henry Boughton, reprinted courtesy of the Billy Graham Center Museum, Wheaton College.

responsibility for seeing that your infant is baptized falls primarily on the child's father. You are likely to be in a state of weakness after delivering the child and not able to tend to such a weighty matter as baptism. Your husband will inform you of the time and place for the baptism.

The baptism must be done by a pastor or deacon by washing or the sprinkling of water, and it must be done in a public place in the presence of a large body of God's people. Although baptism is not a guarantee of salvation, it is the first step you take that makes it possible for your child to share in the riches and glories of Heaven. Through the baptism of your children, you acknowledge that God has given them to you and that you "heartily give back those children to God again: their Baptism is to be the sign and seal of your doing so."

Naming

Your husband will consult with you about the child's name. Like many parents, you may choose to give a daughter your own name, or give a son your husband's name. Or you may wish to preserve the memory of a deceased family member or relative by bestowing upon your children the esteemed name of one who is no longer with us in this world. Many parents name their infant after a sibling who has died as a way of remembering that child.

There are those in the Bible whose life is worthy of our imitation, and their names may be given to your child. Think of Isaac, David, Peter, Hannah, and Elizabeth, and what they mean to us and can thereby mean to your child. Names have special meaning and can have significant bearing on the development of the child's character. Give thought to selecting one that conveys the character traits you want your child to develop. Consider the following: John means "grace of God," Jonathan means "the gift of God," Andrew means "manly," Clement means "meeke," Simeon means "obedient," and Prudens means "wife." Abigail means "Father's joy," and Hannah means "grace."

You may also choose a word itself as a name. It, too, can be significant in the development of character. Think of these names, and what they may impart to your child: Accepted, Faithful, Godly,

Gracious, Humble, Meek, Mercy, Pleasant, Redeemed, Renewed, Thankful, Ashes, Dust, Earth, Increase, Faint-not, and Fear-not. Mercy is a name frequently given: poet Anne Bradstreet's sister is named Mercy Woodbridge. Captain Roger Clap named two children Experience and Waitstill.

Finally, you may name your child after an event that occurred during the birth. For example, Seaborn Cotton was born on a ship traveling here from England.

Education

As your child grows in ability to understand what is being said, you must continue to attend church every Sunday and to talk about the sermon, as you have done from the days of the child's birth. Through questioning, you can determine if your child was attentive throughout the sermon, and you can find out how much he or she understood of it. You may need to help your child remember and understand some parts of the sermon.

In your home instruction, refer often to the child's baptism, explaining that through baptism, children become "listed among the servants and soldiers of the Lord Jesus Christ, and that if they live in rebellion against Him, woe unto them!" (See Plate 5.)

Your son or daughter must learn to read as soon as possible in order to prepare for salvation in the next world. Within our families, it is your husband's responsibility to provide the catechism and instruction in reading. Your husband will cause the child to single out passages of Scripture and commit them to memory. He will question the child frequently about the passage and help the child to better understand God's word. Later on, your child will attend one of our schools, but until then, home instruction is necessary.

You must purchase a Horn book to begin teaching the child the alphabet and the Lord's Prayer. What we call Horn books are not really books, but are simply a thin piece of wood on which a printed page is placed and covered with a thin layer of yellowish horn through which the print can be read. Thread a string through the hole in the corner, so the Horn book can be worn about the child's neck where it is easily available for practice and instruction throughout the day.

Plate 5. A primary responsibility of Puritan parents is the spiritual and secular education of their young children. This Puritan father is leading his family in singing hymns. From *The Whole Booke of Psalmes,* reprinted courtesy of the Folger Shakespeare Library.

We emphasize the need to teach our young children to read so that they may soon be able to read the Scriptures themselves. Without such teaching, children, in a state of ignorance, may invite heresy and damnation. Worst of all, you, as a parent, lay your child open to the evil and power of Satan. Reverend Mather writes:

If there be any Considerable Blow given to the Devil's Kingdom, it must be, by Youth Excellently Educated. . . . Learning is an unwelcome guest to the Devil, and therefore he would fain starve it out.

In addition to the Horn books, there are a number of other books written to assist children in learning to read and also to introduce them to God's words. Cotton Mather has written several, including "Good Lessons for Children, In Verse," "The Life of

Mary Paddock, who died at the age of nine," "The Child's New Plaything," "Divine Songs in Easy Language," and "Praise out of the Mouth of Babes." These little books are significant to your child's early learning, because they contain verses that instruct about God's word.

Discipline

Because children are blessings from God, we welcome them with joyous hearts and indulge them in their first year of life; their days are filled with tranquillity and comfort. This helps to ensure survival during this vulnerable period, and to gain their trust so we can more easily win them over to God's will.

However, by the first birthday, it is time to begin a different sort of parenting. This is when all children begin to need restrictions and limits. Now is when you shall see the behaviors that indicate that your infant was, indeed, born in sin, that all infants are born evil, and thus are the root of rebellion against God and man. Your child will become increasingly mobile and will begin to express his will, which will frequently be at odds with yours. The weeds within will sprout. Your child will lie to you and become stubborn, peevish, and sullen. It is your duty to break and beat down the natural pride and stubbornness that may develop.

However, not all children are alike! Each child has his or her own nature. As Anne Bradstreet tells us:

Diverse children have their different natures; some are like flesh which nothing but salt will keep from putrefaction; some again like tender fruits that are best preserved with sugar: those parents are wise that can fit their nurture according to their Nature.

Knowing the natural inclinations of your child will help you to instruct him or her against natural weaknesses and tendencies to sin. Watch your child carefully, as this careful study will help you intervene when a bad habit begins to develop. You must stop its formation before it becomes entrenched.

Many of our ministers counsel that you win your child over to holiness by kindness rather than force. Apply all your wisdom, moderation, and equity to your child, that you will not alienate the young mind and heart. Reflect on the words of Reverend Cotton Mather, who advises us:

> The first Chastisement, which I inflict for an ordinary Fault, is to lett the Child see and hear me in an Astonishment, and hardly able to beleeve that the Child could do so base a Thing, but beleeving that they will never do it again.
> I would never come, to give a child a Blow; except in Case of Obstinancy: or some gross Enormity. To be chased for a while out of my Presence, I would make to be look'd upon, as the sorest Punishment in the Family...

However, each parent must decide the proper method of disciplining the child. Some turn to the birch rod. Indeed, our esteemed Reverend Cotton Mather instructs us that it is better to whip a child than let him be damned. The gentle rod that breaks neither skin nor bone, with God's blessing, has the power to break the bond of corruption in the heart. However, the birch rod is to be used only as a last resort, when verbal admonishment and demonstration have failed. Be mindful that anger and wrath are cruel, and do not allow them to enter into the discipline of your child. As Reverend Mather has written:

> Never give a Blow in passion. Stay till your passion is over; and let the Offendors plainly see, that you deal thus with them, out of pure obedience unto God, and for their true Repentance.

You must strive to teach your child to have a reverence for you, a holy respect and fear both of your person, and of your words. The child should be fearful of losing your favor, crossing your interests, falling short of your expectations. Call the child to kneel before you twice a day, to show deference to your authority.

All this must be mixed with love and affection, both of the kind you extend to your child and that which he or she returns to you. It is natural that you love your child, and it is the duty of your child to return that love. You must, however, exercise caution. Wise parents will keep a due distance between themselves and their children, knowing that lavish displays of affection and familiarity breed contempt and irreverence.

A World of Babies

Throughout the coming years, as you raise your child up to be a member of God's community, turn often to the words of Cotton Mather that I have recorded here, and heed them:

> Know you not, that your Children have precious and Immortal Souls within them? They are not all Flesh. You that are the Parents of their Flesh, must know, That your Children have Spirits also, whereof you are told, in Heb. 12:9. God is the Father of them; and in Eccles. 12:7. God is the Giver of them.
>
> The Souls of your Children, must survive their Bodies, and are transcendently Better and Higher & Nobler Things than their Bodies. Are you sollicitous that their Bodies may be Fed? You should be more sollicitous that their Souls may not be Starved, or go without the Bread of Life.
>
> Are you sollicitious that their Bodies may be cloath'd? You should be more sollicitious that their Souls may not be Naked, or go without the Garments of Righteousness.

CHAPTER 3

Luring Your Child Into This Life

A Beng Path for Infant Care

Alma Gottlieb

WHO ARE THE BENG?

The Beng are one of the smallest and least known of about sixty
ethnic groups in the West African nation of Côte d'Ivoire, or Ivory
Coast. With a population of approximately 12,000, they live in some
twenty villages located in an ecological border zone between the rain
forest to the south and savanna to the north.

The Beng are surrounded by neighbors who speak different languages from theirs (especially Baule, Ando, and Jimini). Their
language is part of the Southern Mande group of languages that are
spoken far to the west and southwest of the Beng. Most of their
neighbors consider the Beng to be the indigenous population in the
region. However, their history is complex and somewhat mysterious.
Linguistic evidence suggests the current nation of Mali as a starting
point from which the group split off and began a long series of migrations over 2,000 years ago.

The Beng have no memory of the Atlantic slave trade. Perhaps
whenever they felt the threat of slave traders passing nearby, their
ancestors managed to elude the slave hunters by escaping deep
into the forest. Certainly as farmers living in relatively small vil-

lages in or near the rain forest, they knew the forest well, regularly making intense use of its animal and plant resources. They also engaged in long-distance trade in kola nuts, ceramic pottery, bark cloth, and other local products, largely with villagers and long-distance Muslim traders from the north, often using cowry shells as currency.

Their first memories of contact with Europeans are quite recent. The French occupied the Beng region in the early 1890s. As pacifists, the Beng prayed to their ancestors and the Earth for deliverance from the colonizing force but offered no military or political resistance to the French regime, unlike other nearby groups who actively resisted colonization. The French colonizers brutally forced Beng farmers to build roads and to devote much of their time to planting new crops (especially coffee, cocoa, and new varieties of rice and cotton) that the Beng "sold" as taxes to the French to support the colonial empire in West Africa.

The nation of Côte d'Ivoire gained independence from France in 1960. A wealthy Baule plantation owner, Félix Houphoüet-Boigny, became the nation's first president and held that position until his death in 1993. Beng villagers overwhelmingly supported Houphoüet throughout his long reign, even though his final years were marked by increasing national debt, corruption, poverty, urban crime, and repression – and mounting criticism by educated citizens.

The vast majority of Beng people still live in relatively small, rural villages, where they practice a mixed economy of farming, hunting, and gathering. Both men and women work long hours in the fields much of the year, and children – whether or not they attend primary school – are trained in local farming techniques. Even toddlers of two to three years of age help with agricultural tasks to the best of their abilities. In precolonial times, men also hunted game regularly in the forest. However, the growth of a cash economy, with its more labor-intensive farming techniques based on monoculture, has reduced the time available for hunting, and the price of bullets is too high for many men. As a result, the amount of animal protein eaten has declined in recent years. Women, men, and children continue to collect wild plants (especially berries and leaves), as well as a variety of small forest creatures.

Luring Your Child Into This Life

Despite pervasive Western rhetoric about "development in the Third World," as with many other peasant populations of Africa, the Beng have become progressively impoverished under both the French colonial regime and the postcolonial governments. These days, the world market price for coffee is so low that Beng farmers barely make a profit from their coffee harvest, which they developed under the French as their major cash crop. In the 1990s, some Beng families reverted to a virtual subsistence economy. As elsewhere, the implications of this declining economy for children's lives are drastic. Today, many Beng parents cannot even afford childhood inoculations, let alone bus trips to the nearest town (M'Bahiakro) to buy Western medicines for sick children. Moreover, many parents who would like to send their children to school cannot afford the expenses (for uniforms and school supplies) associated with the nominally free school system.

The Beng group their villages into two political divisions, each of which is ruled by a king-and-queen pair (who are considered to be sister and brother). A local court system has an appeals structure built into it; only rarely do people rely on the highest level of appeal – the national government. Indeed, most Beng have endeavored to maintain a certain independence from the state. Until about twenty years ago, many parents refused to send their children to government-run schools. The schools are modeled on the French educational system, with all instruction conducted in the country's official language of French. Even though elementary school is compulsory for six years, most Beng parents, endeavoring to maintain their distance from anything related to the French colonial regime and its aftermath, do not comply with this law. Earlier in the century, some parents who were forced to send their children to school even prayed to local spirits that their sons and daughters fail their exams so they could leave school. However, nowadays more young people are rejecting the conservatism of their elders, and more parents are complying with national law and sending their children to elementary school for at least a few years. Still, the failure and dropout rates of Beng students, even at the elementary school level, remain quite high. For example, in 1993 in one Beng village elementary school, eleven out of thirty-nine first grade students failed, and only thirteen out of thirty-six students in the last grade passed an eligibility test to attend junior high school. As of this writing, a single Beng student is a graduate student in the U.S., and another is a university student in Europe.

Beng families are usually large. In the villages, birth control efforts are generally limited to a taboo on sex until a new baby can walk independently. Although there are many variations, extended families typically consist of a husband and wife (or wives), all their unmarried daughters, all their sons, and their married sons' wives and children. Until the 1960s, extended families generally lived together under the thatched roof of a single large, round house. In the 1960s, the government, citing risk of fire, bulldozed these houses and required smaller, square houses with tin roofs for all new construction. Nevertheless, extended families still manage to live near one another: Family subgroups often inhabit small buildings surrounding an open courtyard.

A "dual descent" system of clans crosscuts the family structure, with each individual belonging simultaneously to two clans – one whose membership is traced exclusively in the female line (matriclans) and another whose membership is traced exclusively in the male line (patriclans). At marriage, neither men nor women change their membership in either of these clans. Until recently, virtually all first marriages of young women were arranged by their families, according to a complex system determined by birth order. This system is still actively maintained, although some women are rebelling against it.

Until recently, virtually all Beng devoutly practiced their own religion. In the past few decades, an increasing number of Beng have become attracted to Islam, and some have endorsed Christianity (both Catholicism and Protestantism). There is now a mosque in one village, and most other villages have at least a significant minority of Muslim Beng (as well as immigrant Muslims of other ethnic groups, especially Julas). However, like many West Africans, most Beng who have endorsed one of the "world" religions continue to practice at least some components of their traditional religion; only a few have completely converted.

The indigenous religion requires people to offer regular prayers and sacrifices to *eci* (sky/god), their ancestors, a variety of bush spirits, and spirits affiliated directly with the Earth. Indigenous religious practitioners are primarily of two sorts – diviners and Earth priests. Diviners, who may be either male or female, use a variety of techniques to communicate with invisible spirits of the bush and of ancestors; they then interpret the spirits' communications to their clients. One of the most common reasons for villagers to consult diviners is to try to discover the cause and/or cure for their children's illnesses. Mothers of sick children frequently consult a secular herbalist first; if the child's symptoms remain after she has carried out the herbalist's orders, the mother then consults a diviner.

Often, the divination indicates that a sacrifice to the Earth is necessary. In this case, the client then consults an Earth priest. These priests, who are almost always male, worship the Earth spirits once every six days (according to the traditional six-day Beng calendar). They offer prayers, as well as sacrifices of palm wine, kola nuts, eggs, and domestic animals, on behalf of people who seek protection against witchcraft, relief from afflictions deemed to have a spiritual cause, or atonement for past sins. They also offer sacrifices on behalf of those who want to give thanks for wishes granted or good fortune experienced.

A divination may reveal that a given illness is being caused by ancestors feeling neglected by their living descendants, who may not be making the desired offerings. As elsewhere in Africa, Beng ancestors are incorporated into daily life. Most adult men and some adult women pray and make offerings (especially palm wine) to their ancestors regularly. For example, before drinking palm wine, beer, or commercial wine, people always spill a few drops onto the ground for their ancestors. Male and female clan heads also make regular offerings to the clan's ancestors on behalf of the entire clan.

Once people die, their souls, or *nining,* are said to become *wru,* or spirits, that travel to *wrugbe,* the land of the dead. As ancestral spirits, the *wru* lead full lives parallel to the daily lives of those on earth. Eventually, the ancestors are reincarnated into this life. All newborns are seen as having just emerged from *wrugbe;* sometimes their ancestral identities are revealed early in childhood.

The "manual" that follows is based on typical Beng village infant care practices. Some Beng mothers now living in towns and cities in Côte d'Ivoire try to replicate these practices in an urban setting. Other Beng women living in town return to the villages when they are pregnant or soon after delivering. Still others have begun to modify or even abandon the infant care practices of their grandmothers in favor of those deemed modern.

Like people in any society, individual Beng villagers offer a variety of perspectives on child rearing. The "manual" that follows highlights two perspectives that are particularly important in Beng villages: that of grandmothers, who tend to offer pragmatic/secular advice based on their years of child rearing and its exhausting labor demands; and that of diviners, who offer herbal cures as well as what might be called "pastoral counseling," based on their communication with the invisible spirits that populate Beng consciousness. However, the distinction between these two voices is not absolute. Diviners may themselves be grandmothers or mothers and offer pragmatic advice on occasion as well. Moreover, like all Beng adults, grandmothers are acutely aware of the spiritual aspects of infancy, even if they do not articulate the subtleties of this awareness as regularly and clearly as diviners do. It is a matter of explicit emphasis rather than of knowledge. Indeed, for Beng villagers, the religious and the mundane are not easily distinguished. The infant care practices that are described in the "manual" that follows illustrate that general principle.

For the "authors" of this "manual," I have constructed two personas who are modeled after individuals I have known in Beng villages. The fictional, non-literate grandmother I have created is inspired by many older Beng women who have shared their child-rearing expertise with me over the years. Her male counterpart, a young, semi-literate diviner, is modeled on a young man (whom I came to know well during my last stay in Bengland) who, despite his youth, was renowned throughout the region and beyond for his knowledge of the spirit world.

LURING YOUR CHILD INTO THIS LIFE

A Beng Path for Infant Care

About the Authors

A GRANDMOTHER

I have lived a long time. My white hair shows I have seen more than two days, and my children have had children; my grandson's wife is pregnant with my first great-grandchild. I have taken a belly nine times, nursed and bathed nine babies, painted nine babies' faces, carried nine babies on my back, made jewelry for nine babies, and kept nine babies from walking too early – and that doesn't include all the grandchildren, nieces, nephews, and neighbors' babies I have cared for. Only two of my little ones died during their first year; the other seven have survived.

Not all elders become wise – some merely become more foolish as they grow older. May our sky/god, *eci,* let me have learned something I can show you before I join the ancestors. Since I never attended school, I do not know paper; I have told what I know to one of my grandsons who has gone to school, and he has written down my words. Through him, I will show you how to raise your child.

A World of Babies

Everyone needs diviners. Most villages have at least one; even animals have the porcupine who wags its tail to answer their questions. We diviners reveal the other world to people of this world.

When I was born, our sky/god, *eci,* gave me the gift of speaking with the spirits. At three, I was already reading cowry shells – the spirits spoke to me through them. Even now, I am still young – my wife and I have only two children – but people often walk from faraway villages for me to show them who or what has harmed them and what they must do to cure their illnesses.

I went to school, but as for books, the rainwater didn't seep into my house – I didn't learn much because I had to leave after three years to help my father in the fields. So I have told my words to a schoolboy who has written them down. May *eci* let him know well the ways of paper.

🌸

SHOWING YOU THE BENG WAY

Since two of us are talking, we may sometimes show you different things to do. If you follow one of our recommendations and it doesn't help, try a suggestion that the other one offers. Better yet, do everything we both show you, and you will not go wrong.

In our villages, girls and women usually take care of babies, so we have addressed this manual to you. Still, we know that some boys and men like caring for babies. There is no shame in this – you too can learn much from these pages.

If you are Beng and were raised in a Beng village, you don't need this paper, for all your mothers – your own mother and her sisters – and indeed all the village's women will be your teachers. We have made this guide mostly for those Beng people who were born or raised in the city, or who have married a Beng person but are not themselves Beng. Wherever you live, it is important to preserve our ways. After all, if you are Beng, you will join our ancestors in *wrugbe* when you die; after staying there some time, you will be reborn –

perhaps into one of the villages. Besides, you know well how few Beng there are. If our children do not maintain our customs, our ways will vanish.

TAKING A BELLY

A Grandmother's Words

If yours was an arranged marriage, you already know that your first duty is to "take a belly" as soon as possible. At your wedding, people undoubtedly blessed you, "May *eci* make it right!" You probably realized that this meant you should have many children. If a few moons go by and you do not see signs of pregnancy, it may be because you are too hot. Try drinking some "raw medicine." Pound together some leaves, add some crumbly white clay to it, and drink the mixture cold. You can ask a healer to recommend good plants for this purpose. (If you married your husband in a love match, you probably won't feel in quite such a rush to take a belly to please your families.)

Once you become pregnant, you must observe many precautions. You should keep your breasts covered when you are walking around the village. If they are exposed, a jealous woman might bewitch you and make your childbirth difficult. Your hair must remain on your head – if you were to shave it off, as we do in mourning, you would die during childbirth.

As your belly swells, the skin becomes tight. If you can afford it, buy some shea butter in the market (or make it from kernels of the shea tree's fruits), and rub it on your belly to keep the skin nicely stretched. Don't wear tight shirts or your baby won't breathe properly.

Be careful not to eat fufu from large bananas or your baby will be too fat. Avoid eating meat from the bushbuck antelope with striped lines, or your baby will have striped or patchy skin. Do not eat purée of boiled yams or leftover foods; if you do, your labor will be difficult, and you will defecate during childbirth – a great embarrassment! Don't drink palm wine during the first few months or your pregnancy will be totally ruined.

While you are pregnant, you should give yourself special enemas every day. If you make an enema using the slippery and shiny leaves of the *vowló* vine, your placenta will be slippery too and will slide out quickly after the birth. If you don't know this plant, ask your mother or mother-in-law to show it to you in the forest, or send for it from a village relative if you are in the city.

If you remain in the village, you must bear in mind another risk. Never eat food while walking along the paths to your fields. Should you forget this, a forest snake may eat the crumbs that fall on the path and will develop a longing for human food. To continue feasting on our delicacies, the snake will switch places with the fetus inside you, and you will give birth to a snake-child. At first the baby may appear human, but as the diviner will explain, its true character will one day be exposed. May *eci* let you escape from this misfortune!

Be careful to stay far away from corpses of people and of dogs – both kinds are dangerous to the baby inside you. If you touched such a corpse, your baby would be born with the disease "Dog" or "Corpse." Just in case you might touch a corpse by mistake, bathe regularly with a decoction of leaves from the *wéé* plant – this should protect against the disease catching your fetus. (Even after birth, your baby will remain vulnerable – if you bring your little one to a funeral and your baby is very near the corpse, it might entice your baby back to *wrugbe.*) Still, if another pregnant woman dies from witchcraft while you are pregnant, you must join in her funeral. The funeral dance in which you must participate would be held outside in the courtyard of the woman who died, but it is really a secret women's dance. The women who dance wear nothing but the old-style bark cloth underwear, and no men or boys may watch.

But enough of such sad affairs. May *eci* grant that you never hear any rotten news! Let us turn to another subject. After you have taken a belly, your actions will determine your baby's character – try to be good so your child will have a good character too. If you steal something while you are pregnant, your child will develop the long arm of a thief; if you bewitch someone, your baby will become a witch. Don't set hunting traps – pregnancy is a time to nurture life, not take it. Try not to offend others. If someone is so angry that they invoke the Earth to curse you, your pregnancy is in jeopardy. You must immediately sacrifice an animal to the Earth to apologize; otherwise you will have grave difficulties during the delivery, truly!

64

Once you take a belly, you shouldn't return to an old boyfriend or take a new lover. If you do, you may suffer a miscarriage, and your lover will suffer for the next seven years. For his part, your husband must observe certain precautions. He should stop hunting, especially at night when it is difficult to see well, because he might kill a female animal that is pregnant. If that should happen, both you and the baby inside your belly would die! Even though the two worlds of people and animals are separated into village and forest, they remain connected; occasionally, they can even switch places. What happens to forest animals can affect what happens to you and the baby inside your belly.

You can continue to have sex with your husband throughout your pregnancy. Any position is fine as long as it is comfortable. Of course, toward the end of your pregnancy, side-by-side will probably be the only position possible. If you prefer not to make love, your husband should not insist.

If you and your husband argue and he threatens divorce, your family should tell him that whether it's good for him or it ruins him, he should remain with you until after the child is born; otherwise you would have a very difficult time during childbirth. For that matter, if you die during the birth, it is your husband who must offer sacrifices – if he has divorced you, who would present the offerings?

Giving birth is dangerous. In the old days, our ancestors had strong medicines to protect us against witchcraft, and we old people say it was rare for a woman to die while trying to give birth. Nowadays there are more witches who may threaten your pregnancy. If you are living in a village or small town and are afraid that someone may bewitch you during your delivery, earn or borrow some money so that before your eighth month you can take a bus to Bouaké or Abidjan to give birth in a doctor's room. May *eci* grant that you reach there safely! It will be difficult for the witches to find you so far away.

A Diviner's Words

If you are having trouble taking a belly, consult a diviner. If the seer throws cowry shells on a mat, one may land on top of another – a sign that you will become pregnant and will carry the baby on your back, just as one cowry shell is carrying another on its back. Two shells landing apart from the rest means you will become pregnant with twins. If the two cowries apart from the rest are stuck to one another, it signifies that there must be twins living in your family who have disrupted your menstrual cycle. All twins are witches, so you must offer the twins a sacrifice to ask their forgiveness. If they accept it, you will become pregnant.

Once you take a belly, before the seventh month of your pregnancy make sure that your husband sacrifices an egg to the Earth of your village. After receiving the sacrifice, the Earth will protect you and your baby through the pregnancy and delivery.

WHEN YOUR BELLY STARTS TO HURT

A Grandmother's Words

When your belly starts to hurt, your baby wants to be born. May *eci* let it be good for you! Tell someone in your compound, and some women in your husband's or your family will come to help. Sit on the floor with your legs outstretched, and one of your companions – preferably someone who is strong and not too old – will support you as you lean back. For your first birth, it's normal for you to be afraid; trust the older women in the room to tell you what to do.

Once the baby has been born, one of the women will cut the umbilical cord with a razor blade. Try to find a new one to use, as the nurses tell us that an old razor can cause "the serious disease" I will tell you about soon. Still, if a witch is determined to kill your child, she will do all she can to find other means.

Once the placenta is out, someone will announce the news around the village. At least one person from every household will soon be at your door. If you live in a large village, the line of well-wishers may be long! One by one they will bless you and ask, "What have you given me?" You can just reply, "A girl" or "A boy," and they will thank you. That way, everyone in the village will feel that they are part of your baby's life, and your newborn will feel welcome to the village.

Luring Your Child Into This Life

A Diviner's Words

If you are having trouble giving birth, may *eci* get you out of it! We diviners know some good herbal remedies. For instance, you should deliver soon after someone rubs the leaves of two particular plants between the palms of her hands and squeezes some of the water onto your head and some into your mouth, then rubs the rest onto your belly.

If you are still having trouble after such treatments, one of your or your husband's relatives should consult a diviner. We may diagnose that either you or a member of your mother's clan has sinned against the Earth. In this case, we will instruct someone in your family to make an offering, usually a chicken, to the Earth right away to apologize. Then the birth should proceed without problem. Or we may hear from the spirits that the baby inside you is not joining this world because no one is calling the baby by the right name – the name the baby wants. One woman I know was having a very difficult childbirth. The diviner said that spirits had named the baby Mo Jaa, and she was waiting to hear her name before coming out. When the women in the room called, "Mo Jaa, come out quickly!" the baby was born right away.

BEFORE THE UMBILICAL CORD STUMP FALLS OFF

A Grandmother's Words

Soon after the birth, if the breast water that will sustain your baby over the next year has not yet poured out, ask female elders of your village for leaves to lay on your breasts to make the water come in. If your breasts are also swollen, witchcraft is the cause. Some healers know other leaves you can heat and apply to your breasts to reduce the swelling.

Meanwhile, start doing *kami* right away. When the baby cries, before offering your breast, get a cupful of cool water from your large ceramic water jar. Cradle the baby in your arms, tilt the head back a little, and give a small palmful of the water. If your little one refuses the water, don't be shy to force it down the throat. You must teach your baby to like the taste of water. That way, when you can't be together – say, you're chopping trees for firewood or collecting water from the well – someone else can satisfy your hungry baby with plain water until you return with breastwater. You know how much work we women have to do, and we can't always take our babies along. If you don't train your baby to do *kami*, your life will be difficult!

A Diviner's Words

Right after the birth, the baby needs a very thorough bath. In the old days, the female head of your mother's clan would have washed your baby in a large wooden bowl; nowadays your mother might bathe the baby, using an enamel basin sold in the market. Remember that your new child has just been living in *wrugbe* with our ancestors, so your mother must wash off as much of *wrugbe* as possible. For the first bath, she should use homemade black soap – the kind we use for washing corpses. This makes sense, since newborns and the newly dead are both moving from one world to the next. (In future baths, you can use the white soap sold in the market.)

Following the first bath, your mother will wash out your baby's mouth with lemon juice; she may also attach a whole lemon to a cotton cord and tie this around your infant's tiny wrist as a bracelet. These, too, will help chase away death and will protect your baby from witches. The lemon is a powerful tree, helping us move from one world to the other and keeping us from the other world when it is not yet our time to go. (At a funeral, people also wear lemon bracelets to protect against witchcraft and death, and they wash corpses with leaves from the lemon tree.)

Your mother will bathe your baby four times a day until the umbilical cord stump falls off, which usually happens by the third or fourth day. To dry out the stump quickly, one of your mothers or grandmothers will dab a tiny bit of an herbal mixture on the dangling cord every few minutes all day long and even through the night. This is a tiresome task, but it is too important to neglect! Until the umbilical cord stump falls off, your newborn has not yet begun to become a person. The tiny creature is still living completely as a *wru* in the other world. If your newborn stops breathing during those first few days, we won't hold a funeral; having never left *wrugbe* at all, the baby hasn't really died.

WHEN THE UMBILICAL CORD STUMP FALLS OFF

A Grandmother's Words

The day that your baby's umbilical stump falls off, you and some female relatives will gather in your dark bedroom and give the baby the first enema. For your first child, your mother will teach you how to crush the leaves of the *kprawkpraw* plant together with a single chili pepper and some warm water, and then put the mixture inside a bulb-shaped gourd that we women grow for this purpose. With the little one lying across your knees, and a basin below, insert the gourd into your baby's bottom hole. You will hear some loud screams, for it is like breaking the hymen the first time a girl has sex. You remember how that hurt, don't you? Still, you will feel proud that you are starting to introduce your baby into this life, since we give ourselves enemas regularly all our lives. Indeed, from now until the baby walks, you *must* administer such an enema every morning and every night (though you can use a rubber bulb syringe sold in the market rather than the old-fashioned gourd). Usually the baby will shit into the basin as soon as you have removed the gourd.

A few hours after the first enema, your mother (or another older woman) will make the baby a simple necklace from savanna grass or the bark of a pineapple tree. After she puts the necklace around the baby, your mother may bless it by saying, "May *eci* let it never rip." Your baby will wear this necklace night and day. Only after this cord is attached can your little one begin to wear jewelry with beads, shells, and other ornaments. That very day, if your baby is a girl, a female elder can pierce her tiny ears, leaving a black cotton thread in the hole until it sets and you can use real earrings.

A Diviner's Words

The day that a baby's umbilical cord stump falls off is important, truly! It shows that your newborn has begun to leave *wrugbe*. As soon as the stump drops off, rub *nunu pléplé* leaves onto the spot.

Along with lemon trees, the leaves from this plant are used at funerals, where they chase away the smell – and contagion – of death. On your baby's belly button, they will help your baby leave the death of *wrugbe* behind. Still, you should know that this is a long, slow process that takes your child a few years to complete. One day you will know that your older children have left *wrugbe* forever when they tell you or your husband about a dream they had, saying that it was only a dream. But that may not happen until your child is older, maybe even six or seven years old.

Until then, your baby will miss certain things from the other life. You should consult a diviner as soon as possible to find out what these are! Our fees are not high – rarely more than fifty CFAs. This is far less than the price of a bus that you will pay going to the city clinic if your baby gets very sick because you did not consult a diviner!

We diviners have several methods. Some swirl milky-white water in a bowl; others dance. Me, I throw cowry shells on a bark cloth mat. Once I water my cowries, the spirits of the bush and the ancestors are drawn to the shells. Since your baby was just living in the other life, your little one can speak to these spirits, which also inhabit *wrugbe*. As I throw the cowries onto my mat, the spirits arrange the shells to speak for your baby, and I read their secrets from the patterns.

Usually we tell you to give a cowry to your baby as a first gift. This is because long, long ago, the cowry was money for our ancestors; it is still money in the other life, so the spirits of our ancestors all like them. Remember, your newborn was just living amongst the ancestors a few days ago, and a shell will remind your baby of that life in *wrugbe*. You can string the shell onto cotton thread that the baby can wear as a bracelet.

YOUR BABY'S NAME

A Grandmother's Words

No matter what your child is named, the baby's grandparents may want to be present for the naming. In the old days we named our babies for spirits in the rivers, hills, and other places. Nowadays, few parents do this. Depending on the day the baby was born, most parents just use the day names we have borrowed from our Baule neighbors. For example, if your daughter is born on a Tuesday, her name will be Ajua (for a boy, Kouadio). Keep in mind that our day ends at sundown, so if your baby is born after dusk, you must use the name of the day beginning that evening. If your daughter (or son) is born the same weekday that an older sister (or brother) was born, add *kro*, or "little," to the baby's day name and *kala*, or "big," to your older child's name. That way they won't both come when you call!

Each of the day names has a somewhat secret name – a "name underneath" – that goes with it. You will find good occasion to use this name with your child – for instance, if you are angry at your child for being naughty, or to calm down your child from being upset. But remember that even though the baby's "name underneath" is shared with all the other people who have that day name, we try to keep these names hidden. Only say it aloud to your child in your own compound, or it won't remain concealed for long! I won't divulge the names here – find out your baby's own "name underneath" from an older relative.

In addition to the day names, if you have twins, a girl will also be named Kolu or Klingo; a boy, Sã or Zi. If you have three daughters or three sons in a row, the third will be named Nguessan; if your next child is another daughter (or another son), the name will be Ndri. If two babies die one right after another, the next child born will be called Wamyã (for a boy) or Sunu (for a girl). With these names, wherever your children go in our world, people will know something about them.

In addition to our black people's names, some parents choose to give French names to their children. In truth, I don't know what these names mean or where they come from, so I can't say more about them. The teachers seem to like calling our children by these names in school. I suppose these names' time has come.

A Diviner's Words

If your baby is born the very same day that a grandparent dies, the little one should be named after that grandparent. Or your baby may be given the same name as a grandparent who is already in *wrugbe.* In both these cases, your baby is a replacement of the baby's grandparent, and many people will call the child Grandma or Grandpa.

Nowadays our naming system is not good. Many of our parents just assign day names without imagining who the baby was in *wrugbe.* This is not realistic! Everyone had another identity in the other life, and many babies prefer us to acknowledge that. Other babies are gifts of spirits and should be named after them, or the spirits will become angry. As I will explain, if you have chosen the wrong name, your baby may become very sick.

PROTECTING YOUR BABY AGAINST SICKNESS

A Grandmother's Words

As a mother, it is your responsibility to keep your baby healthy and find appropriate medicines for sicknesses. Should you neglect this duty, your husband may criticize you. If you are still living in your parents' house, your husband may hold a private family trial requesting that you return to his home so he can make sure you are giving the baby proper treatments.

We have many ways to protect our babies from falling ill. An important one is the long bathing routine. Once the umbilical cord has fallen off, you *must* bathe your baby twice a day – every day – until the child walks. Otherwise, the little one will come down with the very serious disease Dirt, which causes a bad Dirt Cough. This disease is not from the ordinary dirt that sticks to the skin when your baby lies or crawls on the ground; no, it is from another form of dirt that we can't see but that is much more dangerous. This is the dirt that comes from being held – or even touched briefly – by a man or woman who hasn't bathed in the morning after having had sex the night before. All grown people know that we must *always* bathe every morning so that if we had sex the night before, we will not bring the sickness of Dirt to babies we might touch that day. Shame on the person who forgets! Even after your baby is no longer vulnerable to this kind of dirt, keep the child accustomed to bathing twice every day so that as an adult your son or daughter will never forget to bathe the morning after having sex.

The next most important way to keep your baby healthy is to put many strands of jewelry onto the little one. Perhaps you have thought that all the necklaces, bracelets, and anklets that our babies wear are just to make them look beautiful. Some of our men think this! In truth, only a few of the necklaces and waist bands are meant just to embellish our babies; most are to protect them from diseases. I will tell you about some items of jewelry, but keep in mind that we have too many types for me to list them all here.

Your mothers and grandmothers may give you some beads and shells, and you can also buy beads in the market – though some are hard to find and expensive. Still, your baby should wear as many strands as possible – the more jewelry, the better protected against disease (Plate 6). For example, you can guard against Dirt by keeping a Dirt Cord on your baby, made with some of your own hair or from pineapple tree bark and some beads and knots. Don't worry that your baby might strangle from the necklaces – remember, the cords protect your baby, so they can't possibly cause harm.

Another danger to your baby's health is Full Moon. If a baby is caught by the bright light of a full moon, the little one's stomach will become quite round and swollen – like the full moon. At another time of the month, the disease Bird can catch your little one if a rotten bird (such as an owl or a vulture) flies overhead on the night of a new moon. This is even more serious – your child's neck may break and bend backwards, the body will become cold, the elbows stiff, and the eyes white.

You may wonder why the new moon and the full moon – the beginning and end of the moon's cycle – are dangerous to babies. Perhaps it is because babies occupy the beginning and end of our own cycle – the beginning of their stay in this life and the end of their stay in *wrugbe*. Fortunately, a waist band can protect your baby against both Bird (from the new moon) and Full Moon. Make it by tying together a black cord (like the black of a new moon night) and a white cord (like the light of a full moon).

Danger is also associated with daily cycles. One form of fever that can kill your baby quickly is caused by touching dew, which is too powerful for babies. Dew of course appears at the beginning and end of the day (before dawn and after dusk) – a bit like babies themselves, who also occupy the beginning and end of our life's

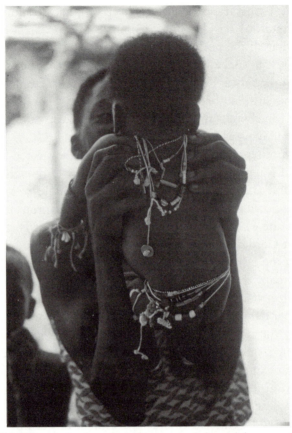

Plate 6. This Beng mother has adorned her young baby with home-made jewelry – necklaces, bracelets, and anklets – to protect the child from disease. This little girl is wearing so many items because she has been sick very often. Photograph by Alma Gottlieb.

cycle. If you put a cotton Dew Cord around your little one's knees or ankles, and maybe running up the shins, the child will be well protected from dew touching a leg on the way to the fields early one morning or late one evening.

All the jewelry I have described must be as clean as your baby's body. Every morning and evening, after you wash your baby's skin, carefully clean each strand with soap, then squeeze the moisture out with a towel. By this time your baby might be very hungry from not having nursed for a while and may start to cry or pull on your breast.

But don't rush washing the jewelry – it must be done properly! As you scrub the jewelry, inspect each strand – if it is frayed, repair it right away, otherwise the beads may fall off and your baby, no longer protected, could fall sick. One of your mothers can show you how to retie the complicated knots.

You can also protect your baby by painting brightly colored medicines onto the face and head (Plate 7). Many babies have an orange dot on their fontanel, which is the end point of a head road that runs down to the throat. If the path becomes blocked, the throat will close, the baby won't be able to nurse or eat well, and the little one may develop a fever or cough. Keep your baby's head road open by painting an orange dot on the baby's fontanel during every morning and evening bath. Make the orange paint by chewing a red kola nut, then spitting out your saliva – which will be bright orange – onto your finger. The kola is a powerful fruit – in the old days it was trading kola nuts that gave us our wealth. Keep applying this orange kola water twice every day until your child starts to walk. At

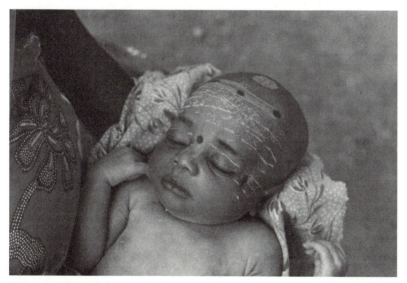

Plate 7. A Beng baby with her face beautifully painted by her mother. Beng mothers paint elaborate designs such as these on their babies' faces every day. Photograph by Alma Gottlieb.

this time, the head road will close up and your little one will no longer be at risk.

In addition to these ways we have for keeping our babies healthy, white people have some useful customs too. Every so often, vans of nurses show up in our villages to inject us with medicines. My school-girl granddaughter tells me that if a woman gets one of those shots, any baby in her belly will be protected against the "difficult disease" that the white people call tetanus. But truly, it takes a lot of courage to line up with your children for the shots. The nurses shout orders in French, and who can understand them? Besides, you have to pay for the needle, and if you don't have a medical record notebook, you'll need to buy one from the nurses. You'd better start saving now!

A Diviner's Words

There is another thing you can do to keep your baby healthy. If your husband offered an egg to the Earth while you were pregnant, this has created a debt. Soon after the baby is born, you or your husband should offer another sacrifice to the Earth – this time, it must be a chicken – as thanks for having protected the baby while still inside your belly. With this second sacrifice, the Earth will continue to watch over your baby.

WHEN YOUR BABY GETS CAUGHT BY SICKNESS

A Grandmother's Words

May *eci* let your baby be healthy! Alas, our babies fall sick quite often. The nurses say it is because of our water and all the insects around us. But we know that a witch will find ways to cause some-one harm no matter how clean the water or how few the insects.

If your baby falls sick, go see a healer. Our healers know many health-giving plants that can cure illnesses. Even the poorest among us can pay a healer. Of course, if the healer is a relative, you won't pay anything.

If your baby's body is hot, one of your mothers can tell you about plants that can bring down the fever. After bathing your baby, lay some leaves on the embers of your hearth fire to wilt them. After a few moments, rub them between your hands to squeeze out their water, then pat the leaf water over your baby's warm body.

If a carrier of the contagious disease Dirt touches your baby, soap will never wash it off. Instead, try bathing your baby with leaves from the *vowlo* liana, which are quite slippery – maybe the disease will slide off the baby. The disease itself is so powerful that you should bathe your baby five or six times a day with this leaf wash. Collect a fresh bunch in the forest for each bath. This disease will keep you very busy! Try and find someone to weed or sow your fields, chop wood, and haul water for you, so your work is not neglected. Another dangerous sickness you can treat with medicinal plants is Corpse. Leaves that touched death can cure your baby if the little one has touched a dead body. If your baby son is caught by Corpse, go to any woman or girl's grave and take some leaves of any plant growing on top. If your baby daughter is sick, have your husband do the same with the grave of any man or boy. Then make a leaf wash that may cure your baby.

Sometime during the first two to three weeks, your newborn may start crying very loudly. If the screams continue and become sharper, the little one's tiny arms and legs get stiff, the back arches, and the baby seems truly miserable, this may be the "difficult disease" (the one white people call "tetanus"). Unfortunately, there is little hope. If you are rich, you can take your baby to the hospital, but the medicines you'll have to buy may still cost more money than you've ever seen. You'll probably need to borrow money from a lot of relatives for the medicines and the bus trip for yourself and one of your mothers or your husband. Plus, the doctor will tell you to stay nearby for a few days to make sure the baby is better before returning home, so you'll have to buy a lot of expensive food in the market. You may also be humiliated by a nurse showing off by speaking French, even if you clearly don't understand a word. If he makes fun of village remedies like the jewelry protecting your baby, ignore it and ask for his medicines. The worst part is that after you endure humiliation and spend maybe a year's earnings, the doctor will tell you that, at best, only half the babies he treats with his medicines survive the "difficult disease." *Aiie,* perhaps after all, it's better for you to save your money to feed and clothe the rest of your family.

Aside from all I've said so far, there may be days when your baby will cry for no obvious reason. It may be that she's not sleeping enough. You know that babies like to fall asleep on someone's back. If you have some work to do in your faraway fields way deep in the forest (or in another section of town, if you live in a city), tie your baby onto your back with your *pagne* cloth and start walking – your baby will sleep well on your back as you walk.

If, despite all your efforts, your baby keeps crying, it's time to consult a diviner.

A Diviner's Words

Remember, babies have just come from the land of the dead, where they were someone else. The younger your baby, the more the little one is still living and thinking with our ancestors, especially the baby's *wrugbe* parents. If *eci* agrees, your baby will leave *wrugbe* behind some day. But this won't happen right away, for babies still hear the language of the other world, and it calls to them. Your little one may miss *wrugbe* and be eager to return. Falling sick or crying is a way to tell you something – what the baby is missing, who the baby was in *wrugbe* – but like most adults, you probably can't understand. When you consult a diviner, your baby will speak to the spirits of the bush and of *wrugbe*; the spirits will then speak to the diviner, who will interpret their words for you.

The diviner may hear from the spirits that the little one is unhappy with the name you have chosen and prefers another one – perhaps the name the baby had while in *wrugbe*, or the name of the spirit who gave you your baby. Offer gifts to these spirits every so often to keep them happy, or they will make your baby sick again. For instance, if your baby was given to you by the Anie spirits that live in one of our sacred pools of water, put some fresh water into a calabash every so often as an offering to those spirits, and call your baby Anie.

In addition to being misnamed, your sick or crying baby may be trying to tell you about some things from *wrugbe* that are missed. Young babies especially miss cowry shells, old French coins, and silver jewelry – the treasures they had while in *wrugbe*. We might recommend a single shell or coin on a necklace, or lots of cowries strung together on a bracelet. In giving your baby this jewelry, you will be showing that you respect your child's memories and desires. As soon as you provide the jewelry and begin using the name the child wants, your little one should stop crying and return to good health. That will show you that we diviners speak the truth!

Another way your child may fall sick is if you, your husband, or someone in your families has violated one of the Earth's taboos and has not yet offered a sacrifice as apology. This is very serious. The Earth may remind you of your debt by making your baby sick. The diviner will tell you what to offer the Earth to apologize. Buy the egg, chicken, or palm wine right away so that you don't delay your child's recovery. Remember, once they fall sick, babies can die quickly.

IF YOUR BABY DIES

A Grandmother's Words

I know it is sad to contemplate, but in our world it is likely that you will bury at least one of your children, perhaps more. Twin babies are especially vulnerable. For example, if a visitor thoughtlessly remarks that one twin is larger than the other, the smaller twin will be very insulted and decide to return to *wrugbe*. If your baby dies, the body will be buried in a muddy patch behind your home. I am sure you and your husband will be too upset to attend the burial.

If this is the first of your children to die, there will be a special *fewa* funeral. Before being buried, your baby's body will be laid out on many layers of special cloths. You and your husband must stay for three or four days in a newly built house without coming out at all, except to go to the bathroom. While you are in the house, two or three ritual specialists will sit with you. These women have paid dearly for their knowledge – to gain the secret information they now possess about how to do a *fewa* funeral, they each had to bewitch a pregnant or laboring woman in their family, whose soul they sold to the ritual specialists who taught them! You should respect them, for power is on them. The oldest among them will sleep in the same

79

room with you and your husband, and for two or three nights, you and your husband must have sex in front of her. If the baby died just a short time after being born, sex will be very uncomfortable for you, but you have no choice.

After this, the old woman will take you and your husband into the forest. There, she will shave the hair on your heads and bodies, wash you with special medicines, and put mourning jewelry on you both. Many other things will happen that I cannot reveal. People who haven't gone through *fewa* themselves can't approach you during these rituals, or their own children – current or future – will be at risk!

Nowadays, some people, especially Christians or Muslims, don't want to bother with this ritual. They say it is too difficult, too humiliating. Shame on them!

A Diviner's Words

There are many reasons that babies die. One is that the mother has not consulted a diviner to discover who the baby was in *wrugbe* or what the baby misses from there. Such babies are so sad that they decide to return to the other world. Another reason is that you are mistreating your baby. If you don't nurse your baby enough or seek good medicines when the baby is sick, your child's *wrugbe* parents will call their suffering one back. Still another reason is that the Earth may be punishing you. For example, you know that when you first married, you were supposed to ritually confess the names of any lovers you had before your husband; if you covered up a name or two, the Earth may kill your baby unless you offer the proper sacrifice. Consult a diviner right away to find out what you should offer the Earth.

If you are unlucky enough to have two babies in a row die, one of them may take pity on you and will return during your next belly as a "Sunu" (if the baby is a girl) or "Wamyā" (if a boy). Sunus and Wamyās are pleased if their mother pats mud over their body every so often, to remind them of the muddy patch in which they had been buried after dying in their previous life.

If your child dies, it may comfort you to remember that the younger the baby, the more the little one was still living in *wrugbe*. Indeed, if the umbilical cord hadn't fallen off yet, the baby hadn't even begun to leave the land of the ancestors, and the village chief won't announce a funeral. If the umbilical cord *has* fallen off, you must wait until the chief announces the funeral to the village before you start to cry.

GOING BACK TO WORK

A Grandmother's Words

For the first two or three months after the birth, you can relax while your mother and other relatives pamper you. Your major job is to nurse and bathe your new one. I always tell mothers to stay a full three months at home, but nowadays women often rush back to their farms after only two months. Start slowly – at first only one or two half-days a week in your fields, then three or four half-days. If you start back working full-time too early, you won't recover properly from the delivery.

All this will be much easier if you find yourself a *leng kuli* – a baby carrier – to care for your baby when you are busy. This is especially important if you have other young children and are living in the village. Your *leng kuli* can carry your child when you walk to the fields balancing a heavy load of crops, farm tools, cooking pots, or firewood on your head. While you're working, she can take care of the baby in the fields, and you'll only need to stop working every so often to nurse.

Try asking an older daughter, a younger sister, or a niece to be your *leng kuli*. If you can't find a relative, look around the village or neighborhood. To interest someone, make sure the baby looks beautiful! After the morning bath, apply your baby's face paints carefully – draw the green medicine lines across the little forehead and down your baby's nose as straight as possible; and chew a kola nut well before spitting out the juice to make sure it's a bright orange for the dot over your baby's soft spot. In addition to the medicine jewelry that your mother has given you or the diviner has prescribed, add a few other items for beauty – a belt of shiny green beads, an anklet of bells. Rub shea butter all over your baby's skin after the bath. The skin will glow, showing off your baby's beads, shells, and bright face paints to great advantage. If your baby is irresistibly beautiful, someone will be eager to carry her for a few hours; if you're lucky, she might offer to be a regular *leng kuli.*

Even a seven- or eight-year-old can be a good baby carrier. Make sure you show her how to tie the baby onto her back firmly with your *pagne* cloth. Of course, if she's young, she won't be able to carry the baby for too long, but at least your little one will get a lot of short naps. If your *leng kuli* does a good job, after a few months you can buy her a pair of earrings at the market. At the end of a year, buy her a dress if you have the money. Then she'll be happy to go on being your *leng kuli* for another year.

AS YOUR BABY DEVELOPS

A Grandmother's Words

It's important to watch for signs that your baby is developing properly. Several steps are especially significant.

Teething

Babies should not be born with teeth! If your baby *is* born with a tooth, this is a bad omen – the baby is in a rush to leave *wrugbe,* and therefore in a rush to trade places with an elder in this life. In the old days, we asked a female elder to drown such a newborn.

When your baby starts to cut the first tooth, pray that it comes through as a lower tooth. If your baby cuts an upper tooth first, this is also a bad omen. In the old days we would drown such a baby as well, or else someone in the baby's family would die.

Nowadays, we don't kill such babies, for we know we could go to jail if the gendarmes heard about it. We just worry and look to see who in the family will die.

Walking

When your baby starts to crawl, you'll be proud, for this is the beginning of learning how to walk. But you must discourage the baby from walking until a full year in this life. (The diviner may show you why this is so important.) You may need to keep the child strapped to someone's back as much as possible, and your husband may have to spank the baby for trying to walk too early. If your child is still determined to walk before the first birthday, string a *lagba* bead onto a cord and tie it around the baby's waist. With this powerful belt, your baby should just sit still.

Nowadays, some young parents don't listen to their elders, and they allow their babies to walk early. Some even look for medicines to *encourage* early walking! Perhaps they are trying to be modern. I hope you don't listen to these people.

On the other hand, if your baby is over a year old but has not yet started walking, you will want to make every effort to find proper medicines to encourage those first steps. After all, having sex is absolutely forbidden for you until your baby can walk properly! This restraint is important to protect your child. If you become pregnant before your baby learns to walk, the new one in your belly will steal breastwater from your baby. The baby will never learn to walk properly, and eventually the poor child will die. If you have a co-wife, it won't be so difficult for your husband to wait until your baby walks before having sex with you. I am sorry to say this, but if you have no co-wives, it would be better for your husband to visit a prostitute than to bother you.

Your Listening and Talking Baby

You will probably talk to your baby from the first day of life in this world. When your baby cries, as you offer a breast, you will look into the little one's eyes and say, "Shush! What's the matter? I'm sorry!" or other such phrases. Doubtless you have seen many mothers talk like this from their babies' first days in this world.

When your baby is a little older, it's important to teach the words for all the relatives. Your baby won't be able to say our elaborate greetings properly until learning this, since we always address each other as Uncle, Big Sister, Little Mama, and so on when we greet anyone. And you know how important it is to say hello to almost everyone in the village every morning and evening to show that we are all part of the community.

After learning to greet politely, the next thing your baby must learn is how to tease certain relatives by tossing dirty names at them. Anyone your little one calls Grandma and Grandpa – not just your parents and your husband's parents, but all their sisters and brothers as well – will tease your baby son by calling him jokingly, "Shit prick!" "Red prick!" "Raw shit scrotum!" or your daughter, "Shit cunt!" "Black cunt!" "Tiny cunt!" Your child will soon learn that this is all in good fun, and you should teach the little one to engage in the repartee by laughingly shouting back dirty insults. There is nothing cuter than a one-and-a-half-year-old shrieking out with delight, "You red balls!" to her doddering grandfather or "You black asshole!" to his old grandmother. Later, when you become much stricter with your children, it will be a comfort to them to have such a relaxed and teasing relationship with their grandparents. They may even seek refuge with them if you chastise or punish them too severely one day.

A Diviner's Words

Some children's character comes from who they were in their last life. For instance, Wamyās and Sunus are sad a lot. Having died as a baby in a previous life, they can foretell a death. If a Wamyā or Sunu appears sorrowful, gets angry easily, or even hits people for no reason, don't be too harsh, or the child may decide to return to *wrugbe*. Remember, the bad behavior you are seeing is simply a sign that your son or daughter is distressed from secretly knowing that someone will soon leave this life for *wrugbe*.

Walking

Grandmother has already warned you that your baby must not walk before the end of the first year. Now I will explain why. As you know, babies are reincarnations of our ancestors. With souls crossing back and forth every day between this world and *wrugbe*, babies and elders are closely connected. They both have only a fragile hold on this life, and it's easy for one to replace the other. An infant who walks before a year walks on the spirit of one of his or her grandparents, and that elder will soon pass to the other world.

As Grandmother mentioned, you must also make sure that your baby doesn't start to walk too late. If your baby does not begin to take some steps soon after a year, it may be because you and your husband started having sex before the baby began to walk. Forbidden sex can cause a very serious condition that we call "split leg," which can prevent a child from ever walking. If this could be your child's problem, you'd better consult a diviner who can pre-scribe the right remedies, or your child will soon depart this world.

On the other hand, if your baby is slow not just in walking, but in other ways as well – perhaps not talking on time – it may be that you committed a serious violation while pregnant. If you ate food while walking along the path to your fields in the forest, your child may actually be a snake. If so, there is no treatment; the child will never be human. If you can afford it, consult a specialist who can offer what appears to be medicine, but is really snake food, to your child in a secret ritual in the forest. If your child ignores the food, it probably means that your son or daughter is actually human, and there is some other reason accounting for developing so slowly. But if the medicine seems delicious, your baby will eat the food and immediately start turning back into a snake, which will slither off into the forest. If you're lucky, the creature won't return the next time you take a belly, and you'll give birth to a person. If you suspect your baby may be snake, you should do this ritual as soon as possi-ble. The longer you wait, the more the ritual specialist will charge, and the harder it is for the medicine to take effect – in the end, you may be left with a snake-child. The creature will never have a fam-ily, for who would marry a snake?

Your Listening and Talking Baby

In *wrugbe,* unlike life in this world, different groups of people live together and understand each other's languages. When a *wru* is reborn into this life, the baby remembers all the languages that were spoken in *wrugbe.* For this reason, your baby will grasp everything that you – or anyone speaking any language – says. As your baby starts to leave the afterlife and join this world, the memory of all those languages will start to fade. Eventually, your child will under-stand only the languages he or she hears in this life.

Until then, your baby understands everything anyone says, so talking may help lure your little one into this life. If you look your baby in the eyes and speak softly, your child will probably babble something back. Doubtless you and everyone else around will delight in such sounds. You should teach your baby to talk real words by speaking *for* him or her. For example, if someone asks the baby, "How are you?" you can hold up the child and answer, "Yes, I'm fine." After a few months of this, your little one will be able to join in conversations.

At the same time, you should train your baby not to interrupt adults' speech, since children must respect their elders. If your baby is interrupting your conversation with another adult, even with adorable noises, you must say firmly, "Stop talking!"

On the other hand, if your very young infant utters a real word or two in Beng or any other language we know, this would be a very bad omen. While babies understand all languages, they *speak* only the language of *wrugbe*. Speaking a language of this world would be a sign that your little baby has already left *wrugbe* completely to enter this world far too early. This is bad – a grandparent will soon die.

TOILET TRAINING

A Grandmother's Words

You and your mothers began to toilet train your baby the day the umbilical cord fell off, and I assume you've continued to give your baby an enema twice a day, every day, since then. By the time the little one is a few months old, you shouldn't have to worry about pooping during the day at all, as long as your baby stays healthy. This is good – then you can give your baby to a *leng kuli* without worry that the baby carrier's clothes will be soiled as she carries the baby, for this would be a great shame on you! Later, when your son or daughter is walking, you can show your child the places we have in the forest for shitting. When you teach your child about wiping with a dried corn cob, emphasize how important it is to use the left hand, *never* the right.

As for urine, it really doesn't matter where a little baby pees – if someone's lap gets wet, they'll just hold up their clothes to let the urine drip off. Once your baby can walk well, you can show the little one to pee anywhere on the village outskirts.

Luring Your Child Into This Life

WHEN TO HAVE ANOTHER BABY

You may be considering how many children to have, but *eci* is the one who decides this. We old women do have secret methods to keep from getting pregnant, but ordinarily they are not for young women with only a few children, so I won't divulge them here.

However, if you have one difficult pregnancy or childbirth after another, a witch may be trying to kill you – perhaps she has sworn a pact to bewitch a pregnant woman in the clan as an entrance fee into one of the women's secret ritual associations. Until she kills another pregnant or laboring woman in your mother's clan, your own pregnancies will not be safe. In this case, do anything you can not to become pregnant again for a while – you can even try to find out about the new methods available in the cities.

AS YOUR CHILD GROWS UP

A Grandmother's Words

As your baby grows, teach the child that being young means having no authority over anyone except those who are even younger. Remember that in our language, one word for "child" really means "little slave." As soon as the little one can walk confidently, don't hesitate to send your child on errands in your village or neighborhood. Even two-year-olds should be able to find their way to Grandma's and Little Mama's houses and back again.

Sending your toddler on an errand – say, to tell your sister you'll carry her baby tomorrow or to give a dish of palm nut sauce to your mother – will accomplish many significant things. Your child will get to know many people early on. This is the most important thing, since our lives are always filled with people. It will especially help the little one learn who is who in the family. For instance, when you tell your child to bring a dish to one of your husband's younger brothers or male cousins, refer to him just as Little Father, but provide hints – the Little Father who lives next to so-and-so, or who has light skin, or who is short. In this way, the baby should soon understand which of the many Little Fathers in the family you mean.

A World of Babies

From doing errands, your child will also become familiar with the neighborhood; by three at the latest, your little one should be able to navigate anywhere in the village (or your *quartier,* if you live in a city). Then, your child will feel confident to join in the groups of children who play together, roaming far and wide around the village or neighborhood when they aren't working for their parents. And of course you will gain a helper − a great boon, considering how much work we women have to do!

A FINAL WORD ABOUT GOOD MOTHERS AND BAD MOTHERS

A Grandmother's Words

Being a good mother isn't something that comes naturally to every woman. Almost all of us will bear children, but that doesn't mean we must raise them. If you show tendencies toward being a bad mother, consider giving your children to others who are more fit for the job. Perhaps your sister is an especially good mother − give her one or more of your sons or daughters to raise with her own. Your and your sister's children are sisters and brothers anyway, not cousins, so this isn't a matter of adoption. If you turn out to be bad at mothering but don't acknowledge it, your relatives and neighbors will let you know. If you beat your children too much, one of your husband's relatives is bound to take the children. Even a frail but loving grandmother is better for children than a vigorous but mean-spirited mother.

Still, being a good mother isn't really difficult or complicated. Of course, you have to make enough money to buy what's necessary for your children. You'll need plenty of soap to bathe them twice a day, and if you buy cooking oil, salt, and occasionally a fish or piece of meat, your children will appreciate your tasty sauces. Other than that, if you are kind, it is enough. Even a madwoman in one of our villages is a good mother, because she manages to feed and bathe her children. If she can raise her children well, you probably can too.

Luring Your Child Into This Life

A Diviner's Words

Bad mothers do not consider that their babies have *nining* – souls that come from another life. These mothers don't consult a diviner to discover the lives that their babies were leading in *wrugbe*. As I've been telling you all along, when your baby emerges from your belly, the little one is leaving behind a life lived elsewhere with another set of parents – in a place that is invisible to you but that your baby can describe to the spirits, who can then describe it to us diviners. One of your main responsibilities is to figure out who your baby is and what your baby misses from *wrugbe*. This is so important, I can't remind you enough times! If you consult a diviner regularly about your growing child, you'll be a good mother.

Everything I've told you, I've learned from the spirits. Have I lied?

CHAPTER 4

Gift from the Gods

A Balinese Guide to Early Child Rearing

Marissa Diener

BALI

Bali, one of the approximately 6,000 occupied islands that constitute the tropical nation of Indonesia, is far better known to the West than are most of Indonesia's other islands. The small but densely populated island (approximately 2.8 million residents) constitutes less than half of 1 percent of the entire nation's population.

Bali's tumultuous political history is known from written records of a series of dynasties dating back to the ninth century A.D. The island's past is strongly intertwined with that of its much larger neighbor, Java; over the centuries, the two islands have frequently been united under the same leader or kingdom. From the fifth century on, traders, priests, and adventurers sailing from India and China brought to Bali and Java a variety of Hindu and Buddhist ideas and practices that were adapted and assimilated into Balinese culture.

Europeans first encountered Bali in the late sixteenth century, during the era of European exploration of the seas and massive expansion of world trade networks. Dutch sailors landed in 1597, inaugurating Dutch involvement in the region's economy that eventuated in a brutal conquest of the islands that became the Dutch East Indies. During the second half of the nineteenth century, as the Dutch gradually obliterated the royal Balinese courts, the Balinese actively resisted the colonizing force. The Dutch completed their conquest of the remaining independent region on Bali in 1908.

During World War II, the Dutch East Indies was occupied by Japan. At the end of the war, led by nationalist leader Sukarno, Indonesia declared independence, an act that the Dutch first resisted with violence but reluctantly recognized in 1949. Sukarno's rule was marked by poverty and chaos, and in 1967 he was ousted by a military regime led by General Suharto. Backed by the United States, the Suharto regime was able to underwrite improvements in basic health care, food, housing, and education, thanks to rapid economic growth based largely on an oil boom. However, Indonesia's economy later plunged into crisis amidst rampant corruption and nepotism, and Suharto resigned in May 1998.

Bali is divided into eight districts, which correspond to former kingdoms. Villages within the districts contain one or more organizational units called *banjar,* of which there are approximately 4,200. The most important role of the *banjar* is to oversee death ceremonies for *banjar* members. *Banjar* also serve other purposes, such as in weddings and various political activities. Indeed, the Dutch colonial regime and then Suharto attempted to turn the *banjar* into efficient units of administration. Members construct and maintain *banjar* property, such as roads, buildings, and temples. The head of a *banjar* passes on central governmental information and directives to the community, and the *banjar* are called upon to enforce governmental laws, settle disputes, and decide upon punishment for wrongdoers in the community. However, the *banjar* also endeavor to maintain a certain level of autonomy and in some cases refuse to follow government directives that conflict with local practices.

Traditionally, the local economy of Bali was based largely on agriculture. Rice cultivation dominates agriculture; bananas, coconuts, and other fruit are also grown as subsistence crops, and coffee, tobacco, oranges, and assorted vegetables are grown as cash crops. Men are generally responsible for plowing and preparing the fields and caring for cattle, whereas women care for household gardens and pigs and may keep snack stalls at village markets. Men and women generally do the manual planting and harvesting together, in large groups. Nowadays, however, more and more Balinese work in government-run schools and offices and other places of paid labor. Tourism, including craft production, is becoming a major source of household income, and in some areas it dominates the economy.

Most Balinese live in villages centered around temples and public buildings. People who have moved to cities in Bali often return to the village in which they were born, to visit and to continue participating in village activities and rituals. Most villages have a market for selling and buying vegetables, fruits, pigs, chickens, and other foods as well as goods such as incense. Larger towns also have markets, as well as goldsmiths, tailors, and other merchants.

Upon marriage, a woman goes to live with her new husband's family. Family planning efforts by the government are resulting in smaller families than previously. Extended families still live together in fenced houseyards that contain several buildings, including the family temple, sleeping and sitting pavilions, a kitchen, and a refuse area where pigs are kept. Houseyards and buildings within villages are arranged so that the temples are nearest Mount Agung, an active volcano on the island thought to be the dwelling place of the gods, while the kitchen and pigsty are placed nearest the sea.

A system of social ranking imported to Bali from India, where it had its roots in the caste system, has been modified to accommodate local Balinese realities. The Balinese version includes four hierarchically ranked social groups, with the lowest-ranked group comprising the majority of the island's population. The rank of a given person is made explicit in all conversations; for example, members of a higher ranked group must be addressed by a title conveying respect by anyone of lower rank. The four groups continue to play important roles today in determining people's marriages, for wives should not rank higher than their husbands. Children generally inherit their fathers' rank (though certain circumstances may permit exceptions). However, the ranking system is somewhat fluid, and many in the lowest-ranked group are now quietly challenging their place in the system by such means as claiming ancestry in one of the two top-ranked groups.

Ninety-five percent of the population of the island practices Balinese Hinduism (although Indonesia is overwhelmingly Muslim).

This version of Hinduism has been influenced both by Buddhism and by indigenous religious practices, such as ancestor worship and the giving of offerings to local spirits. The central tenets of Balinese Hinduism include the beliefs that every act has consequences and that one's soul is reincarnated after each death until a perfect life is attained and one's soul is unified with god. Children are believed to be gifts from the gods and are very highly valued in Balinese society.

Religious rituals are central to Balinese daily life. Cremation is particularly important: The ceremony purifies the soul, which may have accumulated impurities through evil deeds committed during present or past lives. After being purified, the soul can then be released to merge with the ancestors and a god known as Betara Guru. Eventually it is reincarnated into a new family member.

Balinese believe that if rituals are neglected, family members may become ill or suffer misfortune. In some cases, even the entire village might endure disasters such as drought or epidemics. Thus, in addition to the many village temples, each family's living area has a temple in which daily offerings are made to show gratitude toward benevolent beings such as gods and ancestors and to placate demons so they will not cause harm. Religious rituals are considered important enough that children may stay home from school and adults may stay home from work in order to participate in them. Ceremonies generally include many people, ranging from extended families to members of the *banjar*. Some public ceremonies, such as cremations of high-ranking persons, are open to the entire island of Bali and may attract thousands of observers, including many tourists (Plate 8). Both men and (to a somewhat lesser extent) women serve as priests; women are also responsible for preparing offerings used in the ceremonies.

Every Balinese person belongs to several dozen temples, each of which is devoted to a particular concern such as agricultural fertility, irrigation, death, or political loyalty. Certain days are deemed auspicious for holding religious ceremonies. Two different calendars that the Balinese use to count time – a 12-month lunar calendar and a 210-day cycle – both contain auspicious days for ceremonies, as well as inauspicious days on which certain activities should not take place. For example, every 210 days each temple celebrates a "birthday" commemorating the day it was consecrated. At this time,

Plate 8. This Balinese mother and her baby are on their way to an islandwide festival on Kuningan Day – the day the spirits and ancestors return to heaven from a temporary visit on Earth. Religious rituals and ceremonies are central to Balinese life. Photograph by Marissa Diener.

the gods that are worshiped at the temple are said to enter figurines in the temple, where they remain for three days before returning to their homes on Mount Agung. The temple members welcome and then send off the gods with ritualized dancing and music played by a gamelan orchestra.

The aesthetic impulse is well developed in many arenas of Balinese life, including religion but going well beyond; indeed, art permeates Balinese life. Tourists flock to Bali to experience the renowned dances, paintings, dramas, shadow plays, and gamelan orchestras performing music on Balinese xylophones, drums, gongs, and flutes. In some areas of Bali, people are also skilled in gold and silver work, woodcarving, and the manufacture of ritual objects such as musical instruments and masks.

During the last few decades, the government has developed a Western educational system, and primary school attendance is now nearly universal. All education is conducted in the national language of Bahasa Indonesian (although the Balinese also speak their own language). The influence of Western schools and other imports notwithstanding, many child-rearing practices recorded earlier in the century are still observable, especially those concerning infants and young children.

For the "manual" that follows, I propose as the fictive author a male healer, or *balian,* who is trained in traditional Balinese healing arts to cure diseases of both physical and spiritual origins.

GIFT FROM THE GODS

A Balinese Guide to Early Child Rearing

About the Author

I have written this manual because I am a healer, or *balian*. My family is high-ranking, and I have learned to read and write. My father and grandfather were well respected for their knowledge of the spiritual world. They learned what they know by studying the sacred palm-leaf manuscripts – our teachings written in the Balinese script, which developed from writing systems of southern India. Some healers learn their skills from a dream or vision, or they serve as an apprentice to a teacher. I am fortunate to have inherited my knowledge from my ancestors.

As a *balian*, I understand many problems. I can treat illnesses caused by what Westerners consider physical factors, such as infection; but I can also treat illnesses caused by invisible factors, such as spirits, demons and witches, sins of ancestors, and actions of gods. Therefore, in this manual I will offer advice about both physical and mental well-being – which are, in any case, inseparable.

YOU'RE GOING TO HAVE A BABY

Congratulations, expectant mother, on the upcoming birth of your child! This manual will help you prepare for the birth and provide suggestions for child rearing. You will find it especially useful if you are a first-time mother. A single manual cannot contain all the knowledge that many generations of caretakers have acquired, so use this manual as a supplement, not a substitute, for talking about child rearing with family, friends, and a *balian*.

It is wonderful that you are becoming a parent, for your children will be a source of great joy to you, your husband, and your families. There are many other rewards of parenthood. By providing a family for your husband, you show yourself to be a good wife. Had your marriage been childless, your husband might have divorced or left you. If this is your first child, you will find that parenthood changes your political status. Your husband will have more influence in the hamlet and in the irrigation societies, temple congregations, and other organizations to which he belongs.

Sons and grandsons are especially important, for they are responsible for performing the cremation ceremony and purification rituals that will allow your soul to be liberated upon your death. Also, your children will take care of you when you are older, and they will be responsible for keeping up your houseyard temple. Neglecting the worship of one's ancestors at the houseyard temple invites disaster: Family members might quarrel or become ill, or you might lose your job or rice crop, or even suffer premature death. Be sure to make offerings thanking the gods and your ancestors for your pregnancy.

The Miracle of Life

The baby you carry in your womb originated with the intermingling of your and your husband's souls. For about 210 days after being born, your baby will be divine; even after that, your child will continue to be the reincarnation of an ancestor whose spirit came down to inhabit the fetus. Fortunately, the ancestor also remains present in the shrine in the houseyard temple. The reincarnated soul that your child possesses will affect his or her development in many ways, and it will also affect how you raise the child.

Gift from the Gods

What to Expect When You're Expecting

Although pregnancy is an event to be celebrated, you will not need to change your behavior very much. You can and should continue your daily work, whether it be in your yard, at the market, in the rice fields, or at a city job. As long as your pregnancy is problem-free, your life can go on as usual. However, you will want to take some precautions to make sure your pregnancy goes well.

Remember, for every positive force in the world, there is a counterbalancing evil force. So you must be especially careful at this time to make frequent offerings to your ancestors and the gods in order to obtain protection from the *leyak* witches. The *leyak* want to capture your blood and your unborn child to offer them to their spirit patrons, such as the goddess Durga. Placating your ancestors, gods, and the spirits with offerings and thanks will ensure your protection. You would do these things anyway, but be extra diligent about it while you're pregnant. You should also visit a local *balian* to buy a magic charm to wear on your belt or hang on your houseyard gate for extra protection against witchcraft. *Leyak* can transform their spirits into different forms at night, so do not venture outside too late, especially around midnight.

You should also make offerings to the four sibling spirits of your fetus. Four spirits, which we call the "four siblings," protect the fetus from conception until birth and beyond. At birth, the spirits are present in the blood, the amniotic fluid, the placenta and umbilical cord, and the waxy vernix coating the infant at birth. The four siblings will protect and nourish your fetus if they are treated properly.

While you are pregnant, you may have to be a bit more careful in what you eat. For example, you should not eat too much chili pepper, octopus, eggplant, mango, or dishes containing fresh blood or roasted pig. Eating too much of these foods, which we consider to be hot, could create an imbalance between hot and cold, causing you to become ill. Also, never accept food from a person who is ritually impure, such as a menstruating woman or someone who has recently had a death in the family.

When your fetus is about six months old, you should perform the traditional pregnancy ritual in order to anchor the fetus firmly in your womb. First, you and your husband will purify yourselves by undergoing a cleansing ritual. Give offerings, use holy water, and entreat the evil spirits away from the house. Once this cleansing ceremony is completed, you and your husband may enter the family temple and pray to your ancestors to protect and bless you and your unborn child. After this ritual, you and your husband should behave as suggested in the Hindu-Javanese epics – with a pure heart. To produce a powerful child, your husband should be calm and considerate in his thoughts and behavior. He should avoid coarse language, and he must not participate in the washing of a corpse in preparation for a cremation. He may want to let his hair grow until your baby is born (as some of our priests do after they are consecrated), for if your husband cut his hair at this time, it might somehow "cut off" the pregnancy and cause you to miscarry.

Finally, if this is not your first child, now is the time to begin weaning your youngest baby so you will be prepared to nurse your new infant.

A Word Regarding the Sex of Your Child

You are probably hoping to have a boy, knowing how important a son is for ensuring that you have a proper cremation ceremony when you die, enabling your soul to be separated from the body so that it can become an ancestor. This purification ritual will be of the utmost importance to you and your husband. A son is also necessary to maintain the house shrines to the ancestors and to carry on the family line. So, you and your husband will be quite excited if your child is a son, especially if he is your first.

Try, however, not to worry about having a girl. For one thing, worrying is very bad for you. It can weaken your spirit and make you more vulnerable to illness and witches. In the past, having a daughter was less of a problem since women had so many children that at least one was likely to be a boy. Nowadays, many women use birth control, and the government urges us to have only two children, so you might very well have only daughters. If this happens, you might try to adopt a male child, especially a nephew if your husband's brother has several sons. If your families are high ranking, it is especially important that the boy be related to your husband. Another possibility is for your daughter to marry a man who is willing to sever ties to his own ancestral shrine. Through the proper ritual, he can become part of your husband's line and take responsibility for your household shrines and perform your cremation ceremony. In this case, he would inherit your house and property just as though he were your son.

Childbirth

In the past, our young women knew a great deal about childbirth, since they were present at several births before having a child of their own. A woman's husband and other kin, as well as children she already had, were present to witness this joyous occasion. Now, however, most women on Bali give birth in obstetric clinics or hospitals.

Several days before you expect to give birth, you may want to leave your and your husband's sleeping area and move into the area on the seaward side of your compound. This will ensure that you do not defile the sacred buildings in your houseyard with the ritual impurity associated with childbirth.

In earlier times, childbirth took place squatting on a new mat on the floor of the household compound, with the assistance of a *balian* specialized in midwifery. Being on the floor helped ensure the protection and assistance of the earth goddess, Ibu Pertiwi. If need be, the *balian* healer would use spiritual powers to change the position of the infant, to ensure a relatively painless delivery.

Although fewer than half our *balian* midwives are male, there may be advantages to having one. A man has a stronger *bayu*, or spirit/life force, with which to ward off evil during delivery. In addition, *balian* midwives who are women may not perform any ritual activity while they are menstruating or after giving birth, and this could prove to be a problem. Today, many women choose to have a government-trained midwife help them give birth at a clinic. These midwives – who may also be *balian* – are usually women. Your government-trained midwife might convince you to give birth lying on a bed rather than sitting on the floor.

If the four siblings have been properly cared for through offerings and prayers during your pregnancy, they will help during your child's birth. One of the four siblings, manifested in the amniotic fluid, will open the gate of your womb for your baby to enter the world. Two of the other siblings, manifested in the blood and the vernix, will protect the infant on the right and left. The final sibling, manifested in the placenta, will push the infant from behind.

Welcome your baby with offerings. For their first 210 days (a full year in our ritual calendar), children are divine. Therefore, the midwife will speak to your newborn in honorific terms befitting a newly arrived god. The midwife will also put words into your newborn's mouth so your baby can thank the people present for witnessing the birth.

Birth in Wuku Wayang

Just as some days are more or less auspicious for marriage, harvesting, puppet shows, and other activities, certain days are also better or worse for a child's birth. Each day brings its own complications, but some must be dealt with immediately. For example, birth on Saturday in *Wuku Wayang,* the thirtieth week of the 210-day year, is particularly inauspicious. A child unlucky enough to be born on this day may be prone to suffer emotional distress and create trouble for others. For a child born during this time, it is of utmost importance to perform a ceremony involving carefully prepared offerings to the gods. The ceremony should also include a *wayang* shadow puppet show at night, with leather puppets behind a white cotton screen lit by a lamp. The purification ceremony and the *wayang* puppet show are likely to induce the gods to accept your atonement and confer good fortune on your child, despite the unfortunate birth day.

Impurity

Childbirth is a vulnerable time when evil spirits are sometimes able to predominate over good spirits. Although your newborn is a god, your own body, weakened by childbirth, may have become ritually unclean, so you must be isolated to avoid polluting others. After the birth of your child, you will be considered *sebel,* or impure, for a time (between forty-two days and three months, depending on local custom). During this period, you are forbidden to enter any sanctified space, including family temples, and you cannot engage in any ritual activity. If you do, you may incur a divine curse, and you and your family will suffer misfortune. Your husband will also be ritually impure after the birth; in his case, however, it is for a much shorter period – only three days. At the end of your respective polluted periods, each of you will undergo a ritual purification. Following this ritual, you will no longer be *sebel* and will be able to enter temples and resume your lives as usual.

Twins

There is a small chance you will have twins. This is often a sign that the village is "hot" and that a purification ritual is needed. The interpretation of this event depends on several factors, such as how traditional your family priest is. A modern priest is likely to interpret religious texts to fit life today, whereas a more old-fashioned priest will probably adhere to the strict textual tradition and require an elaborate purification.

In the past, twin births (especially of opposite sex siblings) were seen as a form of incest in the womb if the mother was a member of the lowest-ranked group. This type of intimacy in the womb was considered appropriate only for the children of kings and those of high castes. An elaborate purification was required so that the parents and the village members could make amends for this incestuous event. In addition, some priests might point out that having more than one child at a time, as animals do, is subhuman and thus a grave wrongdoing.

Traditionally, the temples of the village were closed, because the entire village had been made impure by the twins' birth. The villagers might have decided to tear down the room in which the birth occurred and carry the wreckage out of the village to the unholy land near the graveyard to be burned. The twins and their parents were banished from their village for a time, generally a month, and lived in a house built specially for them. Many watchmen, perhaps up to 50, stayed with the newborns and their parents, making noise to scare off the witches and evil spirits that live outside the village and inhabit the graveyard so they would not cause harm.

At the end of this period, there was a great ceremony to purify the village and the twins' family and to cancel the curse created by the birth of the twins. This ceremony included many offerings to the gods as well as to the demons and evil spirits. The babies' mother consulted a *balian* for more detailed instructions about the performance of these ceremonies, because any neglect of the proper ritual could bring famine to the land and disease to the village. Following the final ceremony, the twins and their parents were allowed to return to the village and resume their normal life. The temporary house they had occupied outside the village was burnt to prevent the evil from escaping.

This is just a brief outline of what occurred in earlier times at the birth of twins. Recently, our country's Department of Religion has attempted to reform or outlaw ritual purifications after the birth of twins. However, most communities agree that it is more humane to perform some rituals rather than leave the unfortunate people in a polluted state. After all, if this event is not dealt with properly, it could bring disaster on the entire village. If you have given birth to twins, your husband's brother or another male relative should immediately alert the men of the village so they can meet and decide how to deal with the crisis. Unless you are attempting to be truly modern, you will probably agree that, despite the great expense and possible illegality of the ritual, performing some type of purification is the wisest course of action when twins are born.

YOU'RE A NEW MOTHER

Placating the Four Siblings

The four siblings will influence your baby's soul throughout life, for better or for worse. Giving offerings to these spirits will help assure that they continue to protect your child against enemies and evil rather than causing sickness.

To gain the protection of the four siblings, you need to bury the placenta. If you give birth at a clinic or hospital, your husband will collect the placenta. Wash it with flower-scented water and place it, with flowers and ritual money, in a halved coconut. Join the two halves of the coconut, wrap them in a white cloth, and bury this in front of your sleeping quarters (or hang it from a tree, if that is the custom where you live). If your baby is a boy, bury the coconut to the right of the entrance; for a girl, bury it to the left. Put a large rock over the burial site, and build a fire over it. After the fire has burned, your husband, his male relatives, and your male neighbors will build a ceremonial altar next to the burial site. Your female neighbors, sisters-in-law, mother-in-law (and perhaps your sister and mother, if they come to visit) will help you make and arrange offerings for this important ritual. Place the offerings to the four spirits on the altar, and ask them to watch over and protect your child. Treat them with respect. Continue to provide the siblings with food you feed your child by expressing a few drops of breast-milk on the rock where the placenta is buried. When you bathe your child, put bathwater on the burial place. Thank the siblings every morning for guarding your child during the night.

Your Infant as a God

At birth, your child will be divine, closer to the world of the gods than to the human world. Having just arrived from heaven, your infant should be treated as a celestial being. Provide the attention that a god deserves, and address your child with the high language suitable to a person of higher rank. You should hold your newborn high, for gods and members of higher rank should always be elevated relative to their inferiors. For the first 210 days (or 105 days, depending on region and status), never put your baby down on the ground or floor, which is too profane for a god. Until then, your baby should be carried at all times.

If your child is born into a high rank, the ancestor who is reincarnated in the baby is likely to be particularly distinguished, so be sure to treat the child with respect. If you married into a higher ranking group than your own, you will be of lower rank than your child, requiring you to be especially solicitous.

If you don't treat your infant with respect, he or she may decide to leave the human world and return to the world of the gods. In Bali today, about 5 of every 100 infants return to the divine world before the end of their first year. Should your newborn return to the heavens after being born, you will not have to cremate the body. Since the cremation ceremony is a ritual of purification, it is not needed by infants (or young children who have not yet lost their baby teeth), as they have committed no sins or wrongdoing.

Lepas Aon

You won't want to take your newborn infant out visiting right away. Wait until after the *lepas aon,* the ceremony to mark the "losing of the ashes" (when the knotted end of the umbilical cord dries up and falls off). This event signals the newborn's freedom from the impurity associated with being connected to the placenta. Place the umbilical cord fragment and some hot spices in a woven palm leaf container at the foot of your infant's bed. Take care to placate the gods and the four siblings properly. Make offerings such as flowers and betel nut to the evil spirits so that they will not attack the newborn, and to the gods so that they will protect your baby. You may also try putting a slice of onion on your infant's fontanel – the smell will drive *leyak* witches away.

Temperament

Your child's character is your responsibility. An infant's character is manageable and shapeable. Soon after birth, you may want to take your infant to a ritual trance specialist, or *balian matuun,* to find out which of your ancestors' souls is in the child, as well as what kind of personality he or she has. The *balian* will enter a trance so that the ancestor can speak through him or her to indicate any special requests for this lifetime – that is, things that you and your family need to do to ensure your child's successful life. For example, you might need to fulfill promises that were not completed in the previous life, or you may need to make offerings such as a roasted pig to protect against an ancestor's greed or inability to control his or her appetites or anger. If you do whatever the *balian* recommends, your child is more likely to have a good life.

Part of your child's personality and characteristics will be determined by the day of birth. Nevertheless, your baby's character is not completely predetermined. You will want to consult the *pelelintangan* chart that cross-references the five- and seven-day weeks of the Pawukon calendar. On the top of the chart, days of the five-day week are listed, and down the side of the chart, days of the seven-day week are listed. Your child's birthday will fall into one of the thirty-five days in the chart. A *balian* can tell you what the day of the birth reveals about the child's characteristics and personality. If you are having problems with your child's personality (for example, if the child cries often), consulting a *balian* regarding the child's birth day and the spiritual forces associated with that day may help solve the problem. Through appropriately directed prayers and offerings, you may be able to change some of your child's undesirable characteristics. The *balian* can also reveal which animals, birds, and gods correspond to the birthdate, and you can make sure that your child gives preferential treatment to these beings.

Some experts say that the child's four spirit siblings unify after the child's six-month ceremony to become two spirits of the soul: the Kala and the Dewa. The spirit Kala is responsible for the child's bad thoughts, emotions, and behavior, while Dewa is responsible for good ones, as well as calmness.

Another solution to a child's undesirable character is a new name. A name can be too heavy or too light, creating an imbalance in the child's spirit. If your child cries a lot or is otherwise difficult, this might be a sign that your child is protesting an inappropriate name. A *balian* can select a new one.

Another way to improve your child's temperament is to perform a therapeutic ritual of *metubah*. This ritual involves putting a special offering of seafood by a river or under the eaves of the house. It is performed to eradicate bad traits, such as a bad temper or laziness, that have been reincarnated in your child. You may also perform this ritual when your child is older (or even during adulthood) if bad traits emerge then.

INFANCY

Naming

Your child will have several names. Immediately after birth, the appropriate birth order name will automatically be bestowed. Your first child will either be called "Wayan" (for a low-ranked child) or "Putu" (especially for a high-ranked child); your second child will be named "Madé," the third, "Nyoman," and your fourth, "Ketut." If you resist the government's birth control campaigns and have a fifth child, start over with "Wayan" (or "Putu"). Stillborn babies and children who have died are still counted when determining your infant's birth order name.

In addition to the birth order name, a personal name will be bestowed at the infant's three-month ceremony. This is an important rite of passage. You will want to gather all of your relatives for this ceremony so that you can introduce your child to them. This will be a big celebration, so it may be expensive. If you cannot afford to pay for all the rituals that are involved, you can delay some until your child's 210-day ceremony.

At the 105-day ceremony you will announce your infant's personal name. A Hindu priest or a *balian* will obtain various personal names through divination and will write them on pieces of palm leaf. When the leaves are burned, the name that can be seen most clearly from the charred remains or the name that takes the longest time to burn will be your child's personal name.

Although all Balinese have personal names, they are not used much before children grow up, marry, and have children themselves. However, your oldest child's personal name will be used by others to address you and your husband as "Mother of _____" and "Father of _____." How you address your child depends on your relative ranks. If your child has inherited a rank from your husband that is higher than your own, you must show respect by using your child's title plus birth order name. Others of lower rank (both children and adults) than your child must also use the little one's title. If your rank is the same as your child's, then you do not have to add the title to the birth order name, although you may do so to flatter your child or just for fun.

Using a child's birth order name can sometimes be confusing if there are other children nearby with the same name; they might all be tempted to come when you call. To avoid this, you can add your child's personal name to the end of the birth order name.

Caretaking

Emotional upsets, even minor forms of surprise from loud noises or quarreling, can weaken or endanger your child's *bayu,* or life force.

The very young and the old are most susceptible to afflictions of the *bayu,* so you need to treat your baby with extreme care and calm. Any physical discomfort or rough handling will further weaken an infant's already weak *bayu,* leaving the child susceptible to physical illness and evil spirits. Infants and young children are easily overcome by emotion and can become sick from getting upset. Don't let your baby fuss: Offer your breast at the first signs of awakening, before he or she is fully awake and has a chance to cry out. If there is a scary object or person around, cover the baby's face so that he or she does not become frightened.

Your infant will sleep with you at night until at least three years of age. During the day, your baby will be carried by someone most of the time, even after he or she can crawl; it is base for a baby to crawl on the ground like an animal. Hold the baby in your arms or in a sling around your body as you go about your daily business. Your infant can stay in the sling even while asleep, although you may want to pull the cloth over the child's face. If you have to put your child down to do some work, another person – your husband, a sibling, child caretaker, grandparent, aunt, uncle, cousin, or neighbor – should hold the child. Everyone loves to hold a baby.

You will probably carry your child on your left hip, leaving your right hand free. This will pin your baby's right hand to your side, so the little one may try to use the left hand to grab objects or food. You must teach the child from a very young age that the right hand is for food, asking, or offering, while the left hand is only for cleansing oneself. Be vigilant in discouraging improper use of the left hand.

Dressing

Traditionally, parents left their young children naked, wearing only a necklace given to teethe on and some bracelets and anklets for ornamentation and protection against evil. The sling in which the baby was carried would provide enough warmth. Nowadays, you will probably dress your infant in Western pants and a shirt. At first your baby will urinate on you while being held in your sling. This isn't a big deal – just change the pants and your sling, and wash off during one of your two daily baths. When your child defecates, a nearby scavenger dog will clean it up quickly. Eventually, your child will learn that one should defecate only in certain places, and not anywhere in the house-yard. Later, you will want to dress your child in traditional Balinese clothing for ceremonies, temple feasts, and birthdays.

Bathing

Your infant should have a bath twice a day in lukewarm water, once in the morning and once at night, just as you do. If you don't have running water in your household, you can carry water from a spring or river. When your infant is young, the bath can be given in a traditional areca-palm bark container or, the more modern way, in a plastic bucket to be used only for this purpose. Roll up your cloth sling to make a pillow for the baby's head. You may want to put red onion in the water to ward off evil spirits. A newborn will probably get cold in the bath, so be as quick as possible. Later, when your child has learned that bathing is enjoyable, you can spend longer at it. After the bath, dump the bathwater on the place where your infant's placenta is buried. This will show respect to the four siblings, so that they will protect your infant. When your baby can sit alone, the bath can be given in a plastic basin. After your child outgrows the basin, you can pour water over him or her from the tank with a ladle, just as you do when you bathe. Even if you have running water in your house, you might sometimes enjoy a pleasant bath in a nearby river or stream. After all, bath time is a good time for playing with your baby.

Feeding and Weaning

Don't feed your child the first milk that comes from your breasts; it is "hard" and indigestible. Instead, provide a porridge of boiled rice flour. Before beginning to breastfeed, express your breasts to eliminate the bad milk; customarily, this first milk should fall on the house wall. Your milk will not be sufficient nourishment for your newborn, so you will have to provide something else. Pre-chew some food like bananas and force it into your baby's mouth with your finger. Although the baby may resist, this food is a necessary supplement to breastmilk.

Feed your newborn solid food at set times during the day, but breastfeed whenever the baby seems fussy or tired. This is easy to do, since you will be holding and sleeping with your infant anyway. Every time you feed your child, make sure you also put food out for the four siblings.

Try to find a comfortable position for both of you when breast-feeding. Even very young infants can be held in a near sitting position in a sling. This has the advantage of keeping your infant's head high, as befits a god. Since this position places the infant's head well above your nipple, it gives the baby, when a little older, the freedom to nurse whenever he or she wants (Plate 9).

Plate 9. A Balinese baby is a god. As befits a god, the child's head is to be kept high at all times – even while breastfeeding. Photograph by Bernadette Waldis, reprinted courtesy of Urs Ramseyer, Museum der Kulturen Volkerkunder Museum, Basel.

Weaning will be an important milestone for your child. It used to occur around the birth of the next child and marked the new status of "knee baby" – an infant who can climb onto your knee rather than constantly being held. However, with family planning, your children may be spaced further apart, so you will have greater choice about when to wean your baby. There is no particular age that is the "correct time" for doing it. Generally, weaning can be done gradually, and since you will have fed your infant porridge and food in addition to breastmilk from the very beginning, it should not be upsetting. If you need to wean your child in a hurry because you are pregnant and your new baby will come soon, you can coat your breasts with hot or bitter herbs or a mixture of lime and sugar.

If you don't get pregnant again while your child is a toddler, the child may gradually wean him- or herself. For boys, this is likely to happen around three or four years, as they become more independent. Sons of a farmer, for example, start to go to the fields with their fathers at this time. Of course, boys are not always able to work with their fathers these days, since many men now have paying jobs away from the fields. In the old days, girls tended to stay close to their mothers to help with other children, so they continued to breastfeed a bit later than boys. Nowadays, however, many women also have jobs that take them away from the home. If this is the case with you, you may have to wean all of your children early.

Otonan Ceremony

The *otonan* ceremony is performed on the first birthday, which comes 210 days after birth. It marks a very important transition – your child's departure from the divine world and entry into the human world. The main purpose of this ceremony is purification and the provision of spiritual strength. Your infant will be given a cap to protect the fontanel and prevent evil spirits from entering. For the first time, you will place your child's feet on the ground, acknowledging your child's full entry into the human world from the divine world.

Gift from the Gods

Understanding Good Health

Good health depends on a delicate balance between the body and the *bayu*. A strong *bayu* can withstand many illnesses, especially those caused by black magic, but also those resulting from natural factors. As a mother, you need to take good care of your own *bayu* through a properly balanced and composed diet. Too many hot foods (such as meat) will overenergize your *bayu* and throw it off balance. On the other hand, too many cold foods (such as sweet potatoes, sugar, apples, and most vegetables) may stiffen your *bayu* and make it rigid and inflexible. So don't overdo either.

The *bayu* also needs calmness and no worry. Forgetting and not caring provide calm, which will strengthen your *bayu*. Anger, envy, jealousy, and taking offense are morally wrong and will weaken your *bayu* and leave you and your child vulnerable to sickness. Strive to be relaxed, avoid disappointment and anger, and forget bad things.

Children are especially vulnerable to afflictions of the *bayu*, and you actually pose the greatest danger to the health and life of your infant through nursing. A mother's *bayu* flows in her blood, which produces her milk. Anything that is unexpected, startles you, or upsets your balance and composure can be detrimental. Any negative emotion you experience can make your milk too hot and life-damaging for your child, or it may even stop flowing. Children very often die because mothers have been startled, angry, or sorrowful! Even unexpected happiness may endanger your child's life. That is why it is very hard to be a mother, and you must carefully manage your emotions.

If you do become upset or startled, you can do things to keep the harmful emotions you experience from passing on to your child. You can rid yourself of the bad milk by drinking cold water and washing your breasts with cold water. Then empty your breasts three times before feeding your child. You can also try rubbing your scalp and forehead with a special grass known for its cleansing powers. Another remedy is eating *kalisasuan,* a certain spider's web. Should you neglect these remedies, your child may cry, get sick, and lose appetite. If any of these symptoms occurs, seek help immediately from a *balian.*

It is important to realize that your husband's negative emotions can affect the health of your child by making you upset. Encourage him to be happy and calm so that he does not adversely influence your emotions. Avoid all people who express negative emotion.

Curing Illness

If you or your child are ill, you can consult either a medical doctor or a *balian*. A *balian* has many advantages over a doctor. A *balian's* main goal (at least according to some) is to treat illnesses connected with a person's *bayu*. Since *balian* treat both supernatural and physical causes of illness, they have a much better chance of diagnosing and curing illness than medical doctors, who prescribe treatments for symptoms without addressing the underlying cause. Medical doctors are good for the relatively rare ailments that have a purely physical nature, but *balian* take into account the state of the patient's *bayu* and treat invisible forces that cause the symptom, such as the sibling spirits, ancestors, past life issues, gods, demons, witches, and so forth.

Balian also have the advantage that they accept whatever one can pay, and medical doctors are generally five to ten times more expensive. If you decide to consult a doctor, the doctor must actually see your child, but the *balian* can diagnose and cure a child without seeing him or her. This is possible because the *balian* can intervene with the spiritual world on behalf of you or your child. So, if your child is ill, consult either a *balian* alone or both a *balian* and a medical doctor.

The *balian* will identify your child's symptoms, explain what has gone wrong, and prescribe a remedy; depending on the problem, this might be holy water, potions, amulets or charms, or certain foods. In addition, the *balian* will divine what rituals need to be performed to appease angry gods, ancestors, or evil spirits. The *balian* will probably make offerings and pray on your behalf as well.

A special advantage of the *balian* is their ability to determine if your child's illness is actually caused by the faults or bad characteristics of the ancestor who is reincarnated in the child. This could occur if the ancestor's family had failed to perform the *meseh lawang,* the ceremony that erases physical faults or bad characteristics of the deceased so these traits cannot be reincarnated in a baby.

Emotional Control

A very important part of parenting is teaching children how to control their feelings. Being able to manage the heart will help your child solve problems independently, and this will allow your little one to become a productive member of our society.

Your young child will experience strong emotions and may throw tantrums. Your job is to help him or her learn how to remain calm even in the face of upsetting situations. When the child is around 21 months, one thing you can do is to "borrow" a young baby from someone. Play with the baby or even let the baby nurse from your breasts, while your child watches. Of course, this will make your child feel jealous, and a tantrum may ensue. Don't become angry or punish the child – indeed, don't react strongly at all. This will encourage your son or daughter to find a way to deal with the natural feelings of jealousy. Then, the next time you "borrow" a baby, your child may react more calmly and may even play with the little one. Be sure to convey how proud you are of this new, appropriate behavior. This is a first step to becoming emotionally mature and self-confident, and a sign that your child will make a good older brother or sister to your next baby. If you use strategies such as this one, by the age of three or four your child will have developed equanimity in the face of provocations, disappointments, or frustrations.

You can also talk directly to your child about how to express emotions. Encourage your son or daughter to be quiet and polite both at home and in public. Even positive emotions should not be displayed in public. For example, a child who receives an award at school should feel happiness in the heart but not express it overtly. By the same token, if your child is frightened of a stranger or a strange situation, advise your little one not to reveal that fear. Likewise, do not permit children to fight over toys. If a conflict does arise, the older child should always be reprimanded and instructed to give in to the younger one. If your children complain of taunts or mistreatment from other children, tell them to rise above such pettiness and just forget the incident.

In short, you should always encourage calm in the face of trouble, and discourage any display of strong emotions. Explain that not caring about disappointments will produce physical well-being, as well as personal satisfaction and self-respect. This is the greatest gift you can give your child.

CHAPTER 5

Making Babies in a Turkish Village

Carol Delaney

MUSLIMS OF VILLAGE TURKEY

Turkey is a nation of about 63 million people, half of whom live in villages similar to the one I describe in this manual. Not that long ago, a considerable majority of the nation's population lived in villages, but in the past twenty-five years, many villagers have migrated to town and city, as well as to Europe. Formerly, the divide between city and village was enormous; now the urban elite live in close proximity to swelling squatter settlements surrounding large cities. Still, few of the urban elite have ever been to a village. Although some express nostalgia for what they imagine as the simple life, most imagine villagers as dirty, dangerous, and ignorant.

The information for my "manual" comes from my anthropological fieldwork in a village in central Anatolia between 1980 and 1982. Studies of village life in Turkey are very rare, mine being one of only a handful. Although several discuss family structure, marriage, and the sexual division of labor, few describe the intimate details of procreation and child rearing.

Anatolia is the name for the major landmass of Turkey, formerly known as Asia Minor. The complexity of the land reminds me of the

United States, although compressed into a much smaller area. Rather than the "Wild West," Turkey has a "wild east" – an area of high, snow-covered mountains – that is less modernized than the rest of the country. Turkey also has a "midwest" – a large, high, central plateau where most of the grain is grown; this is central Anatolia. The desertlike country in the southeast is complemented by a semitropical climate along the Mediterranean, reminiscent of Florida and southern California. This is the area of citrus orchards, and, owing to a vast network of hothouses, it is also home to a major fruit, vegetable, and flower industry, not unlike the central valley in California, that supplies Turkey as well as Europe. The western part of Turkey along the Aegean, like the east coast of the United States, is the most industrialized and urbanized.

Turkey is a secular democracy, founded in 1923 by Mustafa Kemal Atatürk after the collapse of the Ottoman Empire. Turkish, the primary language, is neither Indo-European nor Semitic, but something quite unusual. Some think it belongs to the Uralic-Altaic group of languages; still others see similarities to ancient Sumerian and even to Navajo because of its agglutinative characteristics. In addition to Turkish, Greek, Armenian, Kurdish, and Arabic are spoken in various parts of Turkey, though only in the home. During the Ottoman Empire, the official language was Osmanlıcı – a very rococo form of Turkish that incorporated a great deal of Persian and Arabic. One historian says that the Turkish of today is as different from the Turkish at the beginning of this century as modern English is from Chaucer's English. Not only are the vocabulary and sentence structure quite different, but so too is the orthography. Osmanlıcı was written in Arabic script, but since Turkish is a vowel harmonic language, this was quite unsuitable. One of Atatürk's major reforms was to switch to Latin letters, making literacy attainable by ordinary, even peasant, Turks. Today, Osmanlıcı is incomprehensible to contemporary Turks; those who wish to learn it must do so as a foreign language.

Although Turkey is a secular state, 98 percent of the people claim to be Muslim. There is also a sizable Jewish population, primarily in Istanbul, a city that is home to the Patriarch of the Greek Orthodox church as well as to the Armenian Patriarch. The Greek Orthodox community lives mostly scattered among the islands in the Sea of Marmara, one of which is home to a working monastery. Syrian Christians live in the eastern part of Turkey around the city of Urfa, near Haran, the home of the biblical patriarch Abraham, known to Muslims as Ibrahim. Jews and Christians are generally unaware that Muhammad's role was not to create a new religion but to call the people back to the one true, monotheistic faith of Abraham.

Even though Turkey is predominantly Muslim, it possesses and protects many spectacular ancient Hellenic and Christian sites and, in recent years, has spent an enormous amount of money developing and making the sites more accessible to tourists. Some of the south coast resorts are as fashionable as any found in Europe, with beautiful beaches, excellent food, boutiques, discos, and thousands of yachts. But this lifestyle is very far removed from that of villagers.

In Turkey the official definition of a village is a settlement with fewer than 2,000 people. Over that number, it becomes a municipality, and then it has a right to certain kinds of infrastructure. Most Turkish villages, however, have between 200 and 400 people. The village in which I lived was fairly large, perhaps because it was relatively remote and people could not commute to work in town. When I was living there from August 1980 until July 1982, the village had about 850 people, half of whom were children up to the age of twenty. Villagers told me that the village had been even larger in the past but that now, many of the young people are marrying out. When I visited in 1998, there were fewer than 400 and most of them were old people.

During the time I was in the village, it had both a primary and a middle school – something quite unusual for a village – though very few children, and even fewer girls, attended the middle school. Today, owing to decreased population and lack of pupils, the middle school has been closed. For villagers, literacy is primarily functional, enough to be able to read formulaic letters sent by a son away for his military service, for example, and an occasional newspaper.

Villagers make their livelihood by farming. Most families own enough land to provide sustenance; wealthier farmers sell their surplus either to the state granaries or in the market. Most families also own sheep and goats, as well as a few cows. These provide milk, butter, cheese, yogurt, and occasionally meat, as well as wool and goat hair. The village diet consists primarily of bread and milk products. Vegetables are usually made into some form of stew, sometimes with bits of meat for flavoring. Tea is the primary drink, and in summer, *ayran* (yogurt mixed with salt and water) is popular. Alcohol is forbidden in Islam, yet a few of the men indulge, normally only when they go to town. Men also smoke cigarettes, though never in front of their fathers; women rarely smoke and the few who do, do so only in private when the men are not at home.

Most houses are made of mudbrick and have flat roofs. Mudbrick is well suited to the climate – providing warmth in winter and coolness in summer. As people began to make more money, some of them built houses of cement blocks with peaked roofs covered with red terra-cotta tiles. The traditional floor plan is called *karnıyarık* (split womb), consisting of a central entry hall-room and two rooms on either side, each of which is multipurpose – for eating, sleeping, entertaining, and other activities. Theoretically, each of these rooms could be for a separate family – ideally for the families of two brothers. Rooms are heated with a cylindrical stove that can burn dung fuel, wood, or coal, or a combination of them. The top of the stove is used for some cooking, for heating large containers of water for washing, and for making tea. For most cooking, people tend to use gas containers to which a burner can be attached. Most houses do not have running water; instead, women get water from one of the three bath/laundry houses that are fed from the water depot located farther up on the mountain. The water depot collects water from several underground steams as well as from rain and, at the discretion of the village watchman, is piped down to the bathhouses. By the time I left the village in 1982, a few people had constructed pipes to bring water to their houses. However, the watchman of the village still controlled *when* water would flow and how much there would be. Some clever people concocted arrangements to collect water in large containers with a spigot, which could make it seem as if they had running water.

Since the 1970s, the village where I lived has had electricity – enough for people to have radios and television sets. By the time I arrived, many already had refrigerators, a few had washing machines, and a fair number had other electrical devices such as a machine to churn butter. Light bulbs, however, were scarce and expensive and rarely above 20 watts – not really enough for reading at night (something probably only I was interested in doing). Although there has been much official rhetoric claiming improvements in the lives of villagers, not very much has happened in this direction during the past twenty years. Instead, I believe that many official planners look forward to the day when villages no longer exist and their land can be "capitalized," that is, made more efficient by large landholdings by capitalist farmers.

The village in which I lived has been served by a rural medical program since the late 1970s. A doctor who works at the government health station in the nearest town visits each village in the area two or three times a year. In addition, the government appoints midwives to live in some villages for periods of two years each; we had the same midwife the entire time I was there.

Although access to modern biomedicine is improving, it brings its own problems, and much of village wisdom about health is being lost. There had always been women who performed the services of midwife long before the government sent its own trained midwives to villages. Many of them had a great deal of practical experience and were very successful. The grandmother I write about in the "manual" that follows was one such woman. This woman continued to practice even after the government-appointed midwife arrived in the village. Village women tended to prefer the traditional midwife since they knew and trusted her – she was one of them – while they distrusted and even disliked the government midwife. However, the village midwife was getting quite old and no other village woman seemed to be picking up her craft.

Since I knew this traditional midwife quite well and visited her often, I have constructed for the childrearing guide that follows a fictive persona of this midwife's granddaughter recording her words – much like the role played by the anthropologist.

MAKING BABIES IN A TURKISH VILLAGE

About the Author

My grandmother has been our village midwife for many years. She has
delivered several hundred babies with a great deal of success.
Traditionally, of course, it was grandmothers who assisted with the
births of their grandchildren; thus, it is not so surprising that the word
for midwife and the colloquial word for grandmother are the same. In
the late 1970s, however, the government began to separate the two
roles. As part of its modernization plan, it created a rural medical program and began to train middle-school graduates in midwifery. These
trained outsiders were intended to be "agents of change" in rural areas.
Yet, even though our current government-appointed midwife received
some training after she completed eighth grade, she has had very little
experience. My grandmother says they should have trained one of our
own girls – then, at least, people would trust her.

Our government midwife does help with some pregnancies and
births, and she records all of them. What she doesn't know is that my
grandmother continues to advise pregnant women and to assist with a
number of births every year. But my grandmother is getting old and

will not be able to continue much longer. She cannot read or write and is worried that much of what she knows and has learned over these years will be forgotten. So she has asked me to write down, in her own words, her wisdom on these matters. She is aware of how quickly our knowledge and traditions are fading, and she thinks it is important to preserve our memory of them. Most of what follows was recorded during our conversations; sometimes she addresses me as if I am a new bride or a pregnant woman.

WHY BABIES ARE IMPORTANT

If you're going to understand anything about babies you have to understand why people want them and why they are important to us. Girls and boys are expected to marry as soon as they are of a certain age. As you know, girls used to be married around fifteen, even as young as thirteen, but now the government wants us to wait until a girl is eighteen and the boy twenty one – or after he completes his military service. Many of us, however, want to see a young man married *before* military service. That will keep his eyes from roving, especially if his wife is pregnant while he is serving. Then his focus will be on home.

A child is expected in the first year of marriage. After all, that is what marriage is for. Why else would you get married? In fact, that is what really makes a marriage. And it is what makes you an adult. Having a child is the supreme task in life for both of you. Also, when you become pregnant, it proves your husband's virility, and he will be very proud. He will be even prouder if you give birth to a son because only a son is able to carry on his family line. As we say, "A boy is the flame of the hearth, a girl its ashes." You will be very lucky if your first child is a boy.

Of course, it is our boys who remain in the house when they marry and who will one day inherit it. Girls, on the other hand, are thought of as guests in their parents' home because they must leave when they marry. The word *çocuk* means both child and boy, while *kız* means girl and daughter. Therefore, when officials ask us how many children (*çocuklar*) we have, we usually tell them only the number of boys. Both the word and the practice imply that boys are the ones that really count and hence the ones that are counted; in any case, that is how it seems.

Today, the government midwife must record all births, including those at which I, not she, assist. But for most of us, birthdays are forgotten. We do not follow the custom of the infidels (Christians) of celebrating birthdays; instead we recognize the day of death and hold a *mevlud* to commemorate the anniversary of a death. I think this is because when a person dies, he or she is returning to *the other world*, which is our true home. When you are born, you come into *this world* where we are only guests.

MAKING A BABY

Our purpose in this world is to increase and multiply; that is Allah's command. Although sexuality is part of Allah's plan and was created for the very purpose of increasing and multiplying, we feel ashamed to talk about it openly or to give any instruction to our children. Your husband will never say he wants to have sex; sometimes he will talk about "making a baby," but more often might simply ask you to perform your ablutions – the required washing that you should do both before and after sex. It is a sign he desires to have sex with you; you cannot refuse, as it is your duty. If you are living with your husband's family, you will have your own room. In fact, today, most married people have their own bedrooms, and the children, even the grown ones, all sleep snuggled up in quilts in the living room on the divans, able to fall asleep even if the adults are still talking or watching television.

Most women I know enjoy sex and find it sweet, even though many of them do not realize that they, too, can reach orgasm. However, one of my male neighbors told me that if the man comes first, the child will resemble him, but if the woman comes first, it will resemble her. I don't know if that is true, but it does indicate that he, at least, knew that women can have orgasms. Of course, that is not possible for those women who are "cut" (who have clitoridectomies); fortunately, we do not practice that in our village. I recently heard on television that some families in Turkey are taking their daughters for virginity checks and sometimes have them "sewn up" (infibulated), but so far I have not seen it myself. Normally, "cutting" (circumcision) is only for boys – I will tell you more about that later.

Once a boy is able to ejaculate, he is ready to produce children – which is another reason he should be married young. A child is in the father's seed. Women are like the nurturant field in which it is planted. Some people say that women, too, have seed, but these people are mistaken – the liquid that women produce during sex is merely a lubricant. If a man can produce seed (semen), we assume that he can produce a child. Therefore, if a woman does not conceive, it is considered her fault. A few people have learned from the medical doctor that a man's seed is just like wheat or any other seed – some of them sprout and others do not; that is, some of his seed is not alive. Yet most people in the village continue to blame the woman if she does not get pregnant or if she produces only girls; it is felt she cannot hold onto the (proper) seed.

Most girls in our village do become pregnant in their first year of marriage, but occasionally that doesn't happen. If you do not get pregnant, you need to think about what may have gone wrong. Perhaps it is a punishment from Allah, or perhaps someone has directed the evil eye toward you. There is not much you can do if it is Allah's punishment or if someone has cast a spell on you. But there are other possible reasons for you not becoming pregnant.

You may have neglected to perform your ablutions after you finished your period. You may perform them at home or at the bathhouse. The water and your prayers are necessary to make your field pure and ready to receive your husband's seed. Indeed, right after your period is the best time to become pregnant.

Another reason you are not yet pregnant may be that you have no blood (a condition our doctor calls "anemic"). If so, you will be unable to hold onto your husband's seed and it will spill out. To correct this, you must eat foods that enrich the blood like the molasses-like syrup made from grapes that we call *pekmez*. We always knew it was good for us; now the doctor has told us it is because it is full of iron, and you need that in your blood. Normally, your mother-in-law will give you *pekmez*; if she doesn't, you must ask for some. Also, a spleen from a recently slaughtered animal (cow or sheep) will help increase and enrich the blood. In general, we say that red foods (like meat and tomato sauce), fried foods, and spicy foods heat up the blood and make it more likely that you will conceive a male child. By contrast, we say that white foods like yogurt, cheese, chicken, and rice encourage the conception of a girl.

PREGNANCY

Everyone is happy when a new bride becomes pregnant. Your husband will be proud, and his mother will achieve a new status in the household and in the village. Your own family will be happy too, for their circle of relations widens. Your pregnancy also justifies the hefty brideprice they received for you. There has been some debate about brideprice, so let me try to set you straight. Some people, usually city people or foreigners, think we are selling our daughters. That is not true. Instead, the brideprice is compensation to the bride's family both for the cost of raising her and for the loss of her contributions to the household. Among close relatives, the brideprice can be quite minimal.

Because you now live with your husband's family, your pregnancy and the birth of your child will occur in their house. Your mother-in-law, not your mother, will oversee the whole process. Since she is a very important person in your new life, your family tried to make sure you would get along well with her.

The first sign that you may be pregnant is that you will miss your period; later on you might begin to feel a little sick in the morning. You may not feel much like eating, but it is important that you eat well – especially foods that enrich and strengthen the blood. Just as soil provides the medium in which seed can grow, so does the rich, luxuriant, and moist climate of the womb provide the ground for the child to grow. Similarly, as the soil passes nutrients to the plant, so does blood pass nutrients to the growing baby by means of the little breasts in the womb. Babies in the womb suck on these breasts and receive the nurture that helps them to grow.

You might notice that you begin to crave certain kinds of food – sometimes it is sour things like pickles, other times it is the kinds of sweets that can only be bought in town. Actually, it is really the child who wants these foods, so your husband and mother-in-law will try to obtain them for you. Ordinarily, your mother-in-law will be especially solicitous of you in many ways since she wants a child as much as you do. She is looking forward to the time when she can play with the baby while you take on more of her household work.

A more specific sign that you are pregnant is when you begin to feel some movement in your abdomen – that is the baby moving, a sign that it is alive. It means the soul has opened or, as some say, that the soul has entered the child. Only Allah really knows. As you know, the word for soul also means "life" – soul and life go together. In the womb, the soul of a boy opens at forty days, that of a girl at eighty days. A boy child develops more quickly in the womb than a girl, while a girl matures more rapidly after birth. Remember that anthropologist who visited our village? She told me that this theory is very similar to what the pagan Greek philosopher, Aristotle, said many, many years ago. In any case, this idea is what helps me know the sex of a child if there is a miscarriage. If the expelled material is just a mass of flesh, I know it was a girl.

Pregnancy is a powerful but also risky time, especially the first forty days when new life is taking root. Most illnesses come from outside, from things in the air, especially from drafts. For example, menstrual blood is full of impurities; when these are released into the air, they can penetrate your body and bring about a miscarriage or deform the fetus. So you must be very careful to avoid noxious smells, menstruating women, and cold drafts. You must also avoid jealous people who might cast the evil eye on you. At the same time, when you are pregnant, you pose a risk to others. Your power is very strong so you must not go near new babies, because you could hurt them or make them ill. In addition, women who are in the midst of making bread or yogurt do not want to see you because your very presence will cause the bread not to rise and the yogurt not to take. It will be up to you to avoid dangerous situations, because most people will not even know you are pregnant.

We consider plumpness in a woman a sign of beauty and prosperity – it means her husband feeds her well – so it is often difficult to tell if a woman is pregnant. In addition, the baggy pants and vests that we women wear disguise our large bellies pretty well. That is good, for we don't want to advertise our pregnancies since they are obvious evidence that we have had sex, and we do not talk about that or even allude to it publicly.

BIRTH

When many months have passed and you begin to feel some regular pains in your womb, then you should quietly leave whatever you are doing and go tell your mother-in-law. She will begin to get things ready for the birth and will send for me or the government midwife. Women in our village usually do not anticipate problems with birth, and indeed, there have been very few problems in recent years. As I always say, "May the baby come out as easily as it went in!"

Birth is an affair for women – no men are allowed. I am quite shocked to hear that in America, husbands now witness births. For us, it is shameful for any man, including the husband, to see a woman's genitals. This is why we do not like to send women to the hospital to have their babies; the doctors (mostly male) will see their private parts. You should hear the stories of the terrible treatment and the embarrassment experienced by the few women from the village who have gone there. They report that the hospital cots of all the women giving birth were lined up in a row and all their private parts were exposed. They were rarely given any anesthesia – not even for sewing up the perineum when it tore. They said that was the most excruciating pain, much worse than giving birth.

In the village, this is how birth takes place. Once you alert your mother-in-law, she will put water on to boil and collect the other items that will be needed: a large, low, round laundry washtub made of tinned copper or, these days, more likely, of plastic; a low stool; and some clean cloths. The stool is placed inside the washtub for you to sit on during labor. When you are pushing, you can extend your legs and press against the sides of the tub for support, gripping the edges with your hands. But for much of the time you can walk around and drink some water, sometimes even eat something for strength. Your mother-in-law and I will try to distract you with jokes and gossip so you can relax. That is very important – if you are too tense, it will be difficult, and you can tear. When it becomes necessary to push, get in the washtub; your mother-in-law will support your back, and I will kneel in front to watch for the baby. I will massage your abdomen to help ease the pain and to try to move the baby into a good position. I only do this on the outside; I never go inside to manipulate the baby, nor do I ever "cut" to enlarge the opening as they do in the hospital. If the baby is not in a good position or if something else seems amiss, then I will send you to the hospital. Fortunately, there are usually one or two cars in the village. If there is no car available, the headman will call to town and have a taxi sent up to get you. But let's hope for the best. Anyway, it is in Allah's hands.

Don't be surprised if the baby comes covered in a kind of oily substance. Even though the government midwife thinks this is very dirty and even ritually unclean, we think it is normal. When the baby is out, most women cry out *"Kurtuldum"* – "I am saved, I am delivered." In my experience this can mean many things. For some, it probably means simply, "I am saved from death." This was especially true a few years back when some women died in childbirth. But it might also mean that she is now saved from the shame of not being able to have a child. She has validated herself in the eyes of her husband's family, and she will have more status. A mother of a son is even more valued, for she has saved her husband's lineage from the danger of dying out. If the child is a boy, she also saves herself, because a woman who has borne a son is less likely to be divorced. In the past, a man who had no sons might take a second wife and try to have a son with her, but today polygamy is illegal in Turkey, yet I know that it still occurs. Personally, I favor the interpretation that the woman is saying she is saved because she has fulfilled the function for which she was created.

AFTER BIRTH AND *LOĞUSALIK*

A little while after the child is born, the placenta comes out. We call it *eş* (partner), because it is a little like a partner – not, of course, a spouse or sibling, but a partner nonetheless. Everyone should have a partner: the child in the womb has an *eş*; an only child must have an *eş*; if there are two girls and one boy, the boy must have an *eş*; and finally when one is married, the spouse is *eş*. The placenta, therefore, should be treated with care. We say it is sinful to feed it to the dogs (though I know some ignorant people who have done that). Instead, it should be buried in the courtyard.

I will wash the baby briefly and wrap it up completely. Then I immediately present it to the father and the paternal grandfather. In our tradition, the grandfather whispers verses from the Qur'an into the baby's ear and bestows its name. Speaking the name makes the child a person. In practice, of course, people have usually been discussing the name long before the child was born. Still, I have also known quite a few babies who went without a name for weeks while the parents vacillated or families argued over it. Although it is customary to name a baby after a relative, especially a grandparent (whether living or dead), or after Muhammad or other important figures in the Qur'an, many younger people are choosing new names, sometimes those of famous movie stars or singers. You know, of course, that none of us had last names until our great leader and first president, Mustafa Kemal Atatürk, decreed them necessary in 1934. Before that, we just referred to each other as so-and-so's son or so-and-so's mother. Even Atatürk, whose name means "Father Turk" or "Father of the Turks," had no last name until the Grand National Assembly bestowed that one on him, clearly acknowledging his role in the creation of our nation. In our village, after the new law was introduced, we were given a list of names to choose from in case we could not make one up for ourselves.

After being named, the baby remains tightly wrapped in cloth. Indeed, we continue to swaddle for several months until the baby seems strong and healthy. Swaddling makes a baby feel protected and helps it to sleep well (Plate 10). You must never put a swaddled baby to sleep on its stomach, for it would not be able to breathe. Instead, put the baby down to sleep on its back. The doctor says it is because we always lie our babies on their backs that the heads of so many Turks are rather flat in the back. In addition, swaddling protects the baby from drafts and thus from illness. I was shocked when the anthropologist who lived in our village told me how Americans dress their babies – it seems that in summertime the little ones are almost naked, wearing little more than a tiny shirt and diaper. Poor

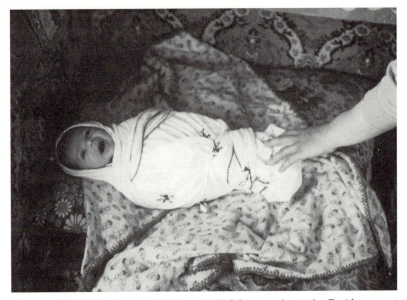

Plate 10. Turkish infants are tightly swaddled for several months. Besides keeping them warm and secure, covering a baby in this way shows everyone that the baby is spoken for – it is "covered by care." Photograph by Carol Delaney.

things, with their little arms and legs flailing around, they must feel quite unprotected.

There is yet one more reason babies are swaddled, and it is perhaps the most important. We say that all valuable and desirable objects must be covered, otherwise they invite the evil eye; babies, like women, are valuable objects of desire, and so they must be covered. Another precaution to ward off the evil eye is to attach a blue bead on top of the swaddling cloth. When you cover a baby's nakedness you show to the world that it is spoken for; it is covered by your care. This is similar to our funerals when children cover and protect the nakedness and vulnerability of their dead parents. After a parent dies, the grown children wash the corpse and wrap it with yards of white cloth just as if they were swaddling a baby, before the body is delivered to the other world.

A child who dies after birth, even without breathing, is wrapped in swaddling cloth. In this case, the swaddling becomes a shroud. The child is buried in the cemetery. As Muslims, we say that since the baby died without sin, it can intercede for you in heaven. Women who have had a baby who died still count that baby; they will say, "I have two children in this world and three in the other world." On the other hand, an aborted or miscarried fetus is not wrapped in cloth and is not buried in the cemetery but rather in the courtyard, like the placenta.

Sometimes babies are born with deformities. If the deformities are serious, the babies often do not breathe but die soon after birth. In our village, as you may have noticed, there are several people who walk with a limp or who have difficulty walking because their hip joint is not working properly. The doctor told us that this condition is due either to our custom of marrying close relatives or to swaddling our babies too tightly. But we have always swaddled our babies, and not everyone has a problem walking. I, too, think it has to do with shared substance – either blood or milk – but not necessarily because of marrying close relatives. The problem arises either because it has been passed down from "grandfather" or because the husband and wife were nursed by the same woman as infants. In this case, we consider them to be "milk siblings," and marriage between them is forbidden. I will tell you more about this when I come to "nursing."

Just as the first forty days of pregnancy are both auspicious and dangerous – when life is literally held in the balance – so too are the forty days after giving birth. This is surely the most precarious time for the new baby, but you, too, face death. In our language, this postpartum period is known as *loğusalık*. We have a saying about this period: *"Loğusanın mezarı kırk gün açıktır"* (the tomb of the postpartum woman is open for forty days). No doubt the "tomb" is open because you are most likely to die during that period, but so is the womb open and therefore open to evil influences and infections. For this reason, you should not have intercourse with your husband, and you should try to stay indoors as much as you can. I suppose you should not even have visitors, but who can stop them? Everyone wants to see the new baby.

Put your newborn baby to sleep in a cradle made of cloth or a handwoven *kilim* rug that is suspended from the ceiling on ropes. A gauze scarf over it will keep off the flies. You can pull on the attached string to rock the baby softly to sleep while you are doing other things.

When the forty days after the birth have passed, it is our custom for you to take a ritual bath. You can invite all your friends to join you – you may even be able to have a *düğün* feast as we have for weddings and circumcisions. Your mother might also come, and, if she can afford it, she might bring you a crib for when the baby gets too big for the hanging cradle. We will make a party for you and everyone will eat, dance, and be merry. After this, you and the baby are free to go out.

In my day, resting during the *loğusalık* was a luxury. Most of us had to get right up after childbirth and start work again. That is why we got old so quickly. You should try to take it easy during the entire *loğusalık* if you can – it will make you healthy and strong again. You should also try not to become pregnant again too soon after a birth. It is true that if the baby is a girl, everyone will urge you to try again for a son. But too many births, too close together, will age you very quickly, and you could lose your teeth, like me.

Still, because children are the gift of Allah, you should accept whatever you are given. Think, too, of how fortunate you are in comparison to the women who are unable to have children. They truly have no status and are hardly considered adults – it is a difficult position to be in, all the more so because there is no formal adoption of children in Turkey, although I do know of several couples who raised their niece or nephew as their own child. While some people think you should accept as many children as Allah gives, we know that there are ways to have only as many children as you want. In the past, the only method we knew, other than total abstinence – which we do not consider acceptable – was for the man to withdraw before he ejaculated. Men still practice this, but today we have better methods of birth control which the doctor can tell you about.

NURSING

Most women in our village are able to nurse their babies and wish to do so. Breastmilk is the baby's most important food, and nursing your infant is part of your role as mother. Nursing also establishes what we call "milk rights." Because you give of yourself for your child, that child should sustain you in your old age – it is our form of insurance.

You should wait a couple of days after birth before giving your baby the breast. You won't have any milk then anyway. During this time the baby should drink only warm sugar water, which will help the stump of the umbilical cord fall off. For the first three days, you should drink only soup or the sugary syrup in which dried fruit has been cooked. You should clean the baby's midriff several times a day with lemon cologne. Someone will probably bring you some as a gift from town – it is the same kind we use to sprinkle on the hands of guests when they visit. After cleansing, wrap the baby's midriff with a clean cloth. On the third day you may offer the baby your breast, and any time thereafter when it cries. We do not believe in letting them be alone or cry for long periods – babies need to be picked up and coddled as much as possible. You don't have to give both breasts at each feeding. Some babies do not suck very well at first but need to be jiggled, gently, to get their attention.

Babies often fall asleep while they are nursing, and then they can be put in the cradle or, if you are visiting, down on the divan next to you. Babies will fall asleep almost anywhere, so don't be afraid to take your baby with you when you go visiting. Besides, everyone wants to see and hold a new baby. There are always people around who are eager to pick up a new baby, even a crying one. Even teenage boys try to get their turn playing with a baby. Grandmothers and grandfathers make good babysitters. I often see grandfathers taking their new grandchild out with them when they go to chat with their friends. They are very gentle with babies and do not seem to feel nervous or demeaned by caring for an infant. I suppose that is because a baby is proof that their family – and, if the baby is a boy, their line – will continue.

If you have a boy baby, you should nurse him for at least two years; if a girl, only about eighteen months. This is because boys take longer to mature after they are born, even though they develop more quickly in the womb. The extra nursing also helps to give them the strength they will need later on to endure military service.

There are, however, cases in which a new mother is simply unable to nurse her baby. Even though she may feel frantic and despondent, she usually does not blame herself but will conclude that someone has placed a curse on her. In the not so distant past, it was usually fairly easy to find someone else to be the baby's "milk mother" – either another woman in the same household or even a woman from another household. Today this still occurs, but less often. When it does take place, we believe it creates a kind of kinship bond not just between the milk mother and the child, but also between that child and any of her own children. That is to say, in the future, none of the children born from the milk mother's womb could marry this child, for they would be "milk siblings." Should they marry without their knowledge of this bond, we believe they would produce *sakat* (unsound, defective, disabled) offspring. For this reason, we try to keep track of which women nursed which babies, so when the times come for them to marry, it is clear which marriages would be forbidden. Today, some women are beginning to use bottles and formula – and not just women who are unable to nurse, but others who think it is modern. I don't advise bottle feeding. For one thing, I know that some women will skimp on the formula because it is expensive; for another, our water is not always clean, so the baby could get sick.

When your baby boy is two or your baby girl is one and a half, and you are tired of this child continually pulling on your legs demanding your breast, you will know it is time to wean. On the day you make that decision, get up early and smear salty tomato paste on your nipples. The baby will not like this at all and will scream and yell, but you must be firm. Sometimes a child will rebel and refuse to eat any white foods – no yogurt, cheese, milk, or white soup, but such rebellion does not last too long. Cutting this tie that binds mother and child is traumatic for both. We say "they are separated" *(ayrıldılar);* it is the same phrase we use when a husband and wife separate.

Although weaning is traumatic, it is fairly short-lived, for by this time other things have begun to distract the child. Older brothers and sisters love to carry babies around and show them off. Most of the time babies are held by someone; we don't usually let them crawl around very much. Indeed, I am not sure all babies even learn to crawl. They are hardly ever put down on the ground outside, because it is just too dirty and they might pick up something dirty and put it in their mouth. In the house, you can let them sit and crawl around on the floor from time to time because the floors are swept clean several times a day. They will find all kinds of things to play with, but you must be careful – I have seen babies playing with knives and scissors, and that can be very dangerous. And when they start walking, you have to be even more careful that they do not try to touch the stove or pull over the tea kettle of boiling water. Nowadays, relatives in town may bring store-bought toys as gifts. But generally, babies are easily satisfied with a spoon, some yarn, or a stick. Mostly, they just like being around people.

THE TIME BEFORE SIN

Sin does not begin to accumulate until puberty. By then, we believe, young adults can distinguish right from wrong and can be held responsible for their acts. Until then, especially up until the age of seven when they enter school, they are freer than they will ever be again. During this brief period we indulge our children. They bring such delight to us. Indeed, I would say that all children, whether girl or boy, bring joy to their familes. Although boys are especially appreciated because they are necessary to continue the family line, and sons stay with their parents all their lives, little girls are loved and indulged too.

If you ask anyone what is necessary for a happy life, most will say, "children." I have heard versions of a story about this on a number of occasions.

There were two couples – one with a child and one that was childless. The couple with a child were always laughing. The other couple could not understand what made them so happy and asked for their secret. They said, "We have a golden ball, and whenever we play with it we are happy." The other couple used up their savings to buy a golden ball, and tossed it back and forth. But that did not make them laugh and after a while they grew weary.

"What are we doing wrong?' they asked the other couple.

"Our child is our golden ball," they said, "it has the flavor of life like fruit."

So you see, without a child, life seems dull and tasteless. Children are both fun and funny; they also strengthen your marriage and make you truly an adult. Notice how important it is for us to know that our president, our prime minister, and even our military generals are fathers; otherwise, I do not think people would take them seriously.

I am sure you will love your child, whether boy or girl, but you must make sure a boy knows that he is *erkek* – a male – so that he will be set on the proper path. Since girls and boys wear the same kinds of clothes when they are small, a little boy must be taught how to display his male pride. Surely, do not let him play with your headscarves as little girls do when they play at being grown-up. If he acts too silly or spoiled, remind him that he is *erkek* and that this should show in his demeanor. Quite early he will connect being male with his penis – which, he soon learns, little girls don't have. So many times I have heard a father or grandfather ask a small boy, while pointing to his penis, "What is it that boys can do that girls can't?" The correct answer is, "Go to the mosque." It is as if that member qualified him for membership in the brotherhood of Islam. Boys learn early on that they have a special connection to Islam and that it confers upon them a sense of superiority.

A boy takes pride in his penis while a little girl learns to be ashamed of her genitals. No doubt the infant boy learns this when his mother kisses it; she also strokes it to get him to urinate. That is how little boys are toilet trained, and it seems to work like a charm. With little girls, you must hold them over the toilet until they go; you should do this several times a day, especially after meals. As for defecation, you can train boys and girls the same way. Begin this training early, around six months at least, so that you will not have to deal with diapers for very long. People normally use gauze scarf material for diapers, but if you don't have this, rags will do. A few people have bought diapers in the store, and I hear that Americans use a diaper once and then throw it away. When a child defecates in his diaper, you can indicate that this is not acceptable by wrinkling your nose at the smell and saying "shameful." Such odors are especially embarrassing and shameful when there are guests.

When your baby's first tooth comes in, you can have another party. We call this party the "tooth bulgur" after the special food, made of bulgur and chickpeas, that is prepared for the occasion. Some say that giving young babies this food helps the teeth come in without pain – or, as we say, softly – since this cooked food is also soft. Another reason bulgur is served at this party is that the wheat from which it is made is also the main ingredient in bread, which is our most important food, our staff of life. For us, wheat also symbolizes virility, which is why it is thrown at weddings – to ensure many children, especially many sons. Perhaps because wheat and maleness go together, the bulgur party is most often held for boy children. Before the party, you must make quite a lot of the bulgur dish, for many women will come, sometimes accompanied by other small children; these women will bring more food and also gifts for you or the baby. You'd better have a music tape on hand because they will want to dance.

BEHAVIOR

When young children do something naughty, it is silly to try to reason with them. Babies and small children do not yet possess reason. Instead, we just say to a child "that is shameful." Usually that will stop the activity. If not, a light slap to the head will do it. Alternatively, our children hate the midwife's needle, so you can threaten them with that. Or you can say, "I will make a *kurban* (sacrifice) out of you." That is usually enough to scare most children. They will have have had time to witness the animal sacrifices performed at the event we call *Kurban Bayramı*, the annual Muslim festival that marks the end of the period for pilgrimage to Mecca and commemorates the willingness of Ibrahim (or, as Jews and Christians call him, Abraham) to sacrifice his son. Children think that if Ibrahim was willing to sacrifice his son, perhaps their own father might be willing to do the same to them.

Children can be annoying at times, but most of us tolerate quite a bit of naughty or spoiled behavior, for it is children's nature; they don't yet know better. Although children make many demands, we generally try to give them what they ask for because it is sinful and greedy to withhold something from a child. Since they lack reason, children cannot be held responsible for unreasonable demands;

therefore, things they are not supposed to have should be covered or hidden. For example, if you are taking food to a neighbor, cover it to keep it from prying eyes. If you have some money in the house, be sure to keep it hidden.

Although all children are indulged, little girls are often spoiled even more than boys are, partly because their lot will be harder when they grow up. From an early age, but especially after they have started school, boys are expected to act with more decorum – they know their value and begin to show it early. They also know they can tell their sisters what to do, even when the sister is older. At the same time, throughout primary school, childhood is a free time – our kids can run around the village and go in and out of people's houses. They might as well run now, because they cannot run when they get older – in an adult, hurrying is unseemly. Although we let children run around the village, they should not go outside it unless accompanied by an adult. You never know what is out there – wolves, strangers, and especially strange men – all could be dangerous for children. Even the sheepdogs that are sometimes outside the village guarding the flock might well turn on our own children.

CLOTHING AND HAIR

Until the age of about seven, boys and girls lead a pretty carefree and happy life. At the age of seven they begin school. Until then, girls and boys are dressed similarly – in pajama-style pants, tops and sweaters, and of course socks and rubbers. As you know, everyone in the village now wears rubbers for daily footwear – they are so easy to put on and take off when going in and out of houses, and they are waterproof. Not only are young boys and girls dressed the same, but people tend to treat them pretty much the same when they are small.

All Turkish children wear uniforms to school. This is felt to be democratic, since all children will be dressed alike and not competing with each other over a particular article of clothing. Of course in the cities, richer people can buy nicer uniforms for their children, while many of our village children wear hand-me-downs. In primary school, the uniforms consist of a smock – formerly black, now

Plate 11. These Turkish mothers and toddlers are gathered in a home in their village. The little girl's head is bare, but when she reaches puberty, her hair must be covered, just like the women in the group. Photograph by Carol Delaney.

blue – with a white detachable collar. Both girls and boys continue to wear pants beneath them. Only in middle school do girls wear jumpers and blouses instead of pants.

Although young girls and boys dress similarly, there is one aspect of their attire that distinguishes them – their hair. Boys have their hair cut beginning when they are around two; from then on, it is kept short. Although some people cut little girls' hair because it gets so tangled, they really shouldn't. A girl's hair is her embellishment and should be kept long and luxurious for the enjoyment of her future husband. At the same time, girls' (and women's) hair triggers desire in men, so it should be covered with a headscarf (Plate 11). "Covering" traditionally begins at puberty, though nowadays it begins routinely at the end of primary school (at the end of sixth grade) whether or not a girl has actually reached puberty. Covering her hair shows that she is a proper young woman, that she recognizes her value, and that she is "covered" or protected by her father. In that way, she controls and displays the honor of the family. As an adult, she may uncover her hair only for her husband. "Covering," however, is not allowed in Turkish public schools. Now that school is mandatory through eighth grade, I don't know what will happen. Some girls cover their hair going to and from school, removing the headscarf only for the time they are in school. But many of our more religious villagers object to this law and do not want to send their daughters to school if they must be uncovered and must attend classes with boys. In their view, boys and girls who have reached puberty should not be together at all. Instead, the older girls of devout families will begin to go separately to the house of the *imam* one afternoon a week to learn the prayers and principles of Islam.

CIRCUMCISION

Another event that distinguishes the sexes is, of course, circumcision. Your son should be circumcised after he is seven but before he is thirteen. Sometimes several boys will be circumcised at the same time. This is a good idea because then the man who performs the circumcision – often a barber – needs to be called only once so it is cheaper for everyone. The Jews also circumcise their sons, but they do it at birth; we say that doesn't take much bravery. For us, being able to endure the operation without crying out is a mark of courage.

Our practice comes from Ibrahim who circumcised Ishmail when he was about thirteen. Not only is it a test of a boy's courage, but it is also performed for reasons of cleanliness. A boy should be circumcised before he has begun to produce semen, which we consider polluting, so it will not collect under the foreskin. But cleanliness represents more than merely a physical condition; it is also a moral quality. As you know, "cleanliness is the foundation of Islam."

Circumcision is a big event. You will have to put on a special party and invite the other villagers. Your son should have a special outfit. Nowadays, this consists of a white suit with a red cape, hat, and sash. No doubt the older boys tell the little ones horror stories about their circumcisions, but you should encourage your son to be brave and tell him that he will receive a lot of money and treats. Still, that is not what they remember. So many of them associate it with the *kurban* (animal sacrifice), since they, too, have come under the knife; perhaps they feel that a part of them *was* sacrificed.

Making Babies in a Turkish Village

Once boys and girls have reached puberty, they are theoretically ready to marry and begin to have children themselves. However, most of us now wait a few years after puberty so the girl can work on her trousseau and the boy can begin to learn a trade, get settled in helping with the farm, or do his military service. After they have finished primary or even middle school, girls help even more with the housework; this means cleaning the house, cooking, doing the dishes and laundry, and helping with the younger children. Occasionally, girls will get together in one another's houses to work on their trousseaux – embroidering prayer rugs, embroidering sheets and pillowcases, making lace, making trim for headscarves, knitting socks and sweaters, and making "covers" for almost everything. Sometimes the girls will take a jumprope and the makings for tea and have a little party up in the hills; occasionally they play a kind of volleyball – but hidden and out of sight. The boys, on the other hand, almost always gather outside; sometimes they play ball in the open field in front of the village, sometimes they loiter outside the men's tea room, sometimes they just loiter. When there is farmwork, they will help their fathers, while some of them are sent to town to learn a trade.

Nowadays, weddings, including the brideprice, are expensive, so a young man is expected to contribute to the cost. The groom and his family are expected to provide the domicile – at first, usually just a room in the father's house, though occasionally an addition added onto the house. They also provide major furnishings such as the bed, an upholstered couch and chairs, a table, buffet, television, rug, sewing machine, and sometimes a refrigerator. The groom also provides his bride with several outfits of clothing suitable for trips to town. People expect to be married, and most young people look forward to their wedding with excitement and anticipation. Indeed, a wedding, which goes on for several days, is something the entire village looks forward to, for it is a break in the normal routine and a time to visit with people you may not see often. And really, it is what our life is all about, as it signals that a new family is being created, and with that, another generation.

You will be happy in your old age if you have raised several children who, when their turn comes, will make babies and provide you with the joy of grandchildren. Then you can train your daughter or daughter-in-law in all I have taught you during our conversations. When your time comes, you can then pass easily into the next world to enjoy all the pleasures awaiting you there.

CHAPTER 6

Infants of the Dreaming

A Warlpiri Guide to Child Care

Sophia L. Pierroutsakos

THE WARLPIRI OF AUSTRALIA

The Warlpiri people constitute one of at least 500 Aboriginal groups living in Australia. Although there has been much debate about Aboriginal history before European contact, it is known that Aborigines have been in Australia for at least 40,000 years and, according to recent archaeological findings, perhaps for as long as 120,000 to 180,000 years. Rock art and stone artifacts were produced at least 5,000 years ago.

When European settlers arrived in the eighteenth century, the Aboriginal population was estimated as at least 300,000. As of 1986, 228,000 Aborigines resided on the continent, constituting only 1.5 percent of the total population of 15 million. Today, the Warlpiri (sometimes spelled Walpiri or Walbiri) number approximately 2,500. They live primarily in settlements in the Central Desert of Australia's Northern Territory. The Warlpiri speak a distinctive language that belongs to the Pama Nyungan language group, but many Warlpiri also speak "Aboriginal English" as well as other Aboriginal languages.

The arrival of Europeans on the continent led to drastic changes in the lives of the resident Aborigines. Beginning in the early nineteenth and continuing into the twentieth century, the British forcibly took control of much of the native lands and established their own modes of agriculture, often ignoring Aboriginal ties to the land. Confrontations between settlers and native groups were often very violent: Thousands of Aborigines were killed in massacres continuing into the 1930s. Deprived of access to land and unable to gather food, thousands more died of starvation. In some regions, as little as 15 percent of the Aboriginal population survived. Many of the survivors moved to cattle stations to work for European colonists; others lived in and around missions and government ration depots.

Discussing the Warlpiri in both the past and the present is challenging for several reasons. First, some scholars have questioned the extent to which various Aboriginal groups are or ever were fully distinct from one another. Second, in addition to the major historical upheavals the Warlpiri and other Aborigine groups have undergone, the experiences of Warlpiri people living in different settlements, missions, and other areas have varied substantially. Third, multiple Aboriginal groups are represented in many of the settlements and towns in which ethnographic research has been conducted. For instance, some Warlpiri live at Warrabri, but the majority of the residents there are Kaytej, whereas Warlpiri constitute the majority population at Yuendumu. Ethnographic accounts do not always make clear whether practices that are common to Aboriginal groups in a general area are shared by the Warlpiri. The practices described here and in the following "manual" have been reported for at least some groups of Warlpiri or in a few cases are regional practices that are likely to be applicable to them.

By the middle part of the twentieth century, the Australian government had adopted a policy of assimilating Aborigines to white European culture. Much of the population was forcibly relocated to government settlements, including Warrabri, Willowra, Nyirri, and Lajamanu. Most of the Warlpiri were settled in Yuendumu. Although the amount of government control and influence varied among settlements, a network of white government officials controlled many aspects of Aborigine life in the settlements, enforcing curfews, imposing compulsory work, and restricting marriages.

Infants of the Dreaming

In the 1960s, Aborigines, often in conjunction with non-Aboriginal people, began to organize protests for citizen and land rights. Australian citizenship was finally granted to Aborigines in 1967, and several government acts restored some land rights. However, conflict continues between European whites, who claim ownership of land from century-old pastoral leases, and Aborigines, who have millennial-old ties to their native lands. As awareness of the injustices committed against the Aboriginal population has increased, the Australian government has begun efforts to facilitate their access to ancestral lands. Aboriginal people are actively pursuing land claims; the Australian Institute of Aboriginal and Torres Straight Islander Studies is supporting their efforts through their very vigorous publication activities.

Today, some Warlpiri live a "modern" lifestyle in the cities but most dwell on the "fringe," living in small towns that evolved from government settlements and missions. Many Warlpiri have successfully fought for rights to their ancestral lands. Currently, nearly half reside on Warlpiri land. Some live in "country camps" consisting of a few families trying to maintain some of the "old law" of "old-time" living.

The Warlpiri have historically been a seminomadic people living in desert areas in the center of Australia, mainly the Tanami Desert of the Northern Territory, but also parts of neighboring Western Australia. Before European colonization, groups of a few families moved within loose boundaries throughout the desert, or bush, according to seasonal fluctuations in weather and the availability of food and water. They gathered fruits, seeds, and roots, and hunted for large animals, such as kangaroo and emu, and small animals, including lizards and small marsupials. When food and water were scarce, they often broke into small family groups to search for food, rejoining other families when conditions improved. Occasionally, several hundred Warlpiri gathered together. In times of serious drought, they congregated at permanent water holes, but they also came together in prosperous times and for annual rituals.

Family units typically consisted of a man, his parents, his wife or wives, and his children, although this varied from place to place. After a circumcision rite that occurred at puberty, a boy was betrothed to an infant girl. The couple became married when the girl

was around nine or ten years old, so there was a substantial age difference between husband and wife. Marriage was not a formal event;
the young bride simply began spending the night in her husband's
camp. A husband and wife would sometimes alternate living at the
camps of their two families. Men often took one or two additional
wives over the years. Women frequently outlived their husbands.
Widows observed a one- to two-year speech taboo, during which
they communicated using a sign language; after this mourning
period, they could remarry. However, arranged marriages, polygyny,
and remarriage are becoming less common as younger generations
of Warlpiri increasingly adopt aspects of a European lifestyle.

Family organization of the Warlpiri, as with other Aboriginal
groups, is considered by anthropologists to be among the most
complex systems in the world. The Warlpiri are divided into eight
distinctly named "subsections" in which membership is based on
both maternal and paternal relationships. Membership in a particular subsection, often called a "skin group," determines the
nature of one's relationships with members of other subgroups. For
example, it determines ideal eligible marriage partners as well as
who must be avoided in daily contact. Both daughters and sons
belong to their paternal grandfather's subsection. All women of a
given subsection often refer to each other as sisters, even though
they may not share biological parents and may be from different
generations; all women of the same subsection are called "mother"
by all the children of these women. Subsections are further grouped
into other levels and based, in part, on the gender and generation of
individuals.

Warlpiri society has very strict rules regarding which relatives
should and should not socialize with each other. For instance,
mothers-in-law should never interact with their sons-in-law, or even
with potential sons-in-law, and a woman has an avoidance relationship with the man who circumcised her son. Such individuals
should not speak or be in each other's company, but they often send
each other certain gifts, such as food, through other relatives.

Kin groups comprise the people with whom one lives and travels.
Such groups may include anywhere from ten to sixty members. The
residential grouping of individuals was often based on men's descent
lines; for instance, two brothers, together with their wives, might

live together. Nevertheless, these groups can change over time as people relocate and travel.

In the past, each Warlpiri had a personal Aboriginal name. This name was sometimes taboo to use in conversation, as when a relative with a similar-sounding name died. Instead, one might be called by terms based on one's subsection and reflecting one's relation to the speaker. Today, most children are given a European first name and a surname, and very few receive a personal Aboriginal name.

In earlier times, when several families joined together during bush trips, each family had an area within the general camp where the husband, his wife or wives, and their children gathered at night. A separate area was designated for bachelors, and another for single women – unmarried women, widows, and married women who were sick, whose husbands were away, or who were seeking protection from their husbands. These separate areas facilitated the maintenance of avoidance relationships. Shelter consisted of low windbreaks, tents, or huts that men and women built and collapsed as the group moved. Today, however, most Warlpiri live in corrugated iron lean-tos.

Religion and ritual, which permeate all aspects of Warlpiri daily life, revolve around the concept of *Jukurrpa,* which has been translated as "the Dreaming" or the "Ancestral Present," an unspecified time that is simultaneously in the past and the present. At that time, Ancestral Beings created the physical and spiritual world and left marks throughout the land as evidence of their life. Their essence is present throughout the desert; they communicate to mortals through dreams. All adults participate in many ceremonies to sustain and be sustained by these ancestors.

The Warlpiri relationship with the spiritual world differs markedly from the common Western notion of honoring or pleasing spirits in order to ensure good fortune. Instead, ancestors' lives are re-enacted through ritual. This maintains the connections with the ancestors' life-giving force and facilitates the conception of future generations. People are believed to have a deep link to the land where they were conceived, and they are responsible for knowing the ritual and history associated with that land. However, land is not privately owned, but belongs collectively to those linked to a particular area. The rights to particular land may be inherited through one's subsection, but there are other ways to acquire these rights as well.

The connection between the past and the present is maintained through ritual, which includes song, dance, drawing, and painting. Songs and storytelling are central to Warlpiri ritual and are especially important during rites of passage, for curing the sick, and to increase fertility. Songs are used to pass ancestral history on to future generations. Communication about past and present life is also accomplished through an elaborate system of designs that are believed to have adorned the bodies of Ancestral Beings and to carry a vital life force. These designs are drawn or painted on the body, in the sand, and – today – on canvas to bring the life force into the present. In recent years, Warlpiri and other Aboriginal art has come into vogue in Western societies, generating controversy over the appropriateness of the commercial display of religious articles.

The conflict between Aboriginal traditions and European influence and control is pervasive. Today, Warlpiri life, and Aboriginal life in general, is a precarious balance between two distinct lifestyles. One Aboriginal woman who has lived both in a settlement town and in a camp on the edge of the town expressed this balance in this way: "We have two different sets of rules at Warrabri. While we are in the settlement, we do *papulanji* [white] way. In the camps we do it *yapa* [Aboriginal] way."

For the childcare "manual" that follows, I have created a (fictional) grandmother who is offering advice about conceiving and raising children based on her own experiences, for the benefit of her own (fictional) granddaughter who is seeking to maintain certain Warlpiri traditions while adopting other Western ones.

INFANTS OF THE DREAMING

A Warlpiri Guide to Child Care

About the Author

I was raised in Warlpiri country according to the Old Law. As a child, I lived in the bush, in the Central Desert of Australia, before the Europeans came here. However, many things have changed since then. I raised my own children during a difficult time; in our contact with Europeans, we have experienced many hardships – losing our land and struggling with alcoholism, domestic abuse, and health problems. Our Law has been violated, and many of our babies have died.

A few years ago, Aboriginal women from throughout the Central Desert met at Alice Springs to discuss our beliefs about "borning," the Aboriginal way of coming into being. We learned that we share many fears and concerns about the "whitefellah way" of giving birth. We also share a desire to return to some of the old ways of the borning process.

In this guide, I direct my advice about the old way of life to my granddaughter. She might have the opportunity to have her baby according to strong Grandmother's Law, the way of her ancestors, while still incorporating some of the ways of the whitefellah. She is now living in a country camp. I am pleased that she will try to have her baby in her own country, at a clinic that respects Aboriginal Law.

These days, few of our young women have a chance to hear the wisdom of their grandmothers, for they rarely live near one another. New mothers are nowadays advised by their mothers or older sisters, but these women do not know the Old Law as I have lived it. I hope that knowing our beliefs and ways will help my granddaughter raise her precious children with an understanding of our history, even in the modern world she now inhabits. By reading this guide, she can learn how our people have always loved children and have helped them understand what it means to live life in Warlpiri country.

❧

THE LAND IS OUR LIFE FORCE

We call the country mother . . . The mother gives us everything, like the land. A woman gives birth on the ground, always on the ground. So when you think of where you were born you think of the country.

This guide is for Warlpiri mothers who want to understand how children were raised according to the Old Law. Some Warlpiri today are raising their babies in a town or settlement area instead of in the bush, and they deal with white Australians on a daily basis. We are constantly faced with European ideas, and our traditions and heritage have been threatened.

These challenges are not experienced by Warlpiri alone. One Aboriginal woman at Warrabri expressed our shared struggle poignantly:

When we lived in the bush . . . we were not frightened of men, our marriages were safe, there was no sickness, there were no jealous fights, no alcohol, no money and we did not starve. Our children were healthy . . .

Today, we are deprived of our land and our water supply. We have even lost many of our precious children, who were taken away to be adopted into European people's homes. Although this horrible practice has stopped, our people continue to struggle with poverty, unemployment, alcoholism, and disease.

Some efforts have recently been made to help us connect with our ancestral lands. Many Warlpiri have returned to the "settle down country" where their ancestors once lived. I am very pleased that you are also doing this. But one cannot go back and undo the damage: Our life before European settlement is gone forever. As a woman in a European world, you cannot live the life we grandmothers did. The drastic changes in our experience make it even more necessary that you are aware of our old way of living. We have been made to feel ashamed of our Aboriginal heritage by white missionaries, white teachers, white tourists, white government officials, and white nurses and doctors, when instead we should feel pride in our tradition. There is no better time for you to explore your heritage than while you await the birth of a Warlpiri descendant.

We know that if we do not maintain our connection with the past, we will surely suffer: We would find no food and fall sick. Unfortunately, in many ways this has come to pass today. I am sure different people would explain this in their own ways, but I doubt many Warlpiri would disagree that distance from our land and our ritual has been harmful in both physical and spiritual ways. Many sites have lost the energy the Ancestral Beings left during their travels. Many of us have managed to return to "our place" in the country; however, this can leave us far from services that are important for our health and survival in today's world.

THE DREAMING AND PARENTHOOD

The advice given here should supplement the wisdom imparted by your own *kapirdi* (older sisters) and *ngati* (mothers). As for sharing what you learn with the child's father, most men do not want to discuss matters such as pregnancy and childbirth, which are considered "women's business." Nonetheless, men do help in many ways with childbirth and contribute to child rearing.

Both men and women are aware of the importance of the Dreaming in our lives and in the lives of our children. We might also call this the Ancestral Present or the Ancestral Times; in our language we call it the *Jukurrpa*. During this time, our ancestors lived and traveled the land. They left their ancestral powers "lodged in the country." In ritual, we connect with this past, bringing it into the present, and thus gain an important life force that sustains us. *Jukurrpa* has many different meanings; for instance, we might use it to refer to the Ancestral Beings themselves, as well as the dreams through which they visit us at night. Of course, the Ancestral Beings of which I speak here are different from the ancestors that lived a few generations before us, such as grandmothers and grandfathers.

Ancestral powers are pivotal in the creation of your child. Neither evil nor good, they simply have power over everything. Although biological conception is necessary, *spiritual* conception is more important. It is made possible by the *kuruwarri,* or "ancestral fertility power," which was left in the ground when our ancestors traveled the earth. (We also use this word to refer to the marks these powers leave on the earth, which we then draw on the sand and on our bodies to stand for them.) The *kuruwarri* animates the fetus inside you, thereby confirming your pregnancy. It then takes residence in some part of the environment, which might be an animal or plant, or an entity such as rain, wind, fire, or yams.

As you become pregnant, a conception spirit, or *kurruwalpa,* enters your body and gives your child a spiritual identity and character. Either your vagina or the soles of your feet can serve as the doorway for this spirit to enter your body.

Your child's life is forever connected to the ancestral site at which you conceive. Therefore, your child should maintain a life-long connection to this land and the Ancestral Beings occupying it. Based on the ancestral site at which you conceive, certain *kuruwarri* designs become an important link to your baby's spiritual heritage. In ritual we recreate the drawings and sand stories that bring the past into the present, thus maintaining the Ancestral Present.

CONCEIVING THE WARLPIRI WAY

As a young wife you may have many questions about conception and pregnancy. In the old days, girls became betrothed before their tenth birthday, but they did not have sex with their husband until after puberty. Nowadays, our women marry later and are more likely to choose their own husbands. Many Warlpiri women are very open about sex and reproductive matters; depending on who is around, some women may be glad to discuss them with you. Listen as older wives and widows share their experiences; learn from their wisdom.

Your husband should participate in fertility rituals. Even though women and men participate in some rituals together, this is not usually true for fertility rituals. Some details of men's ceremonies have been kept secret from women, as have women's from men. I have heard that at Yuendumu, women do not have secret ritual knowledge. In any case, it is often true that men and women know more about each others' rituals than they might admit. It is enough to tell you that men perform "increase ceremonies," which help all living things to reproduce and flourish.

Be sure to participate in female *yawulyu* rituals, which involve singing, storytelling, and drawing designs. I am saddened to see fewer young women go to ceremonies; how else will they learn about our rituals and how to take care of themselves and their families? These ceremonies ensure your connection with the land and keep your relatives healthy.

You can encourage pregnancy by drawing special designs, which are also called *yawulyu*, on your body before having sex with your husband. There are many designs that represent the ancestors and their lives; your mother and sisters, and most importantly, your father's sister, can show you which ones to use. Remember, though, that ritual alone does not lead to pregnancy: You must also have sex with your husband. In fact, you must have intercourse several times; a single instance does not usually result in pregnancy. In my experience, it was my husband who would initiate intercourse. We would get together somewhere outside the camp during the day, for at night there is evil wandering.

Men often minimize the importance of sex for conception. They focus on the importance of ritual, especially their own fertility rituals. We women are usually more willing to acknowledge the role of sex. Still, we all recognize that physical relations alone cannot lead to pregnancy, for a child is composed of both a physical, mortal substance and an immortal spirit. Sex creates the fetus that the *kurruwalpa* enters. This conception spirit gives life to your child.

However, it is the Ancestral Beings and the powers of the *kuruwarri* that make all this possible.

Even though some say that a large family is very desirable, others point out that it is difficult to care for many young children. Especially in hard times, a mother may not have enough milk to breastfeed two babies, and carrying more than one young child while walking long distances is very difficult. Fortunately, our practice of breastfeeding for up to five years seems to keep us from getting pregnant too often; of course, it also provides important nutrition to our children. You can also prevent too many pregnancies by having sex less frequently, since we know that a single sexual encounter does not lead to conception, as well as by practicing the withdrawal method (which one of the older women living near you can explain). An Anbarra woman told me to avoid meat, fish, honey, and eggs soon after giving birth or else I would conceive again. If you become pregnant too soon after your last baby, please accept the situation. To me, abortion is unacceptable. Even though it is legal today, in my day, relatives and friends would shame you for committing such a terrible act; we should not try to control the *kuruwarri*.

Today, young women in some areas are having children at younger ages and closer together. In other places, our women are having children later, in part because they do not adhere to promised marriages: They wait until they are eighteen to twenty years old, and they choose who to marry. As for men, nowadays they marry at a younger age than in the past, at eighteen to twenty-five years old. With all of these changes, many of our babies are sick and must spend time away at a hospital.

Today, you are probably learning about modern methods of birth control. I have heard that today some women use condoms, but I do not know how they work. Hopefully, with both modern and old ways to choose from, you will not have to deal with pregnancies that come too close together.

BORNING

How do you know if you are pregnant? You will notice certain changes in your body: Your periods will stop, and you may feel nausea, or feel pain while you urinate. You will also receive some sign or dream that gives you clues about the child's spiritual lineage. You may first feel ill in the area belonging to the Emu or Ancestral Rain, you may notice the tracks of an ancient creature across your path, or you may see an Ancestral Being in a dream. Relatives, such as your father's mother, your mother's mother, or your mother's father, might dream of an Ancestral Being coming from or sitting on their stomach. The sickness, the tracks, or the dream tell you that you conceived in the land of this particular Ancestral Being: This is where you "found" your child. Your child is tied to the land associated with this being and will always have a claim to this land. He or she inherits a ritual obligation to the land that involves bringing the Ancestral Beings, who live in the ground and other parts of the environment, into the present.

If you are pregnant, it is great news. Pregnancy is an important part of the life of a young Warlpiri woman; it is part of becoming the person you should become. Your child has *palka jarrimi* or has been "brought into being." We also call this beginning the "borning" of the child. For us, borning is the process by which "the spirit of the land and the people come together," beginning with the conception of your child and continuing through the physical birth.

Share the news of your pregnancy with your husband. While the father of the child or other relatives may have dreams about the pregnancy, it is primarily your responsibility to note any signs and tell your family what you have seen. Together with your husband, you should then try to determine where you conceived. However, you will probably not talk much of your pregnancy after that, as this is a very sensitive time for your pregnancy.

It is up to you to watch out for your pregnancy from the moment of conception and to prevent a miscarriage. There are several foods you must never eat while pregnant. For instance, do not eat animals such as anteater, possum, Varanus goanna, or Tiliqua lizard, all of which have spiked or sharp body parts. The meat from these animals, even if you avoid the spikes, can harm your baby while nursing, so stay away from these foods until the baby is weaned. For your baby to develop properly, you must also avoid very strong foods, such as emu, bustard, and rabbit-bandicoot. Of course, these days it is rare for us to find these animals in the bush, so it should not be hard for you to respect this rule. Strong "modern" foods, like eggs and hot tea, are also not advisable while you are pregnant.

Be absolutely certain that you do not harm any specific type of animal that is linked to your baby's spirit. For instance, if your child was conceived in an area known as the land of ancestral dogs – such as on the Warrabri settlement – you must always be very respectful of all dogs. If you or anyone else you know harms or kills one, you may miscarry, or later your child may fall ill or die.

With pregnancy, most of your daily activities do not have to change. Sex with your husband is not taboo as it will not harm anything. You can also continue to work. I remember pregnant mothers in my day continuing to gather food and firewood for their families, walking many miles every day. Today, you must light the fire and buy and gather food. You probably also have to work as a laundry woman or housekeeper, or you might work for the local governing body, the Council. However, if you travel while you are pregnant, you should avoid areas inhabited by dangerous ancestral forces that could harm you. In fact, you may be asked to leave ceremonial ground to ensure your safety.

The nature of the relationship between co-wives during pregnancy can vary greatly. In fact, my relationships with my own two co-wives were some of my strongest emotional bonds. They were both subsection sisters, and I knew them longer than I knew my husband and lived with them after my husband died. They helped with the work that I did every day, including taking care of my babies, doing the wash, and making the fire. It is true that not all marriages work so well – many women I have known feel jealousy and anger toward their co-wives and cannot rely on them for help during pregnancy.

Throughout your pregnancy you will likely be very respected by those around you. The high value we place on childbirth and child rearing is evident in stories that have been passed down and told to us since the time of the Dreaming. Do not forget that as mothers and "daughters of the Dreaming" we deserve respect and dignity.

CHILDBIRTH

Months have passed, and your body has changed dramatically. Soon you will give birth. We Warlpiri women usually mark this life event with some ritual, but in contrast to the Europeans, we do not regard birth as highly stressful or traumatic. Still, it is understandable if you are afraid of the pain of childbirth. Fortunately, I was not alone during labor. However, you will most likely deliver in a hospital and will not have the company you would like for comfort. This can be a very frightening experience, especially if no one in the hospital speaks your language. Fortunately, I have heard that the government may establish a borning center in Alice Springs so that borning according to our Law can be maintained.

In my day, as a woman approached the end of her pregnancy, it was important that she or her mother selected a woman to help her in childbirth. Ideally, this would be her mother's mother. If this was not possible, the pregnant woman could ask her own mother or sister. It was important that the "midwife" be competent and have experience assisting in birth, for she was often the only person who would be at the delivery, since birth is a private affair. In my day, it was improper to offer the midwife any payment; this is a European custom that might have offended her.

Birth was imminent when I felt pain down where the baby would come out. I let my midwife know immediately so she could help me prepare. Someone also let the father of my child know that I was in labor so he could begin his own ritual; he had important things to do.

In old times, the husband would never be present during the birth. He would immediately go to the bachelors' camp, strip completely, and decorate his body with red ochre stripes that would provide strength for his wife and baby. He would then sit alone to ponder the birth. In this way, he could help the birth without being present. This was especially important if the labor was difficult; by speaking with the Ancestral powers, the husband could help the baby come out. Once the baby was born and the midwife had yelled "It is born!" across the camp, the husband would join the other men in the community and resume his normal activities.

If we were on a long hunting or gathering trip with our group when labor came, the pregnant woman and her midwife would stop for childbirth, catching up with the rest of the group later. If we were settled in a camp, the midwife or a few other women would take the pregnant woman to a quiet edge of the widows' camp away from other people. There, the midwife might build a small, temporary shelter.

When the pain intensified, the midwife would then build a fire of acacia leaves in a hole in the ground. This fire provided warmth and kept flies away as the laboring woman lay naked. The smoke from this fire was good for the woman in labor. Sometimes the father was also involved in these preparations, building the fire to "smoke" the mother and the baby.

If a woman was giving birth in the bush, the midwife would help her into a squatting position. By supporting her shoulders and rubbing her belly, she would facilitate delivery. As the pregnant woman squatted, the baby would be delivered directly onto the soil. The land is our mother and provides for all our needs, so it is important that a new life should arrive directly onto her surface.

Assuming a healthy child was born, the midwife cut the umbilical cord with a pointed stick and then tied the cord and packed it with dirt or acacia ashes to prevent bleeding. Our babies are born with very light skin, and coating them with acacia ashes protected against the strong sun. Herbal medicines provided strength for the newborn. We believed it was also important to smoke the young baby; the baby was held over the smoking acacia leaves so that the smoke would surround and give strength to the child (Plate 12).

When I was giving birth, I did not tell the white doctors. Instead, I gave birth with the help of my sisters, according to Grandmother's Law. Today, if you deliver in a hospital, you might take your child to the bush later to have the baby smoked. Of course, this would be more difficult for women not living in country camps and without access to the land.

While the midwife was taking care of my newborn, I squatted over the hole of smoldering leaves. When a woman was not pregnant, this would speed up her menstrual flow; after childbirth, it cleansed her system and helped the body expel the afterbirth. When the midwife was finished preparing the child, either she or the new

Plate 12. An Aboriginal mother smokes her newborn, holding the baby over the smoking ashes to give strength. Drawing by Diana Zion. The drawings in Plates 12 and 13 are modeled after photographs of Warlpiri people performing the actions represented. To respect the Warlpiri taboo against Warlpiri seeing photographic images of their deceased relatives, we have chosen not to publish the original photographs.

mother would bury the afterbirth at the edge of the camp so that dogs could not get to it.

I then prepared a special necklace using hair string and part of the umbilical cord, which I put around my baby's neck. This necklace symbolized the boomerang for boy infants and the digging stick for girls. Both of these objects have important ties to the Dreamtime as they were used both to gather food and in ritual. This necklace would prevent crying and keep the baby from getting sick.

A World of Babies

I did not produce milk the first few days after birth, so I left the breastfeeding to a co-wife or sister who had nursing children. During this time, I stayed in the widows' camp with my baby to rest and regain my strength, being sure to sit over smoking acacia leaves occasionally to help my milk flow. The other women brought me food and helped me care for my baby.

People have had different opinions as to when a woman could join her husband in her family camp and begin caring for the rest of her family. This ranged from a few hours (especially if we were on a hunting and gathering trip) to a few days. My husband decorated the new baby with the same red ochre stripes he drew on his own body during my labor to signify that he accepted the child as his own. Such stripes, drawn from the baby's chest down to the navel, gave children strength (Plate 13). Before returning to your daily

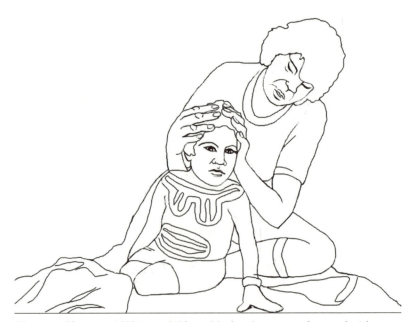

Plate 13. This young Warlpiri child is rubbed with grease and painted with *yawulyu* designs to promote healthy growth. Drawing by Diana Zion.

responsibilities, you will need something for carrying your infant. In my day, we used an oblong, bowl-like baby carrier carved from wood, called a *parraja* or a *coolamon*, lined with blankets. Shoulder straps attached to the ends allowed me to carry my baby comfortably along my side. I found this helpful as I did my chores.

You should hardly ever put your baby onto the ground; instead, you or another person should hold the baby most of the time. I find it unthinkable to leave your baby alone! If you are a young mother, other women should keep an eye on you to make sure you do not mishandle your baby.

Whenever your baby cries, simply offer your breast. If the baby begins to cry while being held by your husband or someone else, take the baby back for feeding. The child should never be denied milk – a crying baby tells others that you are not doing your job well. It was never our way to put babies on a feeding schedule; that was introduced by the Europeans.

Your baby's nutritional needs will be satisfied by your breastmilk, but you should accustom your child to adult foods almost right away. Early on you can let your baby suck on a piece of cloth soaked with dark tea. Later, begin feeding your baby small pieces of lizard, if available, or boiled beef fat.

To ensure fat, healthy babies, the mother or a relative would routinely draw stripes with red ochre on the baby's stomach to encourage the growth of fat (Plate 13). The drawings tell specific stories about the Dreaming. In addition, we rubbed the baby's body and head with grease from the kangaroo, goanna lizard, and/or witchetty grub to encourage growth; today, you can use baby oil or margarine. We also washed our babies with a mixture of a medicinal plant, called *jungarrayi-jungarrayi*, and water, which made them strong.

You obviously have a great responsibility both toward your child and toward the Dreaming. If your brother or the child's father feels you are not adequately conscientious, he has the right to scold or physically punish you. This is unlikely, however, since we are a warm and loving people, as is evident in how we treat our children. Some have claimed that Aboriginal mothers tend to be rough with their young children, but such behavior is the exception, not the rule. You are expected to lavish affection upon your baby. Kiss and nuzzle your child; blow kisses on the infant's stomach. You will both enjoy the experience. You can even wake your baby to pass around to other adults or children for more affectionate treatment.

YOUR TODDLER

Toward the end of the first year, babies begin crawling and walking; even if we could keep them in the wooden sling, they would have outgrown it. In the old days, at this point, it became difficult to bring the child along to search for food. Our husbands were often hunting during the day; in any case, they were not usually responsible for young boys, or for girls of any age. Fortunately, we could count on our female relatives for help. When we needed to gather food, we could leave our child with our sisters, mothers, or grandmothers. Of course, there were times to reciprocate and look after *their* children while they collected food.

In my day, searching for food occupied most of our time every day. This became more urgent once we had children. It was not until their late teenage years that children became full providers of food themselves. Of course, we valued the larger animals hunted by our men, but most of our diet came from the plants, grubs, and small animals that women, older children, and sometimes men gathered and hunted. Indeed, wives often provided a major portion of our nutrition. In some Warlpiri groups, women also prepared and distributed all the food, including the men's hunt, so they had an important role in making sure that people got enough to eat. In fact, before contact with Europeans, we Warlpiri did not consider women's contributions to our society to be inferior to men's.

When we were in camp with everyone else, we did not need to worry about our children wandering throughout the area. Although there were many snakes and animals that could harm our babies inside the camp, there were also many people to keep an eye on them. Even in modern times, it is typical for Warlpiri children to travel throughout the camp or settlement during the day.

Your children are your first priority, and both the mother and father are supposed to nurture and teach them. If your children have already eaten their share of a meal but demand some of your portion, you should give it to them even if this means you will go hungry. By sharing freely with our children, we teach them to share with others. Your toddlers will be spending almost every moment with you. In my day, both my daughters and my sons spent most of their time with me when they were very young. However, as my sons got older and their spirits were strong enough, they began to learn about songs and other aspects of ritual, some of which were kept secret from women. Meanwhile, I taught my daughters the skills I knew. For instance, by watching me, they learned how to gather fruit, tubers, and grubs and how to prepare food.

Some of our rituals help ward off illness, but children do sometimes get sick. At these times, my husband or one of my co-wives would find bush medicine for me, including some plants to rub on us and others to breathe in. Also, women would assemble and sing healing songs. For instance, singing the dreaming song of the rain will reduce swelling. You may also want to visit a local *ngangkayi*, or traditional healer, who has many skills. In addition, today, many women use European remedies such as Vicks menthol rub or aspirin. The best idea, of course, is to *prevent* illness through singing, storytelling, and body decoration.

"GROWING UP" WARLPIRI BOYS AND GIRLS

Warlpiri people know that both men and women's responsibilities are equally important to our survival and that one sex is no less important than the other. It is true that some responsibilities differ for men and women, and some of these differences are experienced from birth and throughout childhood. I "grew up" my children so that they could contribute to and function in their community in whatever way appropriate for their sex.

Mothers and fathers have had very strong relationships with both their male and female children. Starting from infancy, fathers played with and doted on their daughters. They were not hesitant with physical affection and would paint their daughters' bodies. The father was responsible for protecting his daughter from harm, from infancy through adulthood. Even married daughters often turned to their fathers for protection and in times of need. When her father died, a daughter would show respect by immediately wailing and cutting wounds into her head.

Fathers also had very strong relationships with their sons, lavishing affection on them from infancy. The bond grew even stronger when they started spending more time together. The tie between father and son intensified when the boy was circumcised at puberty and began attending male rituals. Sons learned male ceremonies by watching their fathers.

Mothers have typically been very close to their sons; some observers say the mother-son relationship is the most revered relationship in our society. When my boys were babies, I constantly lavished affection on them, blowing kisses on their bodies and using babytalk. My strong relationship with my sons continued into their adulthood. However, throughout my life, I have spent most of my time with my daughters and developed a close bond with them. In the course of daily life, I prepared my daughters to handle their own households when they married.

Parents would make arrangements for their daughter's betrothal when she was still an infant or even before she was born. The mother would never attend the betrothal, however, because of her avoidance relations with her future son-in-law. In my day, a daughter would marry at age nine or ten. Since I married a man in a local group, I continued to see my own mother in the camp, and even spent a few nights a week with her until I felt comfortable with my new husband.

FEELINGS IN WARLPIRI SOCIETY

When we feel sad or happy or mad, we usually express it. You can be free with your happy feelings, expressing your affection and joy to your children of all ages, not just infants. Your children will learn how to express their feelings, as they learn many other things, by watching you. Although we freely cuddle and show affection to our children, it is very unusual for a man and woman to show affection to each other in public. I have seen European couples hold hands in public to show they care for another; I would never have done this with my husband, as it might have hurt the feelings of my two co-wives.

When you are sad and especially if you are in mourning, it is appropriate to make some ritualized outward expression, either by making cuts on your skin or by covering yourself with dust. If you do not express your feelings in these ways, your relatives will nag you to do so. However, when the grieving period is over, it is improper for you to continue to show pain.

Children also learn from adults that if certain rules are followed, terrible feelings can be avoided. We feel fear and shame if we encounter someone we should always avoid. I have seen grown men jump up and run away to avoid meeting their wife's mother.

LANGUAGE

As with so many other aspects of our life, the way we speak is more complicated than it used to be. Today's Warlpiri children typically speak two or even three languages. They often speak English, the language used in government schools, and may also speak the language of another Aboriginal group. The Australian law requires our children to go to school, even though European-style schooling does not blend well with many of our beliefs and practices, not to mention our language. Therefore, parents do not always send their children to school. However, this may get them into trouble with the law.

Let me tell you what I saw of how babies' language developed at the time I raised my own children. Babies make sounds, but not real words, so we often teased and mimicked them, in part to keep them from moving forward in their language before they were ready. Of course, we commonly tease each other and joke about many things so that children become very used to this. They learn to tease back and to participate in the way we talk. It seems that young children talk more freely when we are not around to hear them or tease them. Our children typically do not utter their first understandable words until age two, maybe because our language does not have many very short words. Until they are about five years old and are speaking more clearly, we use babytalk with our children.

The way we speak will continue to change in years to come; the language children hear today is very different from what it was when I was a child. With exposure to television, our children hear and learn to speak more English from an early age. I do not know how this will affect our children's understanding of their own language.

NAMING

Our names link us with our ancestry. To foreigners, our system of kin names seems very complex, and it is true that it takes our children many years to learn the naming system. We typically simplify the names for children so that they can learn them slowly as they mature. It is necessary to learn these names since they are typically used when calling each other.

In the past, children were given an Aboriginal personal name. One of my parents or my husband's parents offered their own proper name for my children. Boys were usually named after a grandfather, especially the mother's father. Girls were named after a grandmother, usually the mother's mother. However, we were free to name the child from either our own family or our husband's. Often, the name referred to an Ancestral Being or a sacred site that was revealed in a dream.

Children were named after their second or third year in a fairly informal ritual; today, this is often delayed until children are around five years old. I was amazed when I heard that in many other parts of the world, children are actually named at birth and called by their proper names throughout life. We should *not* do this in the child's presence! Instead, we use subsection names or a word that describes the child's point in development, such as *warungka*, which means "not yet articulated."

There are strict rules of behavior to be followed upon the death of the relative who has a name that sounds similar to the child's, or for whom the child was named. For about a year after the death of such a person, the child should be called "no name" or *kumanjayi*.

Today, very few children receive Aboriginal personal names. Instead, European first and last names are chosen at birth since they are required by Australian law and used in the schools. Thus, nowadays children and adults are called by a variety of names, including "skin" names and European names, and nicknames based on Aboriginal personal names.

AROUND THE FIRE

Within my group's camp, my own family camp was based around a small structure and my family gathered here to sleep at the end of the day. Together with my husband, my children, and my co-wives and their children, I would sleep on the ground around the fire. We come from the ground, so it is right that we should sleep on the ground.

My young children slept in my embrace until they were about seven or eight years old. I was careful not to sleep too close to the fire so that they would not accidentally roll into it. Be sure that you and your children sleep on your side so that your individual spirits, or *pirlirrpa*, can leave your body through the umbilicus and travel at night in the Ancestral Realm. Take care not to wake your child suddenly; otherwise, the spirit will not have time to return to his or her body.

Today, Warlpiri sleeping arrangements vary, depending on whether families live in or on the edge of cities, in old missions, cattle stations, or settlements. It is most common for our people to sleep outside of their huts or lean-tos near the camp fire. This is probably how you will now sleep at your country camp. This will allow you to maintain your connection with the ground. The land is both a spiritual place and a source of our livelihood. Sleeping on it allows the Ancestral Beings to visit you in your dreams.

CONNECTING WITH THE DREAMING

As I have emphasized, our lives must embody the Dreaming. This is best accomplished through ceremony and ritual that we teach our children. We value our children above all else; the life force of the Dreaming permits our children and our culture to live on. We have an obligation to care for them and each other as best we can, providing them both physical and spiritual nourishment and a full understanding of their ancestry. Your greatest source of support in this effort will continue to be the women in your kin group.

Two hundred years of European colonization have strained our connection with the past, and we struggle to regain and maintain the most basic rights. It seems appropriate to close with a poem written by an Aboriginal poet, Bobbi Sykes, in which pregnancy is a metaphor for the challenges we face:

> We do not always talk
> of our pregnancy
> for we are pregnant
> with the thrust of freedom;
> And our freedom looks to others
> As a threat.

CHAPTER 7

The View from the *Wuro*

A Guide to Child Rearing for Fulani Parents

Michelle C. Johnson

THE FULANI OF WEST AFRICA

The Fulani (also known as the Fula, Peul, and Fulbe) constitute one of the largest ethnic groups in West Africa. Numbering about 10 million, they are distributed across the southern edge of the Sahara Desert in a broad east-west belt of savannah that includes open woodland interspersed with grassland. The largest concentration of Fulani is found in northern Nigeria, where they are intermixed with settled Hausa people, but they also constitute minority groups in most other countries of West and Central Africa, including Mauritania, Senegal, Gambia, Guinea-Bissau, Guinea, Sierra Leone, Mali, Niger, Burkina Faso, Côte d'Ivoire (Ivory Coast), Togo, Ghana, Cameroon, the Central African Republic, and Chad. The Fulani speak Fulfulde (which belongs to the West Atlantic group of Sudanic languages), as well as the languages of their "host" countries. Most Fulani are practicing Muslims.

Because they are scattered over a vast area, inhabiting many different countries and leading somewhat diverse lifestyles, it is difficult to pinpoint exactly who "the Fulani" are. For convenience, the Fulani can be roughly divided into three major groups based on the degree to which they adhere to their traditional, pastoral way of life. The first group comprises the nomadic or pastoral Fulani, who regularly move with their families in search of optimal conditions for their herds of cattle. For example, in the dry season (roughly September to May) the Fulani of northern Nigeria travel south with their herds to avoid drought and to find adequate grazing land. In the rainy season (roughly June to August), their herds are taken north to avoid the dreaded tsetse fly, a source of disease in both cattle and humans.

Their cattle are highly valued by the pastoral Fulani whose sustenance depends on the milk and milk products that provide the bulk of their diet during the rainy season and that are exchanged for grain. Only on special ritual occasions such as the naming ceremony of a child will they slaughter a cow and eat the meat, and they sell cattle only when in dire need of cash.

For pastoral Fulani, cattle are central not only to sustenance, but to their very sense of identity. The cow is such an integral part of their life that it is said to be the father of the Fulani; according to a proverb, "If the cattle die, the Fulbe will die." Being a "good Fulani" is synonymous with being a competent herder, and the nomadic way of life is still considered to be the most "Fulani-like." Their cattle inspire men and herd-boys to compose songs and poems when traveling with them. Cattle are adorned and given names, and herd-boys as young as seven years of age will know the cattle calls, the genealogy of their herds, the types of grasses favored by their animals, and the *gikku* (character) of each.

Settled or sedentary Fulani make up the second group. Most settled Fulani are completely engaged in agricultural production and do not own cattle. Having no herds and hence no need to move, they reside in permanent villages. "Town Fulani," who hold jobs or are students in large cities, also fall into this category.

The largest group of Fulani today are semi-sedentary. They practice a mixed economy of cattle herding and agriculture. Hence, they must strive for both a practical and an ideological balance between herding and farming, constantly weighing the need for seasonal grazing to ensure the health and safety of their herds against the need to stay in one place to tend their crops. Since pastoralism is still highly esteemed and remains central to personhood and identity, most Fulani think of themselves as herders more than farmers and would sacrifice their crops for the well-being of their herds. The manual that follows is based on the lifestyle and child-rearing practices of the semi-sedentary Fulani.

Traditionally, most Fulani of all groups maintain a three-tiered status system of social groups: "free" Fulani (the traditional ruling class), artisans (blacksmiths, bards, woodworkers, and women potters), and descendants of slaves. As among some other West African pastoralist groups, marriage among the Fulani ideally occurs within a limited circle defined by ties between male relatives. Some Fulani are polygymous and, when Islamicized, follow the Muslim limitation of four wives. Favored marriage arrangements unite the children of two brothers or the children of a brother and sister. For all sedentary, semi-sedentary, and nomadic groups, the new wife leaves her own family's compound to reside with the groom's family. Cattle are generally transmitted from father to sons. Among the most Islamicized groups, however, women, including widows, may inherit a share of cattle. Upon marriage, a woman commonly receives one cow from her husband; daughters may also receive a cow from their father at this time.

The semi-sedentary Fulani reside in villages or semipermanent camps. Their basic residential unit is the *wuro*, a term referring both to a physical structure and the particular social group that inhabits it. A *wuro* includes a cattle-owning husband, his wife or wives and their children, and his male relatives with their wives and children. A *wuro* must have at least one resident woman member; otherwise, it is referred to simply as a *suudu,* or a place where one finds shelter.

Everyday life in the Fulani *wuro* is characterized by rigid gender separation. Among all but the settled groups, men are responsible for the bulk of the cattle-herding duties such as daily pasturing, watering, veterinary care, and planning the seasonal migrations. Many older men become quite skilled at curing cattle diseases and maintaining the general health of their herds. Women spend their days caring for their children, cooking, maintaining the *wuro,* milking the herds, making dairy products such as yogurt and butter, and marketing these in exchange for grain products such as rice or millet. In addition to gender, age is another fundamental principle of social organization; elders are shown the utmost respect and deference by younger members of the society.

The most valued traits of Fulani personhood and identity are summed up by the term *pulaaku,* or "Fulani-ness." The desired qualities range from physical and cultural characteristics, such as being light-skinned and slender, to psychological factors, such as having a sense of shame, speaking Fulfulde, and taking good care of one's family and (for all but the sedentary Fulani) one's herds. A proper Fulani should be in full control of his or her own needs and emotions, and should show *seemteende* (modesty and reserve), *munyal* (patience and fortitude), and *hakkiilo* (care and forethought). For most groups, being a good Fulani also means being a good Muslim. Nevertheless, Muslim men and especially Muslim women usually continue to maintain faith in many traditional Fulani religious beliefs, including acknowledgment of the power of ancestors, spirits, and witches. Fulani parents strive to instill these highly valued characteristics and orientations in their children from infancy on.

In the childcare guide that follows, I propose as its "author" a Fulani woman born in a village but schooled in France. I base her character loosely on a young Fulani student from the village of Kapatris (Guinea-Bissau) whom I met while living in Guinea-Bissau. My invented author extends this student's biography into a future of my own imagining. Like this student and my invented author, there are many Fulani woman today who are searching for ways to maintain village practices with which they grew up – especially when it comes to raising their children – while enjoying the benefits of modern, urban life.

THE VIEW FROM THE *WURO*

A Guide to Child Rearing for Fulani Parents

About the Author

This is a guide to child care for Fulani parents. Although the advice is primarily tailored to the needs of parents having their first child, it may also be of use for more experienced parents living in the city who want to get back in touch with our traditional "village" child-rearing philosophy and practices. In this manual, the period immediately following birth and early childhood receives the most emphasis, but there is also some advice concerning young children up to about age ten.

I myself was raised in a small Fulani village where my family both kept cattle and farmed. After attending the village Qur'anic school, I continued my education in the French school in a nearby town. I was especially fortunate for this opportunity, since it is more common for boys than girls to continue their studies. I would often remind myself of this as I made the three-mile walk to and from school under the hot sun. I finished at the top of my class and received an international student scholarship to study psychology and education in France. After completing my studies, I returned to my home country and am now living in the city and teaching classes at the local teacher training college. Having raised my four children in the capital city made me particularly aware of the differences between urban and rural life, and it is my sincere hope that our village traditions will continue to be important to all Fulani and our children. It is for this reason that I write this manual.

I have tried to focus on those problems, events, or precautions that are most central to Fulani village life, including basic child care, the importance of relatives, and how to protect babies against attacks from witchcraft and other dangers and diseases. This manual is designed to assist both mothers and fathers, but due to the nature of our society, mothers will find it of more interest, and so I address women directly in most sections. I hope that this manual will help prepare the way for the often rough but always rewarding journey of parenting, and that it will inspire many generations to come.

As I am still a young woman, let me assure you that I do not claim that the words on these pages have more truth or legitimacy than the words of our elders. Our elders always have the best advice, and it is to them that I dedicate this manual.

❧

MAKING A BELLY AND BEGINNING THE STRUGGLE

Getting Ready

Soon you are going to have a baby – your true introduction to womanhood is about to begin. Childbearing is life's most important task, one that women alone can perform. As you well know from your womanly experience, raising children is a lifelong endeavor. Although it is very hard work and totally consuming, the rewards to you, your husband, and your families make it all worthwhile. The emotional rewards, increased social status, and future cattle that children ensure add immeasurably to the benefits of marriage. With the birth of your first child, you and your husband will become full members of adult society. Before your pregnancy, you were known merely as a *surbaajo*, a young girl, neither a full wife nor a full woman. Becoming a mother sets you on your way to economic independence. At the same time, you must be faithful to your husband, you will no longer be able to spend your nights attending games and dances with the other women, and you must accept your new role as a mother with absolute dedication.

Although this is an exciting time for you, it is important to remain calm and to keep your emotions under control as a good Fulani woman should always do. Pregnancy and childbirth are very unpredictable, and both bring considerable dangers to you, your family, and your baby. In fact, childbirth is probably the most common cause of death for women of childbearing age. Babies also run considerable risk during this joyous yet anxiety-filled time. Since they are delicate and desirable creatures, they are commonly taken prematurely from this world by spirits, witches, and other forest-dwelling creatures. Avoid calling attention to your pregnancy until the birth is imminent, to protect you from greedy spirits, as well as jealous co-wives and barren women of the community. In any case, there is no need to spread the word to your family and friends, since they will probably know of your pregnancy anyway. Young children are especially good at sensing newcomers. If you see them sweeping, handing out straws, or calling out names while looking over their shoulders, they may be signalling a pregnancy.

Your First Pregnancy

If this is your first pregnancy, you should begin making plans to leave your husband's compound and return to your father's compound. Some women prefer to return home as soon as they discover they are pregnant; others may remain at their husband's compound until the third or fourth moon, when their husbands can see that they are "making a belly." This decision should be made by you and your family, but you should most definitely not remain with your husband past the seventh moon of your first pregnancy. Giving birth is a very dangerous time for you and your baby, and it is best to be surrounded by the people you most trust. Your family will protect you and your baby against dangerous forces and uncompromising in-laws. They are also the best source of the affection, generosity, and trustworthiness you need at this important time.

Do not expect your husband to visit you while you are away. In fact, it is important for him not to have any contact with you, your mother, or your father during this time. Don't worry about being away from him and his family. He has relatives, perhaps other wives, and his herds to worry about. More than likely, he will make inquiries concerning your well-being, and he will send gifts of millet and salt to you and your parents. Ignore the frequent demands your in-laws are likely to make for you to return to your husband's compound. Keep in mind that giving birth to your child has everything to do with you and very little to do with them. There will be plenty of time later for them to enjoy the child.

While you are pregnant with your first child, you will be known as "pregnant child," or *boofido*. Staying at your own family's compound will relieve you of your burdensome daily work and will allow you to observe the important precautions and taboos that go along with your esteemed condition. For one, you cannot sleep outside or with your grandmother. Instead, you should spend the night and most of the day inside a *suura*, a special shelter that will be built for you out of branches from the *barkehi* tree. Staying in your *suura* will ensure that you have limited contact with men and cattle. Most pregnant women spend their days inside playing with young children and helping with light household chores. You must arrange your hair in a simple, unadorned style appropriate to your condition, and you should not wear cosmetics or jewelry: unlike other women, a pregnant woman doesn't have to worry herself with beauty.

All you should be concerned with at this time is taking care of your most fundamental needs, relaxing, and observing these precautions and taboos. Don't rush anything. Plan to stay with your family for at least six moons and up to a year after your child is born. After this time, you can return to your husband's compound a new woman.

Later Pregnancies

If this is not your first pregnancy, you should simply carry on with your normal, everyday routines in your husband's compound. A woman doesn't have the time to worry about later births as she does with her first. Since you now know how challenging it is to observe strict rules and taboos for such a long period, you will find your later pregnancies much easier; they simply won't interfere with your life as your first pregnancy did. Even if you don't mention anything to him, your husband may suspect the pregnancy and bring you gifts of meat and groundnut cakes. You and your husband can continue to have sex, and you should continue to fulfill your wifely duties of cooking for him and bringing him bath water.

With later pregnancies, you always have the option of returning home to your natal compound, and some women prefer to do this. If you decide to make the trip home, you should leave around the seventh moon of your pregnancy. If you stay with your husband, however, make sure he leaves the house when the time for birth is near. Have a female companion such as a trusted co-wife sleep with you instead. She will protect you much like your own family did when you had your first child. No men should be around when you give birth, even to later children. Childbirth is not their business – this is the Fulani way.

The Struggle

No doubt many people will remind you what to do and how to do it with regard to giving birth and surviving the first few months. Nevertheless, here are some suggestions to help you know what to expect and hence to ease your transition from girlhood to motherhood. Pregnancy lasts about ten moons, or roughly 280 days. If you are at your husband's compound, you should refrain from all work-related activities about one week before your expected delivery. Have a co-wife take over your routines, and expect to return the favor some day. Be prepared to give birth alone or with a companion. When you feel the pains come – which we call *luuwa*, the "struggle" – light a fire and squat on the floor of your shelter. As you feel the pains intensify, grit your teeth, close your eyes, and take up the kneeling position. Try to keep calm and do everything you can to avoid screaming. It is shameful to show fear of childbirth, and if your co-wives and mother-in-law hear you, you will never hear the end of it. This is one of the reasons that Fulani women like to give birth in their own family's compound!

As the baby emerges from your womb, it is of utmost importance that you make sure he or she comes in contact with the ground. This ensures that the earth will be welcoming to your child, and it establishes a powerful connection between the baby and his or her new home. If this contact with the earth is not made, your child will be less attached to his or her birthplace and may be more prone to leave you later in life.

The cry of your newborn child should signal your female companions to come into your shelter. If the "struggle" continues after you have delivered the baby, forget shame and go ahead and scream, since you may be having twins. If so, you will no doubt need extra assistance. Once your baby has been born, don't be alarmed when you are bombarded with birth attendants, family members, neighbors, and friends (all female, of course). If this is your first child, you might become a bit overwhelmed or nervous when so many people arrive, but you will benefit from listening to the suggestions, directions, and criticisms of the more experienced women around you. Take all insults and teasing as a good Fulani should. After all, proper mothering is not a skill with which women are born; it must be learned, and some women become better at it than others.

After your female companions have joined you in your shelter, an attendant should cut the umbilical cord with a knife or razor blade and rub the area with ashes from the fire. Have someone bury the afterbirth in the same spot where your child first touched the ground, to further strengthen the connection of place and identity that will be so important for you and your child. One of your female companions – most likely your grandmother or an older maternal relative – will heat a pot of water and wash you and your new baby thoroughly with an herbal mixture. Wash the baby directly above the place where the afterbirth was buried, to prevent it from rotting. You and your baby should continue to bathe with warm water morning and night for two moons if your child is a girl and for three if you have a boy.

It is crucial that you and your assistants maintain the fire that you lit before you gave birth; it should burn continuously during the first week of your child's life. Do not let the fire die out under any circumstances until the child's naming ceremony, which should be held on the eighth day.

Once you have had your first child, you and your husband will soon experience a change in social status. To mark this, your relatives will shower you and your child with gifts. For example, you should receive beautiful gowns from your husband's father and bedding materials and a ceremonial set of calabashes from your mother. Your mother must also provide her new grandchild with a decorated calf halter, which she will place around the child's neck. Your husband will give you a few head of cattle and a *danki* mat on which you can display your cooking utensils. Your husband himself will be said to "know his cattle." Having established his own household, he will experience his first taste of freedom from his father. For your part, you are no longer a *surbaajo* nor a *boofido;* you have achieved the elevated status of a *kaabo debbo,* a girl "who has born one." As such, you have earned the right and responsibility of milking your husband's herd, which is the key to gaining your economic independence.

A Note on Complications

So far, I have emphasized what to expect during a problem-free, successful pregnancy and delivery. In doing so, I have probably made everything seem very easy. Sometimes it is, but at other times there can be complications.

First of all, becoming pregnant isn't always as easy as we would like it to be. There is a chance that you could find it difficult to "make a belly," even when your menstrual cycle is regular and there are no obvious problems. Infertility can be a very distressing time for young couples, since there is typically great pressure from everyone, especially in-laws, to have a child. Some fathers-in-law become especially anxious and critical during this time. Although in schools the books we read tell us that fertility problems can be due to either the wife or the husband, in our villages women are most often blamed, so be prepared. Your husband should not become angry at you over this matter, but you must realize that it is only natural for him to be frustrated and to feel shame, especially if you have been married for a couple of years and are still childless. Don't be surprised if your husband speaks of leaving you. While this may seem harsh, you know that among our people, failure to bear a child is grounds for divorce, just as you could divorce your husband if he failed to provide you with enough cattle to milk. However, most husbands do not take such drastic action. Although he may never admit it to you, your husband may even seek herbal medicines and magical remedies to maintain or enhance his sexual vigor and aid in conception.

When you finally do become pregnant, don't be surprised if you have a miscarriage, something that is very common among Fulani women. Early during pregnancy your womb might "spill," and later in the pregnancy the "little one" might "spill." Although this may be frustrating for hopeful young mothers, there is nothing that you can do about it, so there is no use worrying about it too much. Giving birth to a child who never takes its first breath can be more of a shameful experience than womb spilling. If this happens, bury the child right away in your garden and don't make too much fuss. Still unnamed, the child was not actually a person yet. The best thing you can do is to try again for a successful birth to make you and your families happy.

If your problems with infertility and miscarriage continue, consider the possibility that they could be due to witchcraft. Witchcraft is a common danger and should be taken seriously. Failure to make a belly as well as premature deaths of babies can often be traced to the actions of witches. As a pregnant woman, you are especially vulnerable to mystical attacks by postmenopausal women or barren women who, out of jealousy, may resort to witchcraft by "eating" your child before he or she has a chance to be born. Only a specialist can determine whether your condition is caused by witchcraft, so make plans to consult one. If you are a Muslim, do not discuss your suspicions of witchcraft with anyone, especially not with any men, since they will probably tell you that belief in witchcraft is nonsense and incompatible with the doctrines of Islam. They will say, for example, that only Allah can take the life of a human being. Don't let such men alter your views. Listen to your maternal instincts. It is your job to do everything you can to protect your unborn baby as well as yourself, and you will get nowhere if you listen to the easy explanations offered by men.

If you are still not pregnant after a few years and you have tried all of the traditional remedies, it may be time for other measures. You could ask one of your relatives for a foster daughter to raise, or your husband might request a son from his relatives. Or you might want to try another husband.

CARING FOR YOUR BABY

The Naming Ceremony

Your newborn is an uncivilized, incomplete being who has no self-control and is completely at the mercy of his or her needs. After all, your child doesn't even have a name yet! You should make arrangements to name your newborn one week after birth. The naming ceremony is of utmost importance since, without a name, your baby is not a person. This is an important day for you, your husband's family, and the village at large. The baby's father and his relatives will publicly recognize the child, who will indeed be introduced to and accepted by the entire community.

Since this is such an important event, expect everyone to attend: the baby's father, his relatives, your family, former slaves, and members of other Fulani lineages. The ceremony should be held at your parents' homestead. Your husband's family and your father's family must each provide a bull for the ceremony. The bull of your husband's family should be bigger than your father's. After all, your husband is the father of your child, and he should be prepared to demonstrate this fact publicly. In addition, your husband must also provide a sheep of the same sex as your child – according to Islamic custom the sheep should be white. Your husband and his relatives should arrange for a blacksmith to perform the animal sacrifices. Observing these simple rules will bestow good fortune on your child – something all parents want.

Here are some tips to make sure that your baby's naming ceremony is a success. The separation of men and women during the ceremony is important. Let the men do the "men's things," such as handling the distribution of the meat to your relatives, to important guests, and to the women for cooking the day's meal. As for the women attending the ceremony, they will present you with many wonderful things such as kola nuts, pounded millet, meat, and blessings for the health of you and your baby.

Before the actual name is given, your infant's head may need to be shaved completely, especially if you follow Islamic custom strictly. You and your sisters should first arrange for a healer to make sure that it is a good day to shave the child's head and that there is no sign of witchcraft. If the healer suspects something, he may suggest putting off the shaving (and hence the ceremony) until another day, when he can ensure the baby's safety. If your child is a boy, his head should be shaved by your father's brother. For a girl, your brother should shave the baby's head, since your daughter may grow up to marry your brother's son. Once the baby's head is shaved, make sure your sisters (or your husband's sisters) take the hair and hide it to prevent a witch from doing any harm to your child.

After the shaving, your baby should be washed thoroughly with a medicinal mixture of water and herbs. The infant should then be carried around the *wuro* – three times for a boy and four times for a girl. The next step is for the blacksmith to ritually slaughter the sheep (by slitting its throat and uttering the proper Qur'anic verses). Finally, the blacksmith will pronounce the baby's name aloud for everyone to hear. The name that you choose for your baby should be appropriate to his or her gender and birthdate. As you know, each day of the week has at least one masculine and one feminine name associated with it. Remember that your baby can't be named on a Wednesday or a Saturday since we consider these days to be unlucky for holding a ritual. In contrast, Tuesday is a particularly favorable day both to give birth and to hold a naming ceremony. If your child was born on a Tuesday, consider yourself truly blessed; a Tuesday birth will bring good luck to both your newborn child and your family.

The naming ceremony provides an important early contact between your baby, your relatives, and the community, and it plays a crucial role in how your child's identity is formed. Presenting children to the village and giving them a name are important early steps in establishing their social position among family members and in the society at large. After all, knowing one's relatives and one's social position in relation to them is an essential quality of *pulaaku,* or "Fulani-ness."

Recovering from Childbirth

Starting on the day that you give birth, you must observe a forty-day rest period. During this time, you should refrain from working. Let your relatives or co-wives take over your daily duties of milking, fetching water and firewood, cooking and cleaning. If you have other young children, your co-wives or sisters should take care of them. You must not pray, fast, or have sexual relations with your husband. For the next five months, bathe only with hot water.

During your confinement with your newborn, expect lots of visitors. Don't be surprised if you are surrounded by grandparents, other relatives, and young children for most of the day. If your baby is sleeping when visitors arrive, always wake the little one out of courtesy to your guests. One of the most important things in your child's life is the recognition and appreciation of his or her relatives, and this should begin at birth. The presence of so many people is also very good for you, since your baby should be held continuously during the first few weeks of life; as you can imagine, this is hard for one person to do. Take advantage of this period of rest and confinement to concentrate entirely on breastfeeding, caring for your infant, and getting your strength back. Childbirth takes a lot out of a woman, but before you know it you will be back to your normal routines, little one and all.

Once your seclusion period of forty days is over, you should return to your everyday routines. Simply tie your baby to your back by wrapping a large cloth tightly around your waist. That way, you can carry on with your chores of fetching water and firewood, milking, and cooking. Another option is to have an older child (such as a daughter or a niece) carry your baby around for you while you do your work, bringing the baby to you occasionally to breastfeed. Don't try to make your baby conform to any routines or schedules of eating or sleeping: by attempting to order the disordered nature of a child, you would be wasting valuable time and energy that could be spent on milking or cooking.

Protecting Your Baby from Illness and Witchcraft

As a new mother, one of the most important challenges you will face is keeping your child healthy and safe. In the first few years of life, illness is common, but you can increase your chances of keeping your child healthy by observing your postpartum taboos and taking some precautions. Keep in mind that most illnesses (especially serious ones) can usually be traced to attacks by spirits or witches.

Certain spirits, which we call *dyinna*, reside in large trees, termite hills, springs, and some uncultivated areas. Though often invisible to us, they commonly scare babies by pulling on their arms and legs, which is why babies frequently cry for no apparent reason.

Pay extra attention to properly orienting yourself and your baby. Make sure that your sleeping mat is oriented east to west, and always sit or lie on the east side facing west. Although you are probably not accustomed to paying such strict attention to orientation at bed time, it is absolutely crucial that you start doing so now, since this is a time of danger and vulnerability for you and your baby. Remember that dusk is the time of day when the spirits are most likely to try to harm your baby.

During the first week of your child's life, always keep something made of iron – perhaps a knife or a scrap of a knife blade – near your baby at all times, especially while he or she is sleeping, as it will protect your little one by keeping away witches or spirits that desire babies. You should also carry a knife with you for protection at all times. Most mothers keep a *garjaahi*, a small knife used to cut straw, tucked under their skirts. During the first week after birth, you should avoid being alone. Always have a friend or a relative accompany you to the bush when you relieve yourself.

Although these precautionary measures may seem tiresome or excessive, take them seriously. The last thing you want to face at this moment is a life-threatening attack on you or your child by witches or child-seeking spirits. Moreover, even though everyone knows that babies are highly valued and beautiful, direct compliments can be life threatening and must be avoided at all costs. Directly praising your baby can produce a serious condition we call *hunduko*, or "mouth." Comments such as, "What a healthy baby!" or "That's a good-looking, fat baby!" could lead to your infant's death. If anyone says to you, *"Wuuy, suka ma na wooDi"* (Wow! Your child sure is beautiful), you might reply, *"Hunduko ma soppu fuudo maa"* (Your mouth points right to your asshole).

Fear of witchcraft aside, every Fulani wants a beautiful baby, and it is only natural to want to bathe, oil, and mold your baby to conform to the ideals of *pulaaku*, or "Fulani-ness." This is easiest to do after the bath, when the baby's body is flexible. Practice a post-bath beautifying treatment that includes pressing the baby's nose between your thumb and index finger to make it thinner, molding the head, and gently stretching the limbs. This can be very enjoyable for you and rewarding to your child. The mother of a newborn is always proud when her own mother looks at her child and calls him or her "big head." Keep in mind, however, that beautiful babies are also desirable babies. Someone – or something – might take your beautiful baby, causing your little one to fall sick or even die. To avoid this, offset the beautification routine with protective measures. You might try giving your child an offputting nickname such as *Birigi* (Cow-turd) or *Juggal* (Horse-picket). Rolling your child in cow dung is also a good way to fool greedy spirits into thinking that your child is not worth taking. Occasionally, remark to a friend, "Have your ever seen such an ugly baby?" Another helpful tactic is to attach a chip of the *kahi* tree to a string and tie it around your baby's neck. You should also pay a visit to your local blacksmith early on and have him pierce your child's ear or scarify his or her cheek for extra protection from witches and spirits.

In addition, Muslims and non-Muslims alike can also benefit from making a visit to a *marabout*. This Qur'anic scholar and ritual specialist can give you amulets containing Arabic writings to place around your child's neck, wrists, or waist. These amulets will not only protect your child against sorcery, they will also make him or her strong and successful in later life. In addition, you can bathe your child with medicinal herbs and also with water previously used to wash Qur'anic verses off wooden planks by our children studying in Qur'anic school. At the same time that you are caring for your baby in these ways, try to avoid any public displays of affection, especially with a first born. Everyone knows that babies are irresistible, so this is very hard to do. You can enjoy your baby all you want in the privacy of your own home, but to ensure your baby's health and safety, you and your husband should maintain an attitude of reserve toward your child in public.

During your baby's first rainy season, the child is extremely susceptible to the cattle- and child-killing fever we call *omre*. There seems to be a connection between *omre* and a small antelope we call *lewla*, so do not eat *lewla* meat during your child's first year. If you can acquire a *lewla* skin, you can make a protective bracelet from it to place around your child's wrist during this dangerous time.

Feeding Your Baby

Breastfeeding is of utmost importance for both you and your baby. By giving the child your breast, you are not only providing him or her with a source of nourishment, you are displaying total motherly devotion. To ensure success in breastfeeding, there are a few things you should do. Before nursing your baby for the first time, take a purgative gruel to purify your blood. Continue to purge yourself with Bilma salt, and eat a stew of haricots mixed with the leaves of the milk-yielding plant, *agoahe*. This will increase your milk supply. If you have given birth in the cold season when food is abundant and your diet is extra rich, avoid eating too much of foods such as butter, meat, couscous, and cassava, or your baby will suffer from overrich milk.

As the mother of a new child, you should be hypersensitive to your baby's needs. Offer him or her your breast at the slightest whimper – after all, no mother wants to become "deaf" to her child's crying. Responding immediately to your baby is the best way to avoid unwanted criticism from other women. If your mother-in-law is around, be extra attentive to your child, or she will be the first to yell, *"Arr myininmo"* (Come and give him the breast!). This public criticism is embarrassing for a young mother and may bring shame to you and your family. Although your mother-in-law may be too much to handle at times, try to remember that she has good intentions.

You should realize that breastmilk is a powerful substance that can be dangerous. If breastmilk should drop onto your son's penis while he is nursing, he might become impotent later in his life. If breastmilk should drop onto your daughter's vagina while she is breastfeeding, she may have a very difficult time staying married.

Feel free to supplement your own breastmilk with that of the other nursing mothers in your compound. Your sisters-in-law, mother-in-law, and co-wives are your best options. In addition to breastmilk, you can give your child undiluted cow's milk, goat's milk, or butter as early as the first week.

Frequent *basi* treatments are also important for your child's nutrition and safety (Plate 14). *Basi* is a mixture of water and herbs that we give to newborns for general physical and spiritual health.

Plate 14.   From birth, Fulani infants are given *basi*, a mixture of water and herbs to promote general physical and spiritual health. This mother is giving her baby her own special *basi* from a recipe passed down by her mother. Photograph by Paul Riesman, courtesy of Suzanne Riesman.

To give your child *basi*, simply dip your fingers into the pot and once the mixture has cooled, dabble your fingertips onto the baby's lips so that the liquid drips in a little at a time. If she hasn't shared it with you already, ask your mother for her *basi* recipe. All mothers have their own special recipes, usually passed down to them from their own mothers. However, if you are asked by someone from a neighboring *wuro* for your own *basi* recipe, don't give it to her. It's fine for you to share some *basi* you've already mixed, but you should keep your recipe a secret.

You may also introduce *bita* into the diet within your baby's first month of life. To make *bita,* simply mix pounded millet flour and water to make a thin gruel. Add tamarind pods, baobab fruit pulp, red peppers, or sugar for flavor.

Despite all these supplements, you should continue to breastfeed your child until well into his or her second or even third year of life. This is very important for your child's personality development.

Perhaps you've heard the Fulani sayings, "One can understand another's personality by knowing the breast from which one sucked," and "The milk that is nursed is the milk that comes back." Through breastfeeding, you are transmitting not only nourishment, but your own personality traits and idiosyncratic qualities to your child, such as the tendency to be talkative or taciturn or the tendency to eat quickly or slowly.

Most importantly, breastfeeding is an expression of devotion and maternal affection. Babies who are nursed at least two years by healthy mothers with "good milk" will have a closer relationship with their mothers in later life. If you do not breastfeed for this period, you run the risk of your child being less intelligent, less attached to you, and more prone to leave you later on. Of course, no mother wants this.

An additional benefit of breastfeeding for at least two years is that it may help you avoid becoming pregnant again too soon. If you do get pregnant, wean your child immediately. The milk that forms in your breasts belongs now to the child you are carrying, and it would be dangerous for any other child who "steals" it. If you continue to breastfeed your child while pregnant, he or she may develop "weaning disease," accompanied by diarrhea, which can be very dangerous. You can treat weaning disease by giving your child a cooked egg gathered immediately after it was laid by a chicken that has not yet had any offspring.

If your youngster resists weaning once you have made a new belly, you should consider summoning a *marabout* to recite verses from the Qur'an while spitting on some of the child's food. This will help to curb desire for the breast and will set your child on the road to successful weaning. Grandmothers can also be a great help: A drastic but very efficient way to wean a reluctant child is to send the baby to your mother. Away from you, your child will probably lose the desire to nurse. To ease the transition, the grandmother may offer her own breast to the child. This helps pacify the child, but soon he or she will realize that there is no milk and will lose interest. However, be forewarned that some grandmothers feel so sorry for their grandchildren during this difficult time, and experience such deep love for them, that they produce milk themselves! In that case, the *marabout* will be your best solution.

EARLY CHILDHOOD

Toilet Training

Since you will be carrying your child around on your back for the first couple of years, you need to be very aware of your baby's excretory needs. Many mothers find it easiest to give their baby an enema twice daily, once in the morning and once at night (Plate 15). If you do so, your baby will slip into a routine, and it will be easier to train

Plate 15. This Fulani baby has just been given one of his two daily enemas. His mother is jiggling him on her feet to encourage a bowel movement. Photograph by Paul Riesman, courtesy of Suzanne Riesman.

the child later. To administer an enema, fill a rubber bulb with water, lay your child belly-down and crosswise over your lap, and gently squeeze the water into the baby's anus. Next, place the baby in a sitting position on your insteps and jiggle a bit to encourage a bowel movement. If you do not have a rubber bulb (our ancestors did not), you can use your mouth to push the water. If you prefer not to administer an enema, you should place your baby on your insteps to stimulate a bowel movement.

After children can walk independently, they can be trained to go to the bush to relieve themselves. But remember that unlike the *wuro* the bush is a dangerous place, so children should always be accompanied on these outings until the age of six or so.

The Development of *Pulaaku* ("Fulani-ness")

Early childhood is a time of freedom and exploration when children begin to break away from their parents and spend more time in play groups with other children. This period marks the beginning of the qualities we Fulani treasure and believe make us who we are. You are aware of the vital importance of *pulaaku*, which includes *seemteende* (modesty and reserve), *munyal* (patience and fortitude), and *hakkiilo* (care and forethought). As a parent, you must actively encourage the development of these qualities.

All Fulani parents wish to encourage *pulaaku* in their children, but you must remember that this process takes time and requires patience. Don't expect much at an early age. Although your child has been acquiring these qualities gradually since birth, they will not be firmly in place until around age six or so. You will know that your child has reached this crucial stage of development when he or she begins to recognize all the extended family members and to call them by name.

As early as age two or so, begin teaching your child the importance of the family in knowing one's place and one's identity. Encourage your youngster to greet relatives when they come to visit and to share food with them. A good way to test your child's knowledge of his or her relatives, as well as to exercise memory skills, is to ask the child to deliver an object or a message to a certain relative. You should not praise your child directly for successfully completing the task, for such expressions of emotion are not Fulani-like. Nevertheless, you may show your satisfaction indirectly by letting your child overhear you say to another adult, "See how he knows who so-and-so is."

It is also a good idea to begin insulting your child now and then. You might say, "I am older than you and I have seen all of the foolish things you have done." This will help your child learn to accept the authority of adults. Likewise, you must teach your child never to hit or insult any older child. With this training, your child will soon learn to accept insults from parents and elders and may begin to insult younger playmates.

Good language skills are of course necessary. It is important that you begin teaching your child to speak early. Bounce your child on your knee and say words and phrases, playfully encouraging him or her to repeat them.

The Mother's Role

As parents, you and your husband both share the duties of loving and caring for your children always. You must strive to create a strong, basic sense of trust in them, so they grow up to know that the world is generally good and that people can be relied on. They should also grow up knowing that, as your children, they belong with you and that their future is with you. Moreover, you must instill in them the general importance of kinship, including what it means to be a relative, what duties are associated with kinship, and the idea that we Fulani are "all one." In addition to sharing these responsibilities, mothers and fathers also have separate but complementary duties in rearing our children.

As a mother, you are your child's most important supporter and caregiver. Assuming that you come from a well-respected family and lineage, you are by definition suitable for motherhood and your child will receive your good qualities at your breast. As a new mother, you have probably noticed that there is nothing you do that doesn't involve your child in some way. After all, those who are related "through the milk" experience long-lasting feelings of affection and devotion toward one another. Your relationship with your children should be carefree and relaxed – one of intimacy rather than shame. Around your children, you can do things like eating and sleeping that you would be ashamed to do around your in-laws.

As a new mother, you have probably experienced a powerful emotional attachment toward your baby, who has suddenly become the most important thing in your life. For the first few years, you will be completely devoted to your child, maintaining physical contact with him or her day and night. A good Fulani mother should not be separated from her baby for more than one or two hours in a day before the age of two. Although some Fulani consider this intense emotional bond to be a "weakness," it is actually a completely normal and highly valued part of motherhood. Without it, you would be considered a bad mother.

Don't be surprised if you, as a mother, experience a closer relationship with your daughters than with your sons. This is completely normal, especially considering the fact that you will spend more time with a daughter than with a son – or, for that matter, your husband. As she grows up, you will be your daughter's primary counselor, and she will be one of your closest companions. Because of this special relationship between mothers and daughters, it is only natural for you to favor girls over boys. Yet it is important to have and value sons. Remember that when your children grow up and marry, you will rely more on your sons than on your daughters for security and comfort, since your daughters will move away to live with their husbands, while your sons will remain with you.

Raising Girls and Boys

As a mother, it is your job to be a consistent teacher, role model, and companion to your daughter. You must teach her how to be a good daughter and a good sister, and it is also your job to teach her the skills that she will need to be a wife. Most of these skills are centered around the *wuro*. As early as age three or four, you should begin teaching your daughters about child care, cooking, and fetching water and firewood. Around age six, help your daughter learn how to pound grain, weave fans and mats, decorate calabashes, and sew. At this age you can also begin teaching her how to milk cows and make butter, and she can help you sell these products at the market.

Our young girls take on responsibilities and have much less free time to play with other children than boys do. When they do play, you will probably notice your daughters imitating your behavior, practicing the skills that you have taught them. For example, they might pick up small sticks and pretend that they are running after imaginary herds. They may also build miniature camps and wells, play at cooking, and carry around dolls. Encourage this behavior since imitative play is a very good way to learn and will prepare your daughter for her later adult roles.

The daily activities of boys are less routine than those of girls. While your son is two or three years of age, he will spend most of his time in and around the *wuro* with you and his siblings and other young boys and girls. It is up to your husband, however, to teach your son that, as a boy, his life lies primarily outside the *wuro*. Once he is four or five, start encouraging him to spend more time with other young boys his age so he can form lifelong friendships.

You should also encourage your son to spend more time with his father, who will teach him the value and importance of cattle. Many Fulani fathers agree that the best way to start to do this is with a calf of his own as his first gift. Have your son name the calf, teach him to take care of it, and he will soon come to love and cherish it. The calf will later become the basis for your son's first herd. When he is five or six, your husband should begin teaching him how to tend the herds, clear the fields, and raise crops, as well as how to build mud fences around the fields to keep the cattle away from the crops and grain supplies. By the time your son is seven years old, he will be ready to begin spending his days out in the fields with his father, his older brothers, or his uncles. Your son should start accompanying his father on long journeys with his herds in search of water and salt. He should learn how to take care of the goats and cows by himself – how to give them water, graze them, and tie them up at night. By the age of nine, he should be well on his way to being a good herdsman.

Discipline and Education

Parents' disciplinary style should be subtle yet firm. Remember that children are very much like cattle; some stray from the road but eventually rejoin the herd, while others may become lost forever. Whereas much of your child's personality is predetermined by Allah and through the transmission of qualities through breastmilk, it is your job as parents (and most of this responsibility falls to the father) to make sure that his or her behavior does not stray too far from Fulani standards.

Keep in mind that it is the nature of small children to be irresponsible, to make mistakes, and to lack self-control, especially before they have fully developed social sense and *pulaaku*. Thus, you should never become too frustrated or angry with your children when they are very young. You do, however, need to make every attempt to train and to educate them in politeness, good manners, and proper etiquette so they can participate in society. If your child is acting in an inappropriate way, calmly suggest that the child alter his or her behavior. If you are a moral person and come from a good, respectable family, then your child will have received these qualities at your breast and should thus have the intelligence to take your suggestions seriously. If your child is being obstinate and ignores you, then it is up to you as a mature adult to find a solution. Avoid using force.

From time to time, you may become so frustrated that you yell at or threaten your child. This is only normal and is bound to happen occasionally. The job of being a parent is difficult and never-ending. However, you should never threaten to stop loving your children, nor should you try to make them feel guilty.

Although you may have heard experienced parents talk of beating their young children, saying that this is a good way to make them fear and respect adults, you have probably never actually *seen* them do so. This is because other family members usually prevent it. When a parent threatens to hit a child, other family members usually urge the parent to be easy on the child. As you become a more experienced parent, you will come to appreciate the importance of social influence in the education and discipline of your children. This helps maintain peaceful relations among everyone, and it also teaches children from an early age that they can count on others for support and protection. My advice to you is that, as a good Fulani, you should control your anger with your children; do not depend on your relatives to stop you from doing something that would later bring shame to you and your family.

Pulaaku, or "Fulani-ness," holds that one should not be dominated by emotions. Self-control is one of the most important virtues to instill in your young children. Of course, it is ridiculous to expect total emotional control from young children even after they have begun to develop Fulani-like qualities; still, you can show them indirectly that the raw expression of emotion is both useless and meaningless. For example, if your five-year-old child cries because he or she was hurt in some minor way (such as falling down), you should ask the child, "Who hit you?" even if you know that no one did. Teach your child that the only legitimate reason for crying is that he or she was intentionally harmed by another person.

For most of our people, being a good Fulani is inseparable from being a good Muslim, so religious education should be a basic part of your child's upbringing. In the past, parents could choose whether or not their children would study the Qur'an, but Islamic education has recently been made mandatory for all Fulani groups. Therefore, around the age of six, your sons and daughters alike should begin to learn to read Arabic letters. In addition to their formal religious education, encourage your children to pray, since prayer is proof of dedication to Islam.

Circumcision is obligatory for Fulani boys. When I was growing up, circumcision for girls was also a standard practice. There is much variation among different groups of our people in how the rite of circumcision is done for both boys and girls, at what age, by whom, and for what specific reasons. As you know, in recent years our practice of circumcising girls has become controversial. Some parents are changing the way circumcision for girls and boys is done, while others are deciding not to circumcise their daughters altogether. However, many Fulani parents still feel that circumcision is crucial for a girl's social, intellectual, and religious development. As modern parents concerned with both respecting tradition and supporting change, this will be something that you will have to think about carefully and discuss with your husband and family.

A Few Words for the New Father

The birth of your child will be one of the most momentous occasions in your life, establishing your independence as an adult. Your responsibilities toward your child will grow as he or she does. Your behavior toward your children is considerably different from your wife's. Whereas she should show devotion, attachment, and affection toward your children from the very beginning, you should work on maintaining emotional distance. You are the children's principal authority figure, and keeping a certain distance will force them to fear, respect, and obey you. Although it is only natural that you will occasionally want to play with your children, you must not do so too much, or they will never listen to you when you are serious and want them to do something. Much of your verbal interaction with your children should be in the form of giving orders. Another important job you have is to arrange for betrothals, maybe even when your daughters are still infants, to ensure the continuity of your lineage. Just as mothers experience a closer relationship with their daughters, you will play a larger role in the lives of your sons and will tend to favor them. Your position in the village, your virility, strength, and sense of self-esteem all rest on the number of sons that you have.

A Final Note: Keeping the Community in Mind

The advice that I have offered in this manual is far from complete and far from the last word. Remember to include your relatives, friends, and co-wives in making all important decisions regarding the general health and education of your children. If you fail to do so, they may become offended. Worse yet, they may give you unwanted advice and criticize you, causing you shame. It is best to avoid all this by letting them participate in the first place. Keep in mind that parenting is too much work for one or two people alone – it takes an entire community to effectively raise a child.

CHAPTER 8

Never Leave Your Little One Alone

Raising an Ifaluk Child

Huynh-Nhu Le

THE IFALUK PEOPLE OF MICRONESIA

The atoll of Ifaluk includes two tiny inhabited and two uninhabited coral islets of barely one-half square mile located in the Western Caroline Islands of Micronesia, which is in the western region of the north Pacific Ocean. The two inhabited islets, Falalop and Falachig, are separated by a 35-meter-wide channel that is completely dry during low tide and can easily be crossed on foot even during high tide. Ifaluk is about 350 miles east of Yap, the political center of the Western Carolines, and about 400 miles south of Guam, the nearest economic center. As of 1995, the Ifaluk population consisted of slightly over 600 individuals. Woleian is the primary language spoken on Ifaluk and the neighboring atolls of Woleai, Lamotrek, Faraulep, and Eauripik. Many men, but very few women, also speak English. According to Ifaluk legend, the island's first inhabitants came from Yap, although historical accounts identify migrants from Polynesia as the earliest settlers.

Beginning with Spain in the 1600s, for the last few centuries, the Caroline Islands have been under the control of several colonial powers. In 1898, Germany purchased the Carolines from Spain and began to systematically exploit human and agricultural resources. The Germans instituted the practice of "blackbirding," a form of labor recruitment similar to slavery, in which Ifaluk men were taken to neighboring atolls to toil in phosphate mines. When the Japanese took over the islands in 1914, they introduced formal education, sending Ifaluk boys to Japanese-language schools on Yap. Japan lost control over the Caroline Islands at the end of World War II, and in 1947, the United Nations granted Micronesia the status of a strategic trust territory, with the United States as its trustee. In 1975, Micronesia was divided into four separate political entities. Ifaluk is part of one of them, the Federated States of Micronesia, which is a semisovereign nation that, since 1986, has had a "Compact of Free Association" with the United States.

The Ifaluk people are somewhat self-supporting. Their economy is based on fishing, cultivating taro, and harvesting breadfruits and coconuts. However, they have also developed a trading system and maintain close social ties, through marriage and adoption, with neighboring atolls. Resources are shared in the event of typhoons, which are a major threat to life and property. In fact, the channel dividing the two islets is the result of a typhoon in 1907, in which thirty-five people were killed; and another devastating typhoon hit in 1997. The fact that "the highest area of land on Ifaluk is only a few meters above sea level" makes it highly vulnerable and accounts for the concern the people of Ifaluk regularly express "that their island will disappear in a severe storm."

Western currency is obtained through selling dried coconut meat, or copra, which yields coconut oil. A relatively recent way for some men to earn money is through salaried employment. After assuming trusteeship, the United States began paying a few Ifaluk men as teachers in the newly established local elementary school and Head Start program, or as health care workers dispensing first aid and medicine. In 1994 and 1995, only 20 men were employed in these sorts of positions; one paying job was held by a woman.

A division of labor exists between Ifaluk men and women. Men fish and spend time in the canoe house (which is taboo to all females above the age of six), where they make rope, carve canoes, repair fishing gear, nap, and supervise toddlers. Women spend much of their time gardening and cultivating taro patches. They also weave cloth, prepare food, and care for their infants. Men and women typically distance themselves from each other in public in order to avoid gossip: "A woman who sees a man approaching her will swerve off the path."

There are seven clans on Ifaluk, of which five are high ranking. All people know their clan, lineage, and individual rankings in relation to others. People are born into their mother's clan, or *kailang,* and inheritance is through the mother's line. Each clan is headed by a male chief whose role is to keep harmony and to supervise the distribution of food. Ideally, the current chief's successor will be his oldest sister's oldest son.

There are four villages on Ifaluk, two on each of the islets. Each village consists of about five to thirteen matrilocal households or compounds; the thirty-six compounds range in size from one to four houses and from three to thirty-seven residents. A typical household or compound consists of a monogamously married couple, their unmarried children, and possibly some adopted children. The household also includes any married daughters along with their husbands and children, for newly married men move to their wives' residence. The oldest women usually make major household decisions. They decide how the basic resources should be distributed, and they delegate work and authority to the middle-aged women, who in turn delegate work to the younger girls. Sometimes, Ifaluk boys and young men move to neighboring atolls to attend high school, and nowadays a small number go on to higher education on neighboring atolls. Virtually all Ifaluk girls and women, however, remain on the atoll throughout their lives. In recent years, the unequal access of males and females to both school and cash has partially eroded the matriarchal tendencies of the past.

Their indigenous religion is integral to Ifaluk culture, although as a result of the activity of Catholic missionaries who came to Ifaluk in the 1950s, most of the Ifaluk people are "nominally" Catholic. They combine Catholic and traditional Ifaluk rituals. The Ifaluk people believe that the world has always existed, but not the supernatural beings that influence the world. A generic term, *yalus,* is used to describe two kinds of supernatural beings. The high gods, or *alusians,* are the *yalus* of the sky. They include Aluelap, the ruler of the sky and chief of the gods; Saulal, ruler of the nether world; and Autran, who created the people of the Ifaluk atoll and the other Caroline Islands. The second kind of *yalus* are ancestral figures. Everyone becomes this kind of *yalus* after death, when the *ngas,* or soul, travels to the sky. Unlike the *alusians* or high gods, who are all benevolent, the ancestral *yalus* can be either good or bad. If a person is good during life, he or she becomes *alusemar,* a benevolent *yalus;* a person who is evil during life becomes *alusengau,* an evil *yalus,* after death. The term *yalus,* when used alone, typically refers to the malevolent *alusengau.* The Ifaluk people greatly fear these *yalus,* who can cause illness and induce people to fight, steal, and gossip. Because the malevolent *yalus* attack at night, people are afraid to be out alone after dark. If they have to be out at night, they carry a coconut torch, because the *yalus* are believed to be afraid of light. The *yalus* are a major force in Ifaluk life, and many religious practices are concerned with preventing illness and maintaining health.

The Christian god is now a part of the Ifaluk pantheon; it is usually linked with the indigenous spirits and referred to as *yalus,* though sometimes it is called *got.* To date, Christian doctrine has not had a major transforming effect on local religious practice, although the pattern of serial monogamy that was common earlier in the century has been partially replaced by the Catholic idea of marriage for life.

The Ifaluk people highly value the sharing of food and hard work, as well as the personal qualities of gentleness, cooperation, and obedience. In this highly interdependent culture, it is important for people to avoid doing anything that might disrupt social relationships. The good person is described as *maluwelu* (gentle, calm, quiet) and *metagu* (afraid/anxious). In contrast, the bad person *gataulap* (misbehaves) and is *sigsig* (hot-tempered). Children are socialized to adopt these values concerning the experience and expression of emotions.

Children are precious to the Ifaluk people, and everyone shares the responsibility for their upbringing – socialization is not the exclusive domain of a child's parents. If a child does not share food or misbehaves in some other way, any older individual, including a sibling or a nonfamily member, may discipline the child.

The Ifaluk emphasis on cooperation and sharing and the high value placed on children support the practice of adoption, or *aivam,* which is widespread on Ifaluk, as it is on other Pacific Islands. What is meant by adoption varies: it includes a child living with another family for any extended period of time, as well as a child spending his or her whole childhood with another family. Somewhere between 33 percent and 60 percent of Ifaluk children are adopted. (Estimates of adoption rates vary so widely because they come from different time periods, ranging from 1947 to 1983, and because of the different definitions of adoption.)

On Ifaluk, anyone – man or woman – can adopt children, regardless of whether they are married or whether they already have children of their own. Those who wish to adopt a child go to a pregnant woman to whom they are related (through either the husband's or wife's clan) and ask the mother's permission to adopt her (as yet unborn) baby. If the mother agrees to the adoption, then at the age of three, the child moves to the adoptive parents' residence. Nevertheless, the *aivam,* or adoptee, continues to have a relationship with the birth family. The *aivam* shares the resources of both households, sleeps in either house, and receives shelter, protection, and security from both the adoptive and biological parents. In effect, the adopted child has two sets of parents and two sets of family networks. The child can rely on both families, and in turn both families can rely on the child for mutual assistance throughout life.

Because of the extensive changes that took place in the social and political systems of the Ifaluk people between the 1940s and the 1970s, caretaking practices and customs have also changed substantially. In the childcare "manual" that follows, both continuity and change in childrearing customs will be noted.

For this guide, the fictional author I have constructed is modeled on the many old and wise Ifaluk women who have experience helping women in childbirth, raising their own children, and helping to raise other children on the atoll.

NEVER LEAVE YOUR LITTLE ONE ALONE

Raising an Ifaluk Child

About the Author

What could be more important, more precious than a new baby! Like the rest of the Ifaluk people, I love infants and have helped to raise many – my own babies, my grandchildren, the infants of other members of my *kailang* – all the babies of the atoll. I have been an attendant for the birth and three-month confinement of many babies and know full well the importance of proper care during this most fragile time of life. Even on our small atoll, things are done differently than in the past. But there are some things that are too important to change!

This manual is my attempt to make sure that my grandchildren and others of their generation know how to protect their infants from the *yalus*, appreciate the importance of teaching their child to be *maluwelu* and of being *maluwelu* themselves, and understand why a baby should never be left alone.

A NEW BABY FOR THE ATOLL

As parents, you and your husband are so lucky to be expecting a baby, a new king or queen for the Ifaluk people. Your baby will be precious – not just to you but to every Ifaluk person (Plate 16). And many years from now, your child will be able to take care of you and your family.

Plate 16. Babies are precious to every Ifaluk person, including this older sibling, whose presence is keeping the little one from feeling lonely. Photograph courtesy of Laura L. Betzig.

Because babies are so precious, it is important that parents know how to protect and care for them. You can learn a great deal from the women in your family, and anyone else on the atoll who spends much time with children, but I hope this manual will help you understand not just what you should and should not do as a parent, but also why these things are so important. You will find useful information about pregnancy, giving birth, and the early years of life. There is a special section on adoption, since so many of our families either adopt some children or give some children to others to be adopted. This manual is mostly for mothers, since, until recently, we did not allow fathers to care for their infants during the first three months. However, some sections will be of interest to any fathers who are involved in their babies' lives.

PREGNANCY

Nowadays, we understand that pregnancy results from sex alone. Until recently, however, our people believed that pregnancy resulted from the combination of sexual intercourse and the intervention of *Aluelap*, the male chief of the high gods. If a wife and husband loved each other and had sex, *Aluelap* would intervene and permit conception to occur. This happened when the man's semen mixed with the woman's blood, and the fetus was first formed from a mass of water and blood. We say that the fetus becomes a person at the seventh month of pregnancy, because this is the time when the fetus first looks physically human. Also, at some point while inside the womb – some people think it is during the eighth month – the fetus receives its soul, or *ngas*. Other people think that the *ngas* develops like any other organ, or that it enters the embryo through the umbilical cord.

While you are pregnant, there are certain traditional taboos that you as well as your husband should observe so that you will not become sick. For example, neither you nor your husband can cut your hair; perhaps this is because cutting hair is something we do in mourning, to show our grief. Pregnancy is not a time for sadness!

As an expectant mother, you should anticipate some changes in your routine during your pregnancy. For the first seven months, you should perform only light labor because the fetus is weak. It becomes stronger after seven months – possibly because, as some people think, the fetus acquires all of its physical features in this period. In any case, during your last two months of pregnancy, you should resume heavy work, such as working in the taro patches, because manual labor will help you have a rapid delivery.

Some Ifaluk people believe that you can guess the sex of your baby. For example, if you feel your baby moving around in your womb and/or if you crave coconut water, then you will most likely have a boy. Men are the only ones who climb coconut trees – this is probably why we say that coconut water is a sign of masculinity. If you do not have any cravings for coconut water and/or if you only feel slight movements in your womb, then you are probably expecting a girl.

Adoption

As you know, Ifaluk people are expected to share everything, and this extends to our children. When they discover that you are pregnant, some members of your or, more likely, your husband's *kailang*, or clan, may ask to adopt your baby. Such a request should not surprise you, since Ifaluk children are often adopted. (At some points in our history, as many as six out of every ten children on our atoll have been adopted.)

A clan member might seek to adopt your baby for several reasons. Couples or even unmarried men or women who are childless might want your baby because they are lonely without children, and loneliness should be avoided at all costs. Parents who have recently lost a child might ask for your baby to help them cope with their loneliness and sorrow. Another possibility is that couples who have only one child might want yours if your baby is of the opposite sex of theirs. It helps to have at least one boy and one girl in the family, since only females can work in the taro patch and garden, and only males can fish and work in the canoe house.

If you have no other children, you may refuse a request to adopt your child. However, if you do have other children, then you should agree to it; otherwise you will appear stingy, and other people, especially the chiefs, will be angry with you.

Never Leave Your Little One Alone

CHILDBIRTH

Until recently, when a woman first began to feel labor pains, she would go to *Weluar,* the house that is close to the only birth hut that we had on the atoll, which we called *Imwelipen.* The birth hut was used because it is taboo to mix food of the household – which men will be eating – with the blood of the birth hut (or with menstrual blood). When the pain became severe, the woman would leave *Weluar* and proceed to *Imwelipen.* Nowadays, you can go through labor at home, and when you are ready to deliver your baby, you can go to one of the birth houses we now have that we also use for girls' initiation ceremonies and women's work such as cooking. If you should happen to give birth before reaching the birth house, it is important that you go there immediately afterward. Staying home with your newborn could be catastrophic. Make sure a fire stays lit during the entire time that you are in the birth house, to prevent both you and your soon-to-be-born infant from becoming sick.

Usually you will have attendants – your mother, her sister, and your brothers' wives – accompanying you to the birth house. Nowadays, a midwife would typically be with you; our Ifaluk midwives are experts in childbirth who are also trained by the government to help women with their labor and delivery. If you have agreed to let your infant be adopted, then the adoptive mother may also be present, and she may accompany you when you leave after the birth. Your husband will not go with you, because only women are allowed in the birth house; indeed, men may not walk within 50 feet of it. Violating this taboo would cause our food to rot and could even cause a famine on the atoll.

If there are no complications, you can expect to take a very active role in the delivery of your baby. Traditionally, your mother and aunt would just observe the birth process without helping you in any way. Nowadays, our Ifaluk midwives are always present at our births, even if they are not relatives of the woman in labor.

When you have severe labor pangs, your baby is about to be born. Kneel on the mat in the birth hut and extract the baby by yourself. Try not to cry or express pain in any other way; otherwise you will shame both your mother and yourself (although not so badly as would have been true in the past). Being *maluwelu* – calm, gentle, and quiet – is the ideal state for an Ifaluk person at all times, even during childbirth.

After the baby is born, your mother will help you with the care of your *sauwau* (infant girl) or *ligau* (infant boy). She will hold the baby in her arms until the afterbirth is discharged, and then she or the midwife will sever the umbilical cord. Traditionally, a small sea shell was used for this, though nowadays, a surgical instrument is typically used. Your mother will wrap the severed cord in a new cloth and bury it alongside the birth house, and she will do the same with the afterbirth. It is important that the umbilical cord and the afterbirth be buried, because if you happened to see them, you could become ill.

Birth Complications

Sometimes childbirth does not go smoothly. In the old days, if your labor went on into the night, your relatives and your husband's relatives would hold a vigil for you. They would meet at the *Weluar* and remain awake all night to keep watch over you, offering you herbal drinks to facilitate the birth.

If you are having a difficult birth, your attendants or the midwife will help you extract the baby from the womb. If the baby does not breathe after being born, your mother will massage the baby's head, arms, and legs in an attempt to awaken the baby. Sadly, some babies are stillborn. If this happens, the body should be wrapped in a *lavalava* cloth and tied with a fishline. In my day, the body would have been buried next to the birth house – on land rather than in the ocean, because only humans can be buried in the ocean, and a newborn is not yet human. Nowadays, however, all burials take place on land. To show that you are sad and grieving, you and others close to the baby would cut off some of your hair and place it with the body. Then your family and your husband's family would wail loudly for a brief time – the only time it is acceptable to cry for the baby. Since the late 1970s, though, you may hear less crying or wailing for babies who die in the very early days of their life.

After the burial, it is best that you, your husband, and the rest of your family stop thinking about the baby and go on with your lives as if there had never been a birth. Indeed, it is taboo to talk about the dead. Your baby will become an ancestral *yalus*.

INFANCY

Your Baby's First Ten Days

After the burial of the afterbirth, both your and your husband's female relatives will bring you a variety of foods, including coconuts, taro, and breadfruit. While you are eating, your mother will take your baby to the ocean for the first bath. When she returns, she will give the baby the first feeding of water, followed by coconut oil. Then she will give you the baby to breastfeed. However, because you will not have any real milk until the fourth day after the birth, this first nursing is more of an opportunity for you to get to know your infant than to provide nourishment.

After having been fed, your newborn needs to rest. You or your mother or aunt should place the baby on a floor mat covered with a cloth. Then cover the little one completely with another cloth to encourage sweating. If you continue to cover the baby regularly to produce sweat, this will help your baby grow properly. To keep your baby calm, roll a cloth into a ball and wrap it snugly against the belly. If your baby is frightened by someone or something, the cloth will prevent a startle reflex from further frightening the little one. When your child is older, you will teach him or her to remain calm in the face of upsets and how to avoid frightening situations.

Babies need frequent feedings and should be fed whenever they cry. A flat stomach tells you your baby is hungry. If the baby sleeps for a long time, wake the little one so a feeding is not missed.

You and your attendants should set up a regular bathing routine. Take the baby to the channel between the two islands to be washed three times a day – morning, noon, and afternoon. Do not wash your little one in the evening, because it is then that the *yalus* can come and make the baby sick. Babies are especially vulnerable to attacks by *yalus*, even during the day. They should be covered in cloth when outside the home so that the *yalus* cannot see them.

Along with your attendants, you and your newborn should remain in the birth house for ten days after the birth (though nowadays, some mothers are shortening this period a bit). The newborn will be fragile, so it is important that you or one of the attendants be awake at all times. Although any woman can visit the birth house, only you and your attendants have the privilege of holding the baby. Also, none of these visitors can remain in the birth house overnight; they must all return to their own homes to sleep.

No men, not even your husband, are allowed inside or even near the birth house. If your husband and other male relatives want to see the new baby during the first ten days, they can stand on the other side of the channel and catch a glimpse of the baby being bathed.

As a new father, your husband is responsible for two tasks. First, he and your male relatives should catch plenty of fish, since eating fish will help your milk flow. However, only your female relatives can bring you the fish as long as you are still in the birth house. Second, your husband is responsible for making a cradle of wood and rope. The four wooden sides of the cradle are held together with plaited rope that forms the bottom. Another rope is attached to the four corners of the cradle so that it can be hung from the rafters of your house and rocked or swung (Plate 17). It should be waiting for the baby when you leave the birth house to return home.

The Three-Month Confinement at Home

At dawn on the tenth day of your confinement in the birth house, you, your attendants, and your baby will leave for home. When you get there, you should place a pandanus mat in the wooden cradle your husband made, lay the baby on this mat, and then cover the baby with a cloth. At home, you will find a small celebration waiting for all of you. Your husband's and your female relatives will bring food that they have cooked, and they will stay to eat with you. Only at the end of the day will you and the baby be left alone. Although we usually don't allow men to attend this celebration, sometimes we make exceptions – once, a male anthropologist was allowed to participate.

In the old days, your husband would already have made a small pit for a fire to be kept burning in the room where your baby would sleep during the three months that the two of you were confined at home. As it was sacred, this fire could not be used for any other pur-

Plate 17. This Ifaluk chief is gently rocking his baby to sleep in the cradle he constructed of wood and rope before the mother and newborn came home from the birth hut. Photograph courtesy of Laura L. Betzig.

pose. However, times have changed, and we no longer observe this practice.

The first three months of your baby's life are very important because the infant is still quite fragile and in need of the careful attention that women are better at providing than men are. Indeed, women do most of the caretaking for the first two years of their children's lives, and then men take over this responsibility for the next two to three years. As for the first three months, you should be as devoted as possible to resting and staying with the baby. In earlier times, you would not have left the house for that entire period except to wash the baby and yourself in the nearby channel. Even today, although most women don't stay confined for three months, you should still try to limit time away from the house. It goes without saying that you cannot work during your confinement − your female relatives will cook and do other household work for you. If there are no women in your household to help you, a relative from another household should move in during the confinement period. Most of the time, you will sit peacefully on a mat with your baby lying next to you.

If you and your husband have agreed to adopt out your baby, you should expect that the adoptive mother will spend a lot of time in your home with you and your baby during the three-month period of confinement. After that, you and the baby will probably spend many days at the adoptive parents' home. At the end of each day, you and your baby can go back to your own house to sleep.

Only you and your female attendants may care for your baby during the first three months. The baby should continue to receive baths in the morning, at noon, and in the afternoon. The little one may cry during these baths, especially in the morning when it is cold. This is understandable, but you and your attendants should make every effort to prevent crying, since it might call attention to the baby and you, which in turn might attract the *yalus* to harm your baby. Indeed, up until recently, we disapproved of crying at any time except during funerals, for this very reason. If your infant starts crying at other times, the little one is probably feeling uncomfortable, so try to find a more comfortable position. You may also nurse the baby to see if that will stop the crying.

We Ifaluk love to smell babies. As parents, you (and anyone else) can show affection for your baby by picking up the infant and nuzzling the little one's belly and genitals, and smelling it long and deeply.

Feeding

You are the only person who may feed your baby during your period of confinement. Your little one should be fed whenever he or she cries or whenever else you or your attendants think it is necessary. If you find that you do not have enough breastmilk, you can add coconut water to the baby's diet. In the beginning, feeding follows the same routine as in the birth house – first water, then breastmilk. Although we know that many people use infant formula, we have heard that this is not healthy for the baby.

You should hold your baby in your arms when breastfeeding. To make sure that the child's head does not fall back, wrap the little one with a cloth (in the old days, the cloth would have been very stiff). You should also give your infant a special medicine twice a day – once in the morning and once in the evening – for the first three months to ensure a healthy stomach. The medicine is a concoction of water and three types of leaves mixed together. After feeding, return the little one to the cradle.

Sleeping

After the first day at home, your baby may sleep during the daytime either in the cradle or on the pandanus mat made for the baby. You will find that the baby sleeps often during the day. At night, your baby should sleep between you and your husband, as protection from the *yalus*. Your child may continue to sleep with you and your husband until three years of age, or until you have another child.

In earlier times, you and your husband would have been forbidden to have sex during the first two *rag* after the baby is born – this is about one year in the Western calendar. Our ancestors believed that your baby would die if you and your husband violated this taboo. However, nowadays some couples, especially the younger ones, observe this taboo for only a few short months. Be aware that you may become the subject of gossip if you become pregnant within a year of your last childbirth, revealing that you violated this taboo.

Naming Your Baby

In earlier days, a baby would be named at the end of the three-month period of confinement. Nowadays, some people say that a baby should be named upon coming home from the ten-day seclusion in the birth house – when the period of greatest threat to life has passed. Indeed, no one should talk directly about babies until they are several days old, because not until then do we know that the baby will be healthy. After the ten-day period, the child is a complete person.

Anyone who has an interest in your baby can provide a name. Usually it is you or your husband, or the adoptive parents if you've agreed for your child to be adopted, but it can also be the grandparents or even someone who is not related. In any case, your child will be given a unique name – but never that of an ancestor. It is taboo to mention the name of an ancestor for it would call up the ancestor's spirit, and that would make us feel sad and lonely. Still, a newborn's name often contains *parts* of the names of other loved ones.

A World of Babies

The Father

In my grandmother's time, a husband's involvement with his baby formally began at the end of the day that his wife and baby returned home from the birth house. Five days later, he might be given the newborn to hold, but he would not have picked up the baby himself. Indeed, he was not even allowed to approach the baby's mat until the end of the three-month confinement; otherwise the baby would become ill. At the end of the three-month period, the mother prepared a new sleeping mat for the baby. After throwing away the old mat, she gave her husband permission to hold the baby. Only then would the baby's father (and other people beyond the mother's attendants) be allowed to approach the baby directly. However, these days much has changed, and we allow new fathers to approach their babies before the three-month confinement is over.

After the Three-Month Confinement

After the first three months, you are free to leave your home and go back to work in the garden. You should not bring your baby along to work with you, but be sure that you do not leave the baby alone. No one, especially not a baby, should be left alone, for they would feel lonely and sad. Your baby will most likely be taken care of by one or more adults or an older child (Plate 16), perhaps a sibling of the baby, or even someone who is not a relative. You can expect your older children to take care of each of your babies; it is common to find young children playing with their older siblings and following them around. Don't leave your little one in the care of children younger than six, though, because babies are very fragile, and very young children may not know how to care for them. Once children are two or three years old, anyone, including older children, can take care of them.

Young Baby's Basic Nature

Infants younger than two years of age do not have any thoughts/feelings – what we call *nunuwan* – beyond those of eating and playing. Without *nunuwan*, they are not intelligent and do not know right from wrong, so they cannot be held accountable for their actions. For this reason, it's useless to be angry at your baby – you and your husband should ignore or tolerate your infant's silly behaviors, because he or she doesn't know any better. There's no point in talking to babies younger than two, because they cannot understand what you say.

By contrast, infants do feel certain emotions. It is important that you and your husband protect your infant from these emotions, especially from what we call *rus* – panic, fright, or surprise. Too much *rus* can lead to illness. To avoid *rus*, do not expose your baby to loud noises, and you should be very gentle when handling him or her.

It is very important that both you and your husband love and respect your baby. If you do not treat your baby with proper care or fail to satisfy the baby's needs, *Aluelap* may decide you are not good parents, and you will be granted no more children in the future.

EARLY CHILDHOOD

Weaning

There are two stages to weaning your baby from your breast. You begin the process at three months, when you start feeding your baby taro and fish. First chew the food yourself and then give your baby a little bit from your fingers. If you discover that your baby does not like solid food, don't force it – but do introduce solid food routinely until your baby gets used to it and likes it. Meanwhile, you can continue to breastfeed your infant. In earlier times, our children nursed for three or four years, but now we usually breastfeed for just two years. When you are ready to wean your baby totally, you can shame the child by warning that other children will laugh if he or she continues to nurse. If you have another baby, you should definitely stop breastfeeding the older child, because there will not be enough milk for both.

Sleeping

Young children do not have regular sleeping habits. They usually sleep when they are tired, so you and your husband should allow your child to sleep at any time he or she wishes. However, it is important that your child not stay out after dark, when the *yalus* come to capture children and harm them.

After three years of age (or before, if you have another baby), your child will no longer sleep between you and your husband, but next to you. Alternatively, your child may go to sleep with another adult.

Toilet Training

You and your husband should begin toilet training when your child is about two years old and has learned to walk and talk. Both of you should tell your child that defecation is for the lagoon and is not done in the house or on land. If your child is not learning this habit, or rebels (which is very rare), then you and your husband should reprimand and shame the child until he or she obeys. For example, you might warn your child that the chief of the *kailang*, or clan, will be very angry if the house or the ground is polluted. In fact, any other adult who is around, even someone who is not related, can and should teach your child this important form of self-control. As for urinating, we don't make such an effort to teach strict habits. While still young enough not to wear clothes, your child can urinate anywhere outside on the ground, although not in the house.

Teaching Proper Behavior

Your child does not acquire anything approaching adult-like intelligence – what we call *repiy* – until reaching the stage we call *sari*, or childhood, at the age of five or six. At this time, your son will be called a *sari-mwal* and your daughter, a *sari-showbut*. Before then, your child lacks sense – a state we call *bush*.

Nevertheless, at two or three years of age, having learned to talk and to walk, your child is just beginning to have thoughts and can now start to learn things. You and your husband should seriously begin to help your child to acquire *repiy*. Thus, as parents, you should start teaching and even lecturing your child about the proper ways of behaving in Ifaluk society. Although parents have the primary responsibility for teaching their children how to behave, many other people will also help teach your child – and any of the other children on the atoll.

We value obedience greatly, but we say that children only start to obey when, and because, they can understand language. Thus, we prefer lecturing to spanking. Neither you nor your husband should ever impose physical punishment on your child. If you hit your child, the child may become *bush* or mind-less. Fortunately, this rarely happens on Ifaluk. On the other hand, when your child does something right, you, your husband, and anyone else who is around should offer praise.

Parents should actively encourage children to express emotions in the Ifaluk manner. The ideal person is *maluwelu* – gentle, calm, and quiet – and it is parents' joint responsibility to teach this. Your child can learn to manage his or her emotions by watching and learning from your and your husband's behavior, so it is important for your child that you are both *maluwelu* yourselves.

You and your husband should also teach your child to be *metagu* – afraid or anxious – in the presence of large groups of people or strangers who may visit the atoll. By teaching about *metagu*, you can help your child to avoid dangerous situations, including unfamiliar people, physical injury, death, and the *yalus*. In addition, you can help your child avoid social shame or embarrassment. As parents, you may lecture about *metagu*. You might also pretend to call forward a special spirit, the *tarita*, to frighten your child, as a way to teach about being *metagu* in the presence of danger. For example, if your child has misbehaved, you might conspicuously ask another woman of the household to "Come get this child who has misbehaved!" The woman will slip off and then return disguised as a scary spirit of the bush. She will motion the child toward her while pretending to eat, indicating that the *tarita* can eat children. Witnessing this, your child will probably jump into your arms in terror. Through your amusement, you can show your child that you approve of this reaction, teaching your little one that it is appropriate to be *metagu* at scary creatures. This is a valuable lesson for your child to learn!

Indeed, we Ifaluk believe that children who do not regularly feel *metagu* in appropriate social situations will not be able to anticipate or correctly respond to what we call *song*, or justifiable anger. *Song* occurs when someone fails to live up to his or her obligation to share with others. It is important to remind children that other people will be *song* with them if they misbehave or fail to do something that they ought to have done. Your child must learn to recognize and communicate all of the appropriate emotions, including *song,* in order to enjoy harmonious relationships with everyone.

A Final Word on Adoption

If your child is to be adopted, the time to go to live with the adoptive parents is when the child is about three years old and can walk and do things independently. Remember that your child is free to come back and visit you and your family any time; in fact, he or she is always free to spend time, sleep, and live with either family. Such a child is lucky, having close ties with many people – two sets of parents and their families and *kailangs.*

IN CLOSING

Everyone loves babies. Your baby will know only smiling and laughing faces, soft arms, and soft words. Remember, children are precious, and we must all do our best to teach every child to become the ideal person – one who is *maluwelu,* or gentle, calm, and quiet. May you and your loving child be protected from the *yalus!*

Note to Chapter One

In offering four chapters about contemporary societies based on library research, we follow a venerable tradition of anthropologists reinterpreting rich and reliable data collected by highly respected fieldworkers. For example, data on a host of topics collected by Sir Edward Evans-Pritchard working among the Nuer of the Sudan have been reinterpreted by several generations of scholars. Similarly, data collected by Franz Boas among the Kwakiutl Indians of Vancouver has been creatively reinterpreted by later researchers. Undoubtedly the most spectacular use of other people's field data is that of Claude Lévi-Strauss, who not only built his own career based largely on library rather than field research, but reshaped much of the social sciences in midcentury in doing so.

Some fieldworkers sued to claim sole possession of their field sites. Fortunately, this is rarely true any more in anthropology. Moreover, many aspects of the field experience itself are being both theoretically revisited and methodologically revamped. Meanwhile, after over a full century of intensive field research by cultural anthropologists, even the remotest parts of the globe have now been studied by fieldworkers. Given all this, it may be that careful but creative reinterpretations of published data based on respected colleagues' fieldwork will become both increasingly popular and increasingly respected in cultural anthropology. Indeed, we believe that this is a productive use of already existing scholarship that can in turn enrich the ethnographic literature with new perspectives.

In this volume, the four chapters on contemporary societies that are based on library research have also received careful readings from anthropologists who have conducted considerable fieldwork among members of the society in question. Likewise, our chapter on the Puritans has received careful readings by several historians engaged in archival research on the Puritans. (The scholars we have consulted for these five chapters are enumerated by our authors in the Acknowledgments for each chapter.) Our authors have benefited greatly from close, critical readings from these scholars, who are well known for their work in the field and have generously contributed a lifetime of knowledge about the societies in question. This has increased the reliability of our authors' interpretations, and it has ensured that our authors have made use of the latest relevant scholarship.

About the Contributors

Jerome Bruner is University Professor at New York University, where he also serves as Research Professor of Psychology and Senior Research Fellow in Law. Previously, he was the Watts Professor of Psychology at Oxford (1972–1980) and Professor of Psychology at Harvard (1946–1972). He is the recipient of the International Balzan Prize for his "lifelong contribution to the understanding of human nature" as well as Distinguished Scientific Awards from the American Psychological Association, the Society for Research on Child Development, and the American Educational Research Association. His most recent books are *Minding the Law* (2000, with Anthony Amsterdam), *The Culture of Education* (1996), and *Acts of Meaning* (1990). He has studied children's growing up among the Wolof of Senegal (West Africa), is Senior Advisor to the famous preschools of Reggio Emilia in Italy, and was one of the founders of Head Start in the U.S.

Carol Delaney is Associate Professor of Cultural and Social Anthropology at Stanford University. Her most recent work is *Abraham on Trial: The Social Legacy of Biblical Myth* (1998), which was a finalist for the National Jewish Book Award. She is also author of *The Seed and the Soil: Gender and Cosmology in Turkish Village*

About the Contributors

Society and co-editor (with Sylvia Yanagisako) of *Naturalizing Power: Essays in Feminist Cultural Analysis.* She has held several fellowships, including three Fullbrights and one from the National Science Foundation. She has been a Fellow at Harvard Divinity School, the Stanford Humanities Center, and the Center for Advanced Study in the Behavioral Sciences in Palo Alto, California. (With a daughter and two grandsons, child rearing has been of more than academic interest).

Judy S. DeLoache is Professor of Psychology and the Beckman Institute for Advanced Science and Technology at the University of Illinois at Urbana-Champaign. Her current program of research, which is funded by the National Institutes of Health, focuses on symbolic development in infants and very young children. She has published numerous journal articles and chapters in developmental psychology journals and books. She has been a Visiting Scholar at Stanford University and Oxford University, has held a Senior International Fellowship from the Fogarty Foundation of NIH, and has been a Fellow at the Center for Advanced Study in the Behavioral Sciences in Palo Alto, California.

Marissa Diener is a developmental psychologist and an Assistant Professor in the Department of Family and Consumer Studies at the University of Utah. She conducts research on early socioemotional development and parent–child relationships. She has published research on the transition to parenthood in the *Journal of Family Psychology* and the *Merrill-Palmer Quarterly,* and work on parenting competence among adolescent Latina mothers in the *Journal of Research on Adolescence.*

Alma Gottlieb is Professor of Anthropology at the University of Illinois at Urbana-Champaign. She is the author of *Under the Kapok Tree: Identity and Difference in Beng Thought* and *Parallel Worlds: An Anthropologist and a Writer Encounter Africa* (co-authored with fiction writer Philip Graham), which won the Victor Turner Prize in Ethnographic Writing, and she is currently completing *The Afterlife Is Where We Come From: Infants and Infant Care in West Africa.* She has also written a *Beng-English Dictionary* (with M. Lynne Murphy) and has edited *Blood Magic: The Anthropology of Menstruation* (with

About the Contributors

Thomas Buckley), which was listed as one of the year's best anthropology books for 1988 by *Choice*. She has held fellowships from several agencies, including most recently the John Simon Guggenheim Memorial Foundation.

Michelle C. Johnson is a cultural anthropologist specializing in West Africa, with interests in ritual, Islam, and the life cycle. She has conducted extensive fieldwork among the Mandinga people of Guinea-Bissau and with Mandinga as well as Fulani refugees and immigrants from Guinea-Bissau now living in Portugal. Johnson is the author of a forthcoming article on Mandinga religious identity and female circumcision in *Female "Circumcision" in Africa: Culture, Change, and Controversy* (edited by B. Shell-Duncan and Y. Hernlund). She has held a Fulbright-Hays Fellowship from the U.S. Department of Education, and two fellowships from the Social Science Research Council. Johnson is currently completing her doctorate in anthropology at the University of Illinois at Urbana-Champaign.

Huynh-Nhu Le is a Postdoctoral Scholar in the Health Psychology Program at the University of California at San Francisco. Her research interests include understanding the relations among culture, personality, depression, emotion socialization, and prevention of major depression. Le has worked with diverse populations across community, research, and clinical settings. She recently co-authored an article on emotional disturbances in *Well-being: The Foundations of Hedonic Psychology* (edited by D. Kahneman, E. Diener and N. Schwartz). Currently, she is collaborating on a longitudinal project aimed at preventing depression among low-income, English- and Spanish-speaking pregnant women and young mothers.

Sophia L. Pierroutsakos is an Assistant Professor of Psychology at Furman University in Greenville, South Carolina. She specializes in the cognitive development of young children, specifically infants' understanding of pictures and other symbols. She has co-authored chapters appearing in the 1998 edition of the *Handbook of Child Psychology,* the *Annals of Child Development,* and *Multiple Perspectives on Play in Early Childhood Education.* She is also co-author of articles in *Psychological Science* and the *Journal of Cognitive Development.*

About the Contributors

Debbie Reese is a specialist in education whose research focuses on representations of ethnicity in children's literature, with a special interest in images of Native Americans. She is an associate editor of Native American children's books for *Counterpoise,* a publication of the American Library Association's Social Justice Roundtable, and she serves on the advisory board for the ERIC Clearinghouse on Elementary and Early Childhood Education. She has published book chapters on authenticity in children's books about Native Americans, and articles that critically examine ideology in children's books. She is a regular reviewer for *Horn Book,* a children's book review journal. Reese is currently completing her doctorate in education at the University of Illinois at Urbana-Champaign.

Authors' Acknowledgments

Chapter One by Judy Deloache and Alma Gottlieb

We are very grateful to several friends, colleagues, and kin who offered extremely helpful comments on earlier versions of the manuscript for this chapter: Nancy Abelmann, Kathy Anderson, Jerome Bruner, Ben Clore, Jerry Clore, Carol Delaney, Philip Graham, Alejandro Lugo, Sarah Mangelsdorf, Harry Triandis, and Tom Weisner. Reference librarian Carol Penka at the University of Illinois at Urbana-Champaign kindly provided emergency assistance. We also appreciate the assistance of Kathy Anderson, Dana Loschen, and Sophia Pierroutsakos in putting the finishing touches on the manuscript.

Chapter Two by Debbie Reese

I am grateful to the following scholars of colonial New England: Dr. John Demos at Yale University and Dr. Philip Greven at Rutgers University for reading and commenting on the manuscript; and Dr. Helena Wall at Pomona College and Dr. John Pruett at the University of Illinois for answering many questions. I am thankful for the patience and love of my husband George, and our lovely daughter, Elizabeth.

Authors' Acknowledgments

Chapter Three by Alma Gottlieb

After collaborating with my fiction writer-husband Philip Graham on a nonfiction memoir of our time among the Beng, I have been inspired to continue alternative forms of writing. It was Philip who suggested adapting the manual format to write about child rearing among the Beng. After some initial social scientist's nervousness, I accepted the challenge and composed a pair of hypothetical manuals for a hypothetical Beng mother frustrated by her colicky infant. From that brief article came the idea for this book. I am forever grateful to Philip for encouraging me to see the possibilities of truth in fiction – something he teaches me daily through the wisdom of his own writing.

I have been lucky to receive exceptionally careful readings and challenging comments on this chapter from Philip Graham, Michelle Johnson, Bertin Kouadio, and Alejandro Lugo. To all, I express my deep gratitude.

This chapter is based most directly on fieldwork among rural Beng in Côte d'Ivoire that I conducted in summer 1993 and, more indirectly, on previous fieldwork in 1979–1980 and summer 1985. For intellectual support during my research, I owe a continuing debt, which I always strive in vain to repay, to my dear friends Véronique Amenan Akpoueh and Yacouba Kouadio Bah. Other Beng friends who shared with me their insights into Beng infant culture during summer 1993 include Kouakou Bah and the late Kouassi Kouassi, as well as dozens of Beng women, young and old, whose struggles with motherhood in the face of grinding poverty I found humbling. That summer, Véronique Amenan Akpoueh, Augustin Kouakou, Dieudonné Kwame Kouassi, and Bertin Kouadio also served as wonderfully able assistants. Bertin continued to serve as a research assistant as he made the transition to student at the University of Illinois.

For support of my research in and about Bengland over the years, I am very grateful to the John Simon Guggenheim Memorial Foundation, the National Endowment for the Humanities, the Wenner-Gren Foundation for Anthropological Research, the Social Science Research, the United States Information Agency, the Woodrow Wilson Foundation, and the American Association of University Women, as well as several units and individuals at the University of Illinois: the Center for Advanced Study, the Research Board, International Programs and Studies (for a William and Flora Hewlett Faculty Award), Paul Zeleza at the Center for African Studies, Dean Jesse

Authors' Acknowledgments

Delia of the College of Liberal Arts and Sciences, and Janet Keller at the Department of Anthropology.

Chapter Four by Marissa Diener

I am grateful for the help that many people have given to provide me with information and inspiration for this chapter. Three scholars of Indonesia have been very generous with their expertise and time. Michael Bakan read a previous draft of this manuscript and provided very useful comments and perspective. Edward Bruner read and made very helpful suggestions on the introductory section of the chapter. I am especially indebted to Margaret Wiener and extend my heartfelt thanks to her for reading several drafts of this manuscript and giving me detailed feedback and information on contemporary practices in Bali. I also thank my parents for making possible a brief trip to Bali in 1996. Finally, I thank my daughter, Caroline, for showing me that the Balinese are right – babies are a gift from God.

Chapter Five by Carol Delaney

I wish to thank the villagers who so graciously accepted me into their lives and put up with my questions and strange ways in good humor for two years. Although she was able to visit me in Turkey a few times, my daughter had to endure my absence from home in a time before laptops and E-mail. I am forever grateful. The best reward is that all the relationships have survived and thrived. Now, years later, I also thank my two grandsons for giving me a more than academic interest in the topic of this book.

Chapter Six by Sophia L. Pierroutsakos

I am especially grateful to Françoise Dussart, at the University of Connecticut, for having been extremely generous with her time and providing extensive and very helpful comments and suggestions. I would also like to thank Libby Coates, at the Australian Institute of Aboriginal and Torres Straight Islander Studies, for her very kind and timely assistance, as well as Julie Ward at the National Library of Australia. I am eternally grateful to Garth for his encouragement throughout this project.

This chapter is dedicated to the memory of my beloved father, Leo Pierroutsakos.

Authors' Acknowledgments

Chapter Seven by Michelle C. Johnson

I offer my heartfelt thanks to Professor Margúerite Dupire at the Laboratoire d' Anthropologie Sociale of the Collège de France/ Université de Paris for carefully reviewing an earlier version of this chapter, on the basis of her own research among the Fulani. Her insightful comments and bibliographic suggestions were invaluable to me and are very much appreciated. I am also indebted to Maimouna Barro, a graduate student at the University of Illinois at Urbana-Champaign. Her personal experience as a Fulani woman and new mother, shared with me during the course of this project in both formal interviews and friendly conversations, filled in several gaps and greatly enriched my understanding of Fulani perspectives.

An eleven-month period of ethnographic fieldwork in Guinea-Bissau (West Africa) was generously funded by an International Predissertation Fellowship from the Social Science Research Council. Although I was working primarily with the Mandinga people, I benefited greatly from discussions with Fula friends and acquaintances, often when traveling to and from villages on *kandongas* or bush taxis. I have also worked with Fulani in the course of conducting a ten-month research project primarily with Mandinga people from Guinea-Bissau now living in and around Lisbon, Portugal. I am grateful for an International Doctoral Research Fellowship from the Social Science Research Council, and a Fulbright-Hays Fellowship from the U.S. Department of Education, which supported this project. I would like to thank the many Mandinga and Fulani people I have worked with for sharing their knowledge and experiences with me.

I dedicate this chapter to the memory of Paul Riesman, premier ethnographer of the Fulani whose work on infancy and childhood was particularly insightful, providing a major foundation not only for this chapter but for the discipline of anthropology at large. I am very grateful to Suzanne Riesman both for reading this chapter and for generously supplying the photographs that appear in it.

Chapter Eight by Huynh-Nhu Le

Three ethnographers of Ifaluk have been very generous in sharing their expertise with me in the writing of this chapter. I wish to offer my deepest thanks to Catherine Lutz of the University of North Carolina for all her encouraging and extremely helpful comments on

Authors' Acknowledgments

earlier drafts of this chapter. I especially appreciate her gracious willingness to help with the final set of questions right at the deadline. I am also grateful to Laura Betzig of the University of Michigan for generously sharing her wonderful photographs of Ifaluk families. Finally, special thanks to Rich Sosis of the University of Connecticut who very kindly and unhesitatingly made his work on Ifaluk culture available to me.

Citations and Sources Cited

Foreword

Citations

The numbers in the citations below refer to the numbered references in the immediately following Sources Cited section for this chapter.

Page

ix   child's reliance on caregiver – 2.
xi   change in Western child-rearing practices – 1; change in American legal statutes – 6; no legal protection for black slave families – 3; "maternal qualities" of the black nanny – 5.
xii   systems of law change swiftly – 4.

Sources Cited

(1)   Ariès, P. (1962). *Centuries of childhood.* Translated by R. Baldick. New York: Alfred A. Knopf. [Original French edition, 1960.]
(2)   Bruner, Jerome. (1972). The nature and uses of immaturity. *American Psychologist, 27,* 687–708.
(3)   Davis, P. C. (1991). *Neglected stories: The Constitution and family values.* New York: Hill & Wang.

(4) Geertz, C. (1983). Local knowledge: Fact and law in comparative perspective. In C. Geertz, *Local knowledge: Further essays in interpretive anthropology*. New York: Basic Books.

(5) Jacobs, H. (1987 [1861]). *Incidents in the life of a slave girl: Written by herself.* Cambridge, MA: Harvard University Press.

(6) Woodhouse, B. B. (1992). Who owns the child? MEYER and PIERCE and the child as property. *William and Mary Law Review, 33*(4), 995–1122.

Chapter One. If Dr. Spock Were Born in Bali

Citations

The numbers in the citations below refer to the numbered references in the immediately following Sources Cited section for this chapter.

Page

2   Cadogan on swaddling – 12.

5   Geertz on common sense – 21; Dr. Spock's original book title – 72.

6   common parental challenges – 53, infant mortality rates – 90.

7   Shona study – 20; inadequate diet and poverty – 64.

8   wet nursing: in the ancient world – 18, in Europe – 18, in Paris – 40, in Europe pre-World War I – 18; milk kin and marriage – 16, 44; breastmilk substitutes and death in London – 18; length of nursing – 76.

9   rates of breastfeeding: in U.S. – 79, in Philippines and Guatemala – 80; "half of the world's mothers" – 36; food taboo and malaria – 5.

10   infant care by other children – 82; poverty, infant care, and mortality in Brazil – 67.

11   Brazilian infant deaths – 67, p. 279; increasing poverty – 52, 85.

12   variety of adoption practices – 46, 47; sibling care and emotional ties – 82, day care and attachment to teachers – 34.

13   Baganda naming ceremony – 43, individualistic and collectivistic values and goals – 19, 44, 78.

14   Japanese and American mothers and infants – 14; Mayan apprentices – 66; teaching simple tasks to young children: in Africa – 87, in Polynesia – 60.

15   unintended consequences of education – 37, 42.

16   social sleeping – 69, 70; most common infant sleep pattern – 88; length of co-sleeping: in Guatemala – 59, in Japan – 2, 13; most common U.S. sleep pattern – 55.

17   isolation of sleeping babies – 70; U.S. pediatricians' sleep advice –
      56; ethnic differences in sleep in U.S. – 55, 89; Appalachian sleep
      pattern – 1; study of Euro-American and Mayan mothers – 59;
      nightly isolation of infants as neglect – 69.
18   co-sleeping and sex – 25, 69.
19   new social forms – 58; family as source of advice – 86.
20   study of child-rearing information sources – 32; business of infant
      and child care manuals – 27, 83; earlier advice manuals: in China-3,
      70, in Renaissance Italy – 9; sales of Spock's manual – 77; 2,000
      "how-to" books – 77.
21   revolutionary advice in Spock – 57; Berry Brazelton – 11; Penelope
      Leach – 49, 50, Spock's advice on dressing and outdoors – 73,
      pp. 95–97.
22   ethnographies of infants – 33, 54; recent anthropological work on
      infants and young children – 10, 30, 31, 43, 45, 48, 61.
23   article spoofing Spock – 24.
25   Spence – 71; infant "diary" – 74; novel about West African
      immigrants – 75; ants – 35; Japan – 63; Eudora Welty quote – 84, p.58.

Citations for Note to Chapter 1

The numbers in the citations below refer to the numbered references in the
Sources Cited section for the Note to Chapter 1.

Page

221   reinterpretation of Evans-Pritchard's Nuer data – 17, 26, 38, 39;
      reinterpretation of Boas' Kwakiutl data – 23, 81; example of
      claiming possession of field sites – 68, pp. 135–169; recent
      reconsiderations of nature of field experience – 15, 22, 28, 29,
      62, 65.

Sources Cited – Chapter 1

(1)   Abbott, S. (1992). Holding on and pushing away: Comparative
      perspectives on an Eastern Kentucky child-rearing practice. *Ethos,
      20*(1), 33–65.
(2)   Abelmann, N. (1999). Personal communication, May 21, 1999.
(3)   Anagnost, A. (1997). The child and national transcendence in
      modern China. In K. Lieberthal, S.-F. Lin, & E. Young (Eds.),
      Constructing China: The interaction of culture and economics.
      Ann Arbor: Center for Chinese Studies, University of Michigan,
      Michigan Monographs in Chinese Studies no. 78.

(4)   Arens, W. (1983). Evans-Pritchard and the prophets: Comments on an ethnographic enigma. *Anthropos, 78,* 1–16.

(5)   Beidelman, T. O. (1966). The ox and Nuer sacrifice: Some Freudian hypotheses about Nuer symbolism. *Man* (n.s.), *1,* 453–467.

(6)   Beidelman, T. O. (1968). Some Nuer notions of nakedness, nudity, and sexuality. *Africa, 38,* 113–131.

(7)   Beidelman, T. O. (1971). Nuer priests and prophets: Charisma, authority, and power among the Nuer. In T. O. Beidelman (Ed.), *The translation of culture.* London: Tavistock.

(8)   Beidelman, T. O. (1981). The Nuer concept of *thek* and the meaning of sin: Explanation, translation, and social structure. *History of Religions, 21,* 126–155.

(9)   Bell, R. (1999). *How to do it: Guides to good living for Renaissance Italians.* Chicago: University of Chicago Press.

(10) Bonnet, D. (1988). *Corps biologique, corps social: Procréation et maladies de l'enfant en pays mossi, Burkina Faso.* Paris: Ed. de l'ORSTOM, Mémoires n° 110.

(11) Brazelton, T. B. (1969). *Infants and mothers.* New York: Delacorte.

(12) Cadogan, W. (1749). *An essay upon nursing, and the management of children, from their birth to three years of age (3rd ed.). By a Physician.* London: J. Roberts. Reprinted in Kessen, W (1965). *The child.* New York: John Wiley & Sons.

(13) Caudill, W., & Plath, D. (1966). Who sleeps by whom? Parent–child involvement in urban Japanese families. *Psychiatry, 20,* 344–366.

(14) Caudill, W., & Weinstein, H. (1969). Maternal care and infant behavior in Japan and America. *Psychiatry, 32,* 12–43.

(15) Clifford, J. (1988). *The predicament of culture: Twentieth-century ethnography. literature, and art.* Cambridge, MA: Harvard University Press.

(16) Delaney, C. (1991). *The seed and the soil: Gender and cosmology in Turkish village society.* Berkeley: University of California Press.

(17) Evens, T.M.S. (1989). The Nuer incest prohibition and the nature of kinship: Alterlogical reckoning. *Cultural Anthropology, 4*(4), 323–346.

(18) Fildes, V. (1995). The culture and biology of breastfeeding: An historical review of Western Europe. In P. Stuart-Macadam & K. Dettwyler (Eds.), *Breastfeeding: Biocultural perspectives.* New York: Aldine de Gruyter.

(19) Fogel, A., Stevenson, M. B., & Messinger, D. (1992). A comparison of the parent–child relationship in Japan and the United States. In J. L.

Roopnarine & D. B. Carter (Eds.), *Parent–child relations in diverse cultural settings.* Norwood, NJ: Ablex.

(20) Folta, J., & Deek, E. (1988). The impact of children's death on Shona mothers and families. *Journal of Comparative Family Studies, 19*(3), 433–451.

(21) Geertz, C. (1983). Common sense as a cultural system. In C. Geertz, *Local knowledge: Further essays in interpretive anthropology.* New York: Basic Books.

(22) Geertz, C. (1988). *Works and lives: The anthropologist as author.* Stanford, CA: Stanford University Press.

(23) Goldman, I. (1975). *The mouth of heaven: An introduction to Kwakiutl religious thought.* New York: John Wiley & Sons.

(24) Gottlieb, A. (1995). Of cowries and crying: A Beng guide to managing colic. *Anthropology and Humanism, 20*(1), 20–28.

(25) Gottlieb, A. (n.d.). *The afterlife is where we come from: Infants and infant care in West Africa.* Unpublished book manuscript.

(26) Gough, K. (1971). The Nuer: A re-examination. In T.O. Beidelman (Ed.), *The translation of cultures.* The Hague: Mouton.

(27) Grant, J. (1998). *Raising baby by the book: The education of American mothers.* New Haven, CT: Yale University Press.

(28) Gupta, A., & Ferguson, J. (Eds.). (1997a). *Anthropological locations: Boundaries and grounds of a field science.* Berkeley: University of California Press.

(29) Gupta, A., & Ferguson, J. (Eds.). (1997b). *Culture, power, place: Explorations in critical anthropology.* Durham, NC: Duke University Press.

(30) Harkness, S., & Super, C. M. (1983). The cultural construction of child development: A framework for the socialization of affect. *Ethos, 11* (4), 221–231.

(31) Harkness, S., & Super, C. M. (Eds.). (1996). *Parents' cultural belief systems: Their origins, expressions and consequences.* New York: Guilford.

(32) Harkness, S., Super, C., Keefer, C. H., Raghavan, C. S., & Campbell, E. K. (1996). Ask the doctor: The negotiation of cultural models in American parent-pediatrician discourse. In S. Harkness & C. M. Super (Eds.), *Parents' cultural belief systems: Their origins, expressions, and consequences.* New York: Guilford.

(33) Hewlett, B. (1991). *Intimate fathers: The nature and context of Aka Pygmy paternal infant care.* Ann Arbor: University of Michigan Press.

(34) Howes, C., & Hamilton, C. E. (1993). The changing experience of child care: Changes in teachers and in teacher–child relationships and children's social competence with peers. *Early Childhood Research Quarterly, 8,* 15–32.

(35) Hoyt, E. (1996). *The earth dwellers: Adventures in the land of ants.* New York: Simon and Schuster.

(36) Joseph, J. (1998, April 10). Breaking the baby-bottle code [Homepage of ABCNEWS.com:Health & Living], [Online]. Available: http://more.abcnews.go.com/sections/living/DailyNews/ babyformula980409.html [1998, April 10].

(37) Jourdan, C. (1995). Masta Liu. In V. Amit-Talai and H. Wulff (Eds.), *Youth cultures: A cross-cultural perspective.* New York: Routledge.

(38) Karp, I., & Maynard, K. (1983). Reading *The Nuer. Current Anthropology, 24* (4), 481–503.

(39) Kelly, R. (1985). *Nuer conquest: The structure and development of an expansionist system.* Ann Arbor: University of Michigan Press.

(40) Kessen, W. (1965). *The child.* New York: John Wiley & Sons.

(41) Khatib-Chahidi, J. (1992). Milk kinship in Shi'ite Islamic Iran. In V. Maher (Ed.), *The anthropology of breast-feeding: Natural law or social construct.* Oxford: Berg Publishers.

(42) Kilbride, P. (2000). *Street children in Kenya: Voices of children in search of a childhood.* Westport, CT: Bergin and Garvey. In press.

(43) Kilbride, P., & Kilbride, J. (1990). *Changing family life in East Africa: Women and children at risk.* State College: Pennsylvania State University Press.

(44) Kitayama, S., & Markus, H. R. (1995). Culture and self: Implications for internationalizing psychology. In N. R. Goldberger & J. Veroff (Eds.), *The culture and psychology reader.* New York: New York University Press.

(45) Lallemand, S. (1977). *Une famille Mossi.* Paris: CNRS. Recherches voltaïques, n° 17.

(46) Lallemand, S. (1993). *La circulation des enfants en société traditionnelle: Prêt, don, échange.* Paris: L'Harmattan.

(47) Lallemand, S. (1994). *Adoptions et transferts d'enfants.* Paris: L'Harmattan.

(48) Lallemand, S. (Ed.). (1991). *Grossesse et petite enfance en Afrique noire et à Madagascar.* Paris: L'Harmattan.

(49) Leach, P. (1977). *Your baby and child: From birth to age five.* New York: Alfred A. Knopf.

(50) Leach, P. (1983). *Babyhood.* 2nd ed. New York: Alfred A. Knopf.

(51) Lepowsky, M. (1987). Food taboos and child survival: A case study from the Coral Sea. In N. Scheper-Hughes (Ed.), *Child survival: Anthropological perspectives on the treatment and maltreatment of children.* Dordrecht: D. Reidel/Kluwer.

(52) Lerer, L. B. (1998). Who is the rogue? Hunger, death, and circumstance in John Mampe Square. In N. Scheper-Hughes & C. Sargent (Eds.), *Small wars: The cultural politics of childhood.* Berkeley: University of California Press.

(53) LeVine, R. A. (1988). Human parental care: Universal goals, cultural strategies, individual behavior. In R. A. LeVine, P. M. Miller, & M. West (Eds.), *Parental behavior in diverse societies.* San Francisco: Jossey-Bass.

(54) LeVine, R., Dixon, S., Levine, S., Richman, A., Leiderman, P. H., Keefer, C., & Brazelton, T. B. (1994). *Child care and culture: Lessons from Africa.* New York: Cambridge University Press.

(55) Litt, C. (1981). Children's attachment to transitional objects: A study of two pediatric populations. *American Journal of Orthopsychiatry, 51,* 131–139.

(56) Lozoff, B., Wolf, A. W., & Davis, N. S. (1984). Cosleeping in urban families with young children in the United States. *Pediatrics, 74,* 171–182.

(57) Maier, T. (1998). *Dr. Spock: An American life.* New York: Harcourt Brace & Co.

(58) Malkki, L. (1995). *Purity and exile: Violence, memory, and national cosmology among Hutu refugees in Tanzania.* Chicago: University of Chicago Press.

(59) Morelli, G., Rogoff, B., Oppenheim, D., & Goldsmith, D. (1992). Cultural variation in infants' sleeping arrangements: Questions of independence. *Developmental Psychology, 28,* 604–613.

(60) Morton, H. (1996). *Becoming Tongan: An ethnography of childhood.* Honolulu: University of Hawaii Press.

(61) Munroe, R. H., & Munroe, R. L. (1980). Infant experience and childhood affect among the Logoli: A longitudinal study. *Ethos, 8*(4), 295–315.

(62) Olwig, K., & Hastrup, K. (Eds.). (1997). *Siting culture: The shifting anthropological object.* New York: Routledge.

(63) Plath, D. W. (1980). *Long engagements: Maturity in modern Japan.* Stanford: Stanford University Press.

(64) Pollitt, E., Golub, M., Grantham-McGregor, G., Levitsky, D., Schurch, B., Strupp, B., & Wachs, T. (1996). A reconceptualization of the effects of undernutrition on children's biological, psychosocial, and behavioral development. *SRCD Social Policy Report, 10,* 1–21.

(65) Pratt, M. (1986). Fieldwork in common places. In J. Clifford & G. Marcus (Eds.), *Writing culture: The poetics and politics of ethnography*. Berkeley: University of California Press.

(66) Rogoff, B. (1990). *Apprenticeship in thinking: Cognitive development in social context*. New York: Oxford University Press.

(67) Scheper-Hughes, N. (1992). *Death without weeping: The violence of everyday life in Brazil*. Berkeley: University of California Press.

(68) Schneider, D. (1995). *Schneider on Schneider: The conversion of the Jews and other anthropological stories*. Ed. R. Handler. Durham, NC: Duke University Press.

(69) Shweder, R., Jensen, L., & Goldstein, W. (1995). Who sleeps by whom revisited: A method for extracting the moral goods implicit in practice. *New Directions for Child Development: Cultural Practices as Contexts for Development, 67,* 21–39.

(70) Small, M. F. (1998). *Our babies, ourselves*. New York: Anchor Books.

(71) Spence, J. D. (1978). *The death of woman Wang*. New York: Viking.

(72) Spock, B. (1945). *The common sense book of baby and child care*. New York: Duell, Sloan & Pearce.

(73) Spock, B., & Parker, S. (1998). *Dr. Spock's baby and child care*. 7th ed. New York: Pocket Books/Simon & Schuster.

(74) Stern, D. (1990). *Diary of a baby*. New York: Basic Books.

(75) Stoller, P. (2000). *Jaguar: A story of Africans in America*. Chicago: University of Chicago Press.

(76) Stuart-Macadam, P., & Dettwyler, K. A. (Eds.). (1995). *Breastfeeding: Biocultural perspectives*. New York: Aldine de Gruyter.

(77) Talbot, M. (1999). A Spock-marked generation. *New York Times Magazine,* January 3, 1999, 6, 20; 3.

(78) Triandis, H. C. (1996). The psychological measurement of cultural syndromes. *American Psychologist, 51,* 407–415.

(79) U.S. National Center for Health Statistics. (1997). *Fertility, family planning, and women's health: New data from the 1995 National Survey of Family Growth*. Vital and Health Statistics Series 23, no. 19.

(80) Van Esterik, P. (1989). *Beyond the breast-bottle controversy*. New Brunswick, NJ: Rutgers University Press.

(81) Walens, S. (1981). *Feasting with cannibals: An essay on Kwakiutl cosmology*. Princeton, NJ: Princeton University Press.

(82) Weisner, T. S., & Gallimore, R. (1977). My brother's keeper: Child and sibling caretaking. *Current Anthropology, 18,* 169–189.

(83) Weiss, N. (1978). The mother–child dyad revisited: Perceptions of mothers and children in twentieth century child-rearing manuals. *Journal of Social Issues, 34* (2), 29–45.

(84) Welty, E. (1984 [1972]). "The interior world": An interview with Eudora Welty; Charles T. Bunting/24 January 1972. In P. Prenshaw (Ed.), *Conversations with Eudora Welty.* New York: Pocket Books.

(85) Whiteford, L. M. (1998). Children's health as accumulated capital: Structural adjustment in the Dominican Republic and Cuba. In N. Scheper-Hughes and C. Sargent (Eds.), *Small wars: The cultural politics of childhood.* Berkeley: University of California Press.

(86) Whiting, B. (1974). Folk wisdom and child rearing. *Merrill Palmer Quarterly, 20,* 9–19.

(87) Whiting, B., & Edwards, C. (1988). *Children of different worlds: The formation of social behavior.* Cambridge, MA: Harvard University Press.

(88) Whiting, J. W. (1964). Effects of climate on certain cultural practices. In W. H. Goodenough (Ed.), *Explorations in cultural anthropology.* New York: McGraw-Hill.

(89) Wolf, A. W., Lozoff, B., Latz, S., & Paludetto, R. (1996). Parental theories in the management of young children's sleep in Japan, Italy, and the United States. In S. Harkness & C. Super (Eds.), *Parents' cultural belief systems.* New York: Guilford.

(90) World Bank. (1993). *World development report 1993: Investing in health.* Washington, DC: Oxford University Press.

Chapter Two. A Parenting Manual, with Words of Advice for Puritan Mothers

Citations

The numbers in the citations below refer to the numbered references in the immediately following Sources Cited section for this chapter.

Page

29   stereotypical Puritan characteristics – 44; intellectual and humanistic society – 24, 44.

29–30   Puritans purged Catholic influence – 27, 44.

30   "Common corrupcions of this euill world" – 48, p. 3; corruption of seventeenth-century England – 31; "Citty upon a Hill" – 48, p. 5; "doe more seruice to the Lord" – 48, p. 3; Puritans' goals in New World – 27; Puritans as English – 30, 38; extreme temperatures – 34; room functions variable – 13; nuclear families common – 3; birth and death rates – 3, 13; women's marriage and child-bearing patterns – 3, 22; Anne Bradstreet's children – 9; Roger and Johanna Clap's children – 8; population of New England, 1630–1640 – 38.

31   "Moreover, if thy brother..." – 7; "brotherly correction" – 7, Matt.
      XVIII:15; excommunication for misbehavior – 44; Puritan society
      should continue – 40.

32   parents fined for illiterate children – 13; child rearing too mundane to
      write about – 3, 13; "A virtuous woman wrote..." – 43, p. 218; Puritan
      writings often anonymous – 44; continuing influence of Puritans in
      U.S. – 5, 6, 23, 35; influence of Puritanism on capitalism – 46.

36   take notes on sermons for later home study – 43; avoid pleasure for
      its own sake – 32; Indian parents overindulge children – 15.

37   selectmen remove children from home if parents neglect spiritual
      education – 14, 32; "When thou dost cast thine eyes" – 28, p. 34;
      pray for conception – 9, 20, 13; "act of generation" – 13, p. 95; duty
      to pray without ceasing – 20.

38   abortion as murder – 39; aborted child avenged by God – 12; family
      or village may be punished for abortion – 9; high birth rate February
      to April – 8; breastfeeding reduces pregnancy – 14; average woman
      has eight children – 21; fertility as God's will – 39; Bible forbids wine
      while pregnant – 20; "Behold, thou fhalt conceiue..." – 7, Judg.
      XIII:7; violent passion or motion may produce miscarriage – 20;
      husband must provide for wife – 32; neglectful husband responsible
      for miscarriage may be punished by God – 20.

39   child bearing is blessing from God (Mather) – 26; childbirth as
      untying of knot between mother and child – 9; seek midwife not
      accused of witchcraft – 18; women gather in "borning room" – 3,
      14; birthing room closed and dark – 16; husband does not witness
      birth – 36; "exceedingly hard & Dangerous Travail" – 42, p. 131;
      herbs and prayer during childbirth – 43; planets' positions as signs
      of child's nature – 17; put silver and gold in newborn's hand – 16;
      offer drink and cake to visitors – 16.

40   four weeks of postpartum confinement – 36; feast for midwife and
      other helpers, gifts for newborn – 17; fetus dies within womb – 13;
      children as pledges from God – 26; biblical mothers breastfed – 19;
      Puritan mothers should breastfeed too – 20; breastfeed immediately
      and exclusively – 11, 14.

40–41 "God has given to women..." – 20 p. 511.

41   breastfeeding reduces infant death and illness during winter – 20;
      breastfeed frequently, according to infant's desire – 3, 16, 36;
      bleeding nipples, inverted nipples – 20; cream to prevent cracked
      nipples – 4.

42   desired traits of wet nurse – 11; appropriate foods for healthy
      infants – 17; sickly, squeamish child – 12.

42–43 baby removed from parents' bed by six months – 14, 16, 48.

43 "Cradle Hymn" – 17; bathing infant – 1; harden infant with cold baths – 1; wean by separating from infant – 19, 43.

44 swaddling – 33, 36; stomach band to prevent umbilical rupture – 1; washing diapers – 1; making diapers, optimal number of diapers – 33; diaper cover – 43; shirt for baby – 3.

45 cap, hand-me-downs – 33; fancy clothes do not serve God – 12; corsets for children – 36; late walking – 36; go-cart, standing-stool – 17; community health advice – 16, 36.

46 plant and animal cures – 18; "Wash a peck of garden snails... "– 16, pp. 6–7; bloodletting, ague, colic – 18.

47 stomach ache, stye – 25; teething necklace – 17; gum treatments for teething – 16.

48 train young child in God's ways early – 32; importance of daily prayer – 31; father leads prayers and singing – 32; baptism and christening blanket – 16, 47.

49 pastor or deacon baptizes – 23, 44; "heartily give back those children ... "– 28, p. 13; name child after deceased relative – 3; name infant after dead sibling – 41.

49–50 name for biblical personage or development of character – 4, 17, 43.

50 name after birth event – 17, 43, 40; children at sermon – 32; "listed among the servants..." – 29, p. 16; importance of early reading – 31; father tutors child in Scriptures – 29; Horn book – 17.

51 young children read Scriptures – 31; parents risk child influenced by Satan – 32; "If there be any Considerable Blow..." – 28, p. 4.

51–52 Cotton Mather's books – 17.

52 babies indulged during first year – 3, 43; evil nature, willfulness, sullenness, lying emerge after first year – 3, 9, 12; "Diverse children... "– 9, p. 273; parent's duty to observe and combat child's bad habits – 31, 32.

53 "The first Chastisement..." – quoted in 32, p. 105; whipping better than damnation – 27; whipping as last resort after lecturing – 32, 37; discipline child after anger has passed – 20, 37; "Never give a Blow" – 28, p. 25; child must respect parents – 32; affection also necessary for child rearing – 37; excess affection not recommended – 32.

54 "Know you not..." – 29, pp. 9–10.

Sources Cited – Chapter 2

(1) Alcott, W. A. (1839). *The young mother, or, management of children in regard to health.* Boston: George W. Light.

(2) Ariès, P. (1962). *Centuries of childhood: A social history of family life.* New York: Alfred A. Knopf.

(3) Beales, R. W., Jr. (1985). The child in seventeenth-century America. In J. M. Hawes & N. R. Hiner (Eds.), *American childhood: A research guide and historical handbook.* Westport, CT: Greenwood Press.

(4) Bel Geddes, B. (1964). *Small world: A history of baby care from the stone age to the Spock age.* New York: Macmillan.

(5) Bercovitch, S. (1975). The Puritan origins of the American self. New Haven: Yale University Press.

(6) Bercovitch, S. (1978). *The American Jeremiad.* Madison: University of Wisconsin Press.

(7) The Bible. (1969). Geneva version, a facsimile of the 1560 edition. Madison: University of Wisconsin Press.

(8) Blake, J. (1982). A short account of the author and his family [*re* Captain Roger Clap]. In S. Bercovitch (Ed.), *Puritan personal writings: Autobiographies and other writings.* New York: AMS Press.

(9) Bradstreet, A. (1967). *The works of Anne Bradstreet.* Ed. Jeannine Henseley. Cambridge, MA: Belknap Press of Harvard University Press.

(10) Clap, R. (1982). Memoirs of Captain Roger Clap. In S. Bercovitch (Ed.), *Puritan personal writings: Autobiographies and other writings.* New York: AMS Press.

(11) Cone, T. E. (1981). History of infant and child feeding: From the earliest years through the development of scientific concepts. In J. Bond, L. J. Filer, G. Leveille, A. M. Thomson, & W. B. Weil Jr. (Eds.), *Infant and child feeding.* New York: Academic Press.

(12) Courtwright, D. T. (1987). New England families in historical perspective. In P. Benes (Ed.), *Families and children: The Dublin Seminar for New England Folklife Annual Proceedings 1985.* Boston: Boston University.

(13) Demos, J. (1970). *A little commonwealth: Family life in Plymouth Colony.* New York: Oxford University Press.

(14) Demos, J. (1973). Infancy and childhood in the Plymouth Colony. In M. Gordon (Ed.), *The American family in socio-historical perspective.* New York: St. Martin's Press.

(15) Demos, J. (1994). *The unredeemed captive.* New York: Alfred A. Knopf.

(16) Earle, A. M. (1893). *Customs and fashions in Old New England.* New York: Charles Scribner's Sons.

(17) Earle, A. M. (1983). *Child life in colonial days.* Darby, PA: Folcroft Library Editions.

(18) Eggleston, E. (1901). *The transit of civilization*. New York: D. Appleton & Co.

(19) Fildes, V. (1986). *Breasts, bottles, and babies*. Edinburgh: Edinburgh University Press.

(20) Gouge, W. (1976). *Of domestical duties*. Amsterdam: Norwood.

(21) Grabill, W. H., Kiser, C. V., & Whelpton, P. K. (1973). A long view. In M. Gordon (Ed.), *The American family in socio-historical perspective*. New York: St. Martin's Press.

(22) Greven, P. (1973). Family structure in Andover. In G. M. Waller (Ed.), *Puritanism in early America*. Lexington, MA: D. C. Heath & Co.

(23) Greven, P. (1977). *The Protestant temperament*. New York: Alfred A. Knopf.

(24) Hall, D. (1968). *Puritanism in seventeenth-century Massachusetts*. New York: Holt, Rinehart & Winston.

(25) Hawke, D. F. (1988). *Everyday life in early America*. New York: Harper & Row.

(26) Hiner, N. R. (1985). Cotton Mather and his female children: Notes on the relationship between private experience and public thought. *Journal of Psychohistory, 13,* 33–49.

(27) Lockridge, K. A. (1973). Dedham, Massachusetts. In G. M. Waller (Ed.), *Puritanism in early America*. Lexington, MA: D. C. Heath & Co.

(28) Mather, C. (1995). The Duties of PARENTS to their Children. In C. Mather, A Family Well-Ordered, or, An Essay To Render Parents and Children Happy in one another. Handling Two very Important CASES": I. What are the Duties to be done by pious PARENTS for the promoting of piety in their Children. II. What are the Duties that must be paid of CHILDREN to their Parents, that they may obtain the Blessings of the Dutiful. Boston: B. Green & J. Allen. Reprinted in C. K. Shipton (Ed.), *Early American Imprints: 1639–1800*. Microprint Evans Number 875. Worcester, MA: American Antiquarian Society, 1955.

(29) Mather, C. (1995). Education of Children. In C. Mather, A Family Well-Ordered, or, An Essay To Render Parents and Children Happy in one another. Handling Two very Important CASES": I. What are the Duties to be done by pious PARENTS for the promoting of piety in their Children. II. What are the Duties that must be paid of CHILDREN to their Parents, that they may obtain the Blessings of the Dutiful. Boston, MA: B. Green & J. Allen. Reprinted in C. K. Shipton (Ed.), *Early American imprints: 1639–1800*. Microprint Evans Number 875. Worcester, MA: American Antiquarian Society, 1955.

(30) Miller, P. (1968). The marrow of Puritan divinity. In S. V. James (Ed.), *The New England Puritans*. New York: Harper & Row.

(31) Moran, G. F., & Vinovskis, M. A. (1986). II. The great care of Godly parents: Early childhood in Puritan New England. *Monographs of the Society for Research in Child Development, 50,* 24–37.

(32) Morgan, E. S. (1966). *The Puritan family: Religion and domestic relations in seventeenth-century New England.* New York: Harper & Row.

(33) Nylander, J. C. (1987). Clothing for the little stranger. In P. Benes (Ed.), *Families and children: The Dublin Seminar for New England Folklife: Annual Proceedings.* Boston: Boston University.

(34) Palfrey, J. F. (1966). *History of New England during the Stuart Dynasty.* New York: AMS Press.

(35) Peacock, J. and Tyson, R., Jr. (1989). *Pilgrims of paradox: Calvinism and experience among the Primitive Baptists of the Blue Ridge.* Washington, D.C.: Smithsonian Institution Press.

(36) Pollack, L. (1987). *A lasting relationship: Parents and children over three centuries.* Hanover, NH: University Press of New England.

(37) Sather, K. (1989). Sixteenth and seventeenth century child-rearing: A matter of discipline. *Journal of Social History, 22,* 735–743.

(38) Schlatter, R. (1969). The Puritan strain. In M. McGiffert (Ed.), *Puritanism and the American experience.* Reading, MA: Addison-Wesley.

(39) Schucking, L. L. (1970). *The Puritan family: A social study from the literary sources.* New York: Schocken Books.

(40) Sommerville, C. J. (1978). English Puritans and children: A social-cultural explanation. *Journal of Psychohistory, 6,* 113–137.

(41) Thompson, R. T. (1985). Popular attitudes towards children in Middlesex County, Massachusetts, 1649–1699. *Journal of Psychohistory, 13*(2), 145–158.

(42) Ulrich, L. T. (1977). Vertuous women found: New England ministerial literature, 1668–1735. In A. T. Vaughan & F. J. Bremer (Eds.), *Puritan New England: Essays on religion, society, and culture.* New York: St. Martin's Press.

(43) Ulrich, L. T. (1982). *Good wives: Image and reality in the lives of women in northern New England 1650–1750.* New York: Alfred A. Knopf.

(44) Vaughan. A. T. (1972). *The Puritan tradition in America, 1620–1730.* Columbia: University of South Carolina Press.

(45) Wall, H. M. (1990). *Fierce communion: Family and community in early America.* Cambridge, MA: Harvard University Press.

(46) Weber, M. (1976 [1904–05]). *The Protestant ethic and the spirit of capitalism.* T. Parsons (Transl.). New York: Scribner's.

(47) Whipple. S. L. (1929). *Puritan homes.* Salem, MA: Newcomb & Grauss Co.

(48) Winthrop, J. (1973). A modell of Christian charity. In G. M. Waller
      (Ed.), *Puritanism in Early America.* Lexington, MA: D. C. Heath & Co.

Chapter Three. Luring Your Child into this Life

Citations

The numbers in the citations below refer to the numbered references in the
immediately following Sources Cited section for this chapter.

Page

55   Beng history and language – 3, 8.

56   reaction to French occupation – 14; French colonial regime in Africa
      – 10; independence of Côte d'Ivoire from France – 10.

57   increasing poverty of African peasants in colonial and postcolonial
      periods – 11; increasing poverty of African children – 12, 13;
      political structure of Beng region – 1; Beng parents' prayers for
      schoolchildren's failure – 3, pp. 137–138.

58   precolonial and contemporary housing patterns in Beng villages – 3;
      dual descent and arranged marriage systems – 3; rebellions against
      arranged marriage – 7; eclecticism of African religions – 6; Beng
      religion – 3, 7.

59   ancestors incorporated into daily life in Africa – 9; Beng babies as
      reincarnated ancestors – 4, 5.

60   Beng grandmothers' and diviners' child-rearing advice – 2;
      inextricability of religious and daily life in Beng villages – 3.

65   connection between village and forest – 3.

69   slow process of leaving *wrugbe* – 4.

Sources Cited – Chapter 3

(1) Gottlieb, A. (1989). Witches, kings, and the sacrifice of identity; or,
     The power of paradox and the paradox of power among the Beng of
     Ivory Coast. In W. A. Arens & I. Karp (Eds.), *Creativity of power:
     Cosmology and action in African societies.* Washington, DC:
     Smithsonian Institution Press.

(2) Gottlieb, A. (1995). Of cowries and crying: A Beng guide to
     managing colic. *Anthropological and Humanism, 20*(1), 20–28.

(3) Gottlieb, A. (1996). *Under the kapok tree: Identity and difference in
     Beng thought.* Chicago: University of Chicago Press.

(4) Gottlieb, A. (1998). Do infants have religion? The spiritual lives of
     Beng babies. *American Anthropologist, 100*(1), 122–135.

(5) Gottlieb, A. (n.d.). *The afterlife is where we come from: Infants and infant care in West Africa.* Book manuscript in preparation.

(6) Gottlieb, A. (In press). Le religioni in Africa Occidentale (Religions of West Africa). In B. Bernardi (Ed.), *Enciclopedia Italiana: Storia del Secolo XX* (vol.: *Filosofi, Religioni e Teleologie*). Rome: Istituto della Enciclopedia Italiana/Fondata da Giovanni Treccani.

(7) Gottlieb, A., & Graham, P. (1994). *Parallel worlds: An anthropologist and a writer encounter Africa.* Chicago: University of Chicago Press.

(8) Gottlieb, A., & Murphy, M. L. (1995). *Beng-English dictionary.* Bloomington: Indiana University Linguistics Club.

(9) Kopytoff, I. (1971). Ancestors as elders in Africa. *Africa, 41*(2), 128–142.

(10) Manning, P. (1999). *Francophone Sub-Saharan Africa, 1880–1985.* 2nd ed. New York: Cambridge University Press.

(11) Rodney, W. (1975). *How Europe underdeveloped Africa.* Washington, DC: Howard University Press.

(12) Scheper-Hughes, N., & Sargent, C. (Eds.) (1998). *Small wars: The cultural politics of childhood.* Berkeley: University of California Press.

(13) Stephens, S. (Ed.) (1995). *Children and the politics of culture.* Princeton, NJ: Princeton University Press.

(14) Weiskel, T. C. (1980). *French colonial rule and the Baule people: Resistance and collaboration, 1889–1911.* Oxford: Clarendon Press.

Chapter Four. Gift from the Gods

Citations

The numbers in the citations below refer to the numbered references in the immediately following Sources Cited section for this chapter.

Page

ceremonies – 7; priests – 37; women prepare offerings – 25; temples – 11; two calendars – 14, 37.

94–95   temple "birthday" – 15.

95–96   aesthetic impulse and varieties of artistic expression – 6, 12, 16, 31.

96   educational system – 19.

97   writing systems – 25; inheritance of knowledge – 8, 41; inseparability of physical and mental well-being – 18, 20.

98   importance of children to marriage – 4, 18, 20; changes in political status – 11, 22; importance of sons – 10, 24; children's care of parents – 18; care of temple – 4; neglect of ancestor worship – 13, 37; make offerings – 37; baby is divine reincarnation of ancestor – 18, 32, 37; ancestor also present in shrine – 37.

99   positive and evil forces – 10; *leyak* – 37; offerings for protection – 9, 10, 20; diligence when pregnant – 21; magic charm – 9, 18; *leyak* at night – 10; "four siblings" protect fetus – 25, 36; spirits present at birth – 10, 18, 20, 29; avoid "hot" foods – 9, 18, 40; reject food from impure person – 18; pregnancy ritual to anchor fetus in womb – 10, 18.

100   pray in temple – 18; husband should be calm and considerate – 36, 37; husband's hair – 18, 37; importance of son – 24, 37; having a girl – 11; worrying is bad – 41; try to adopt male child – 9, 37; adopted boy should be related to husband – 24, 37.

100–101   daughter's husband – 24, 37.

101   presence at childbirth – 9; birth in clinics or hospitals – 18; leave sleeping area before birth – 18; earlier times birth on floor – 8; *balian's* powers to ensure painless delivery – 41; male *balians* – 8; reasons to prefer male *balian* – 8, 18; midwives – 8, 18, 37.

102   help of four siblings during birth – 10, 18; offerings for new baby – 18; for 210 days infants are divine – 18, 32; words for baby to thank those present – 2; auspicious days – 10, 14, 20; birth in *Wuku Wayang* – 14, 17, 20, 37; purification ceremony and *wayang* puppet show – 17, 20; evil spirits and childbirth – 8, 9; impurity after childbirth – 24, 37; divine curse – 8.

103   resumption of life after purification – 18, 41; twins as form of incest or subhuman – 1, 5, 24; entire village made impure by twins – 5, 24.

103–104   neglect of ritual – 5.

104   purification ritual more humane, wisest – 1, 5, 24, 36; four siblings – 3, 20, 24, 36; placenta in coconut – 18; bury coconut – 9, 10, 18, 20, 24.

104–105   ceremonial altar – 21.

105   help with offerings – 37; offerings and thanks to four spirits – 10, 18; infant as divine – 10; address with high language – 27; hold newborn high, never on ground or floor – 10, 18, 20, 34; rank of child – 32; 5

of 100 infants return to divine world – 19; cremation ceremony not needed for baby – 3, 10, 34.

106 *lepas aon* – 1, 10, 18; umbilical cord in palm leaf container – 10, 18; placate four spirits – 10; infant's character – 37, 41; take infant to *balian matuun* – 10, 18, 21, 33; ancestor speaks through *balian* – 10; fulfill promises or make offerings – 37; do whatever *balian* recommends – 33; some personality and characteristics determined by day of birth – 10, 35, 36.

106–107 *balian* can tell what birth day reveals – 24.

107 animals, birds, and gods that correspond to birth day – 10; Kala and Dewa – 20; a new name – 9, 33, 41; *metubah* ritual – 41.

107–108 naming system – 10, 11, 24, 37.

108 count dead infants and children – 9; naming ceremony – 9, 10; announce personal name – 1, 11; *balian* will write names on palm leaf and burn – 11, 24; personal names not used much – 11; used to address mother and father – 10, 24; rank and names – 37; add personal name to birth order name – 37.

109 emotion and baby's *bayu* – 41; sleeping and carrying – 20; crawling on ground is base – 10; hold in arms or sling – 20, 28; others can hold baby – 10, 37; everyone loves to hold a baby – 37; teach proper use of right and left hands – 2, 28, 37; traditionally infants were naked – 28, 37; urination and defecation – 37.

110 traditional clothing – 10; carry water – 37; baby's bath – 28, 41; dump bathwater over placenta – 10; bath in basin, with water from tank, in river – 37; supplement to breastmilk – 2, 9; solid food and breastfeeding – 20.

111 food for four siblings – 10, 18; position for baby during breastfeeding – 2.

112 weaning – 9; family planning and weaning – 37; wean gradually – 9; weaning in a hurry – 9, 28; child may wean him- or herself – 28; many men now work away from fields – 37; women also have jobs – 37; *otonan* ceremony – 10, 18, 24.

113 good health depends on balance – 40, 41; emotion and mother's *bayu* – 40, 41; mother and nursing as threat to infant's *bayu* – 38, 39, 40 41; remedies for harmful emotions – 40.

114 husband's negative emotions can affect child – 40; advantages of *balian* over medical doctor – 20, 37, 41; *balian* can intervene in spirit world – 8; *balian* will divine needed rituals and make offerings – 37.

115 teach children to control feelings – 20, 28; "borrowing" a baby – 2; convey how proud you are – 20; development of equanimity – 20, 27; expression of emotions – 20.

116 not caring produces well-being – 41.

Sources Cited – Chapter 4

(1) Barth, F. (1993). *Balinese worlds.* Chicago: University of Chicago Press.

(2) Bateson, G., & Mead, M. (1942). *Balinese character: A photographic analysis.* New York: New York Academy of Sciences.

(3) Belo, J. (1980). The Balinese temper. In J. Belo (Ed.), *Traditional Balinese culture.* New York: Columbia University Press.

(4) Belo, J. (1980). A study of a Balinese family. In J. Belo (Ed.), *Traditional Balinese culture.* New York: Columbia University Press.

(5) Belo, J. (1980). A study of customs pertaining to twins in Bali. In J. Belo (Ed.), *Traditional Balinese culture.* New York: Columbia University Press.

(6) Bruner, E. (1996). Tourism in the Balinese borderzone. In S. Lavie & T. Swedenburg (Eds.), *Displacement, diaspora, and the geographies of identity.* Durham, NC: Duke University Press.

(7) Bruner, E. (1999). Personal communication, May 1999.

(8) Connor, L. H. (1983). Healing as women's work in Bali. In L. Manderson (Ed.), *Women's work and women's roles: Economics and everyday life in Indonesia, Malaysia, and Singapore.* Canberra: Australian National University.

(9) Covarrubias, M. (1937). *Island of Bali.* New York: Alfred A. Knopf.

(10) Eiseman, F. B. (1989). *Bali: Sekala & Niskala.* Berkeley, CA: Periplus Edition.

(11) Geertz, C. (1973). Person, time, and conduct in Bali. In C. Geertz (Ed.), *The interpretation of cultures.* New York: Basic Books.

(12) Geertz, C. (1980). *Negara: The theatre state in nineteenth-century Bali.* Princeton, NJ: Princeton University Press.

(13) Geertz, H., & Geertz, C. (1985). *Kinship in Bali.* Chicago: University of Chicago Press.

(14) Goris, R. (1960a). Holidays and holy days. In W. F. Wertheim (Ed.), *Bali: Studies in life, thought and ritual.* The Netherlands: W. van Hoeve Ltd.

(15) Goris, B. (1960b). The temple system. In W. F. Wertheim (Ed.), *Bali: Studies in life, thought and ritual.* The Netherlands: W. van Hoeve Ltd.

(16) Grader, C. J. (1960). Pemayun Temple of the Banjar of Tegal. In W. F. Wertheim (Ed.), *Bali: Studies in life, thought and ritual.* The Netherlands: W. van Hoeve Ltd.

(17) Hinzler, H.I.R. (1981). *Bima Swarga in Balinese Wayang.* The Netherlands: The Hague.

(18) Hobart, A., Ramseyer, U., & Leemann, A. (1996). *The peoples of Bali.* Cambridge, MA: Blackwell.

(19) Hull, T. H., & Jones, G. W. (1994). Demographic perspectives. In H. Hill (Ed.), *Indonesia's new order: The dynamics of socio-economic transformation*. Honolulu: University of Hawaii Press.

(20) Jensen, G. D., & Suryani, L. K. (1992). *The Balinese people: A reinvestigation of character*. Singapore: Oxford University Press.

(21) Josefowitz, N. (1981). The psychology of politeness among the Javanese. In G. B. Hainsworth (Ed.), *Southeast Asia: Women, changing social structure and cultural continuity*. Ottawa, Canada: University of Ottawa Press.

(22) Lansing, J. S. (1974). *Evil in the morning of the world: Phenomenological approaches to a Balinese community*. Ann Arbor, MI: Center for South and Southeast Asian Studies.

(23) Lansing, J. S. (1983). *The three worlds of Bali*. New York: Praeger Publishers.

(24) Lansing, J. S. (1995). *The Balinese*. Fort Worth, TX: Harcourt Brace College Publishers.

(25) McCauley, A. (1993). Balinese. In P. Hockings (Ed.), *Encyclopedia of world cultures, Vol. 5: East and Southeast Asia*. Boston: G. K. Hall & Co.

(26) Mackie, J., & MacIntyre, A. (1994). Politics. In H. Hill (Ed.), *Indonesia's new order: The dynamics of socio-economic transformation*. Honolulu: University of Hawaii Press.

(27) Mead, M. (1955). Children and ritual in Bali. In M. Mead & M. Wolfenstein (Eds.), *Childhood in contemporary cultures*. Chicago: University of Chicago Press.

(28) Mead, M., & Macgregor, F. C. (1951). *Growth and culture: A photographic study of Balinese childhood*. New York: Putnam's Sons.

(29) Niehof, A. (1992). Mediating roles of the traditional birth attendant in Indonesia. In S. Van Bemmelen, M. Djajadiningrat-Nieuwenhuis, E. Locher-Scholten, & E. Touwen-Bouwsma (Eds.), *Women and mediation in Indonesia*. Leiden: KITLV Press.

(30) Phalgunadi, I. G. P. (1991). *Evolution of Hindu culture in Bali*. New Delhi: Sundeep Prakashan.

(31) Picard, M. (1996). *Bali: Cultural tourism and touristic culture*. Singapore: Archipelago Press.

(32) Suryani, L. K. (1984). Culture and mental disorder: The case of *Bebainan* in Bali. *Culture, Medicine and Psychiatry, 8*(1), 95–114.

(33) Suryani, L. K. (1995). Cultural factors, religious beliefs, and mental illness in Bali: Indonesia. In I. A1-Issa (Ed.), *Handbook of culture and mental illness: An international perspective*. Madison, WI: International Universities Press.

(34) Swellengrebel, J. L. (1960). Religious practices of the family and the individual. In W. F. Wertheim (Ed.), *Bali: Studies in life, thought and ritual.* The Netherlands: W. van Hoeve Ltd.

(35) Warren, C. (1993). *Adat and dinas: Balinese communities in the Indonesian state.* Oxford: Oxford University Press.

(36) Wiener, M. J. (1995). *Visible and invisible realms: Power, magic, and colonial conquest.* Chicago: University of Chicago Press.

(37) Wiener, M. J. (1998/1999). Personal communication.

(38) Wikan, U. (1987). Public grace and private fears: Gaiety, offense, and sorcery in Northern Bali. *Ethos, 15*(4), 337–365.

(39) Wikan, U. (1988). Bereavement and loss in two Muslim communities in Egypt and Bali compared. *Social Science and Medicine, 5,* 451–460.

(40) Wikan, U. (1989). Managing the heart to brighten face and soul: Emotions in Balinese morality and health care. *American Ethnologist, 16*(2), 294–312.

(41) Wikan, U. (1990). *Managing turbulent hearts: A Balinese formula for living.* Chicago: University of Chicago Press.

Chapter Five. Making Babies in a Turkish Village

Citations

The numbers in the citations below refer to the numbered references in the immediately following Sources Cited section for this chapter.

Page

117   studies of village life – 2, 7, 8, 9, 10; discussion of marriage and families – 7, 9, 10, 11; discussion of procreation and child rearing – 1, 2, 3, 4.

118   modern Turkish different from early Turkish – 6.

119   Muhammad's role – 5.

Sources Cited – Chapter 5

(1) Delaney, C. (1987). Seeds of honor, fields of shame. In D. Gilmore (Ed.), *Honor and shame and the unity of the Mediterranean.* American Anthropological Association, Special Publication, no. 22.

(2) Delaney, C. (1988). Mortal flow: Menstruation in Turkish village society. In T. Buckley & A. Gottlieb (Eds.), *Blood magic: The anthropology of menstruation.* Berkeley: University of California Press.

(3) Delaney, C. (1991). *The seed and the soil: Gender and cosmology in Turkish village society.* Berkeley: University of California Press.

(4) Delaney, C. (1994). Untangling the meaning of hair in Turkish society. *Anthropological Quarterly,* 67: 159–172.

(5) Delaney, C. (1998). *Abraham on trial: The social legacy of biblical myth.* Princeton, NJ: Princeton University Press.

(6) Henze, P. (1982). Turkey on the rebound. *The Wilson Quarterly,* 6(5), 108–135.

(7) Kolars, J. F. (1963). *Tradition, season and change in a Turkish village.* Chicago: University of Chicago Press.

(8) Makal, M. (1954). *A village in Anatolia.* Trans. W. Deeds; Ed. P. Stirling. London: Vallentine Mitchell. [1950.]

(9) Pierce, J. E. (1964). *Life in a Turkish village.* New York: Holt, Rinehart & Winston.

(10) Stirling, P. (1965). *Turkish village.* London: Weidenfeld & Nicolson.

(11) Stirling, P. (1993). *Culture and economy: Changes in Turkish villages.* London: Eothen Press.

Chapter Six. Infants of the Dreaming

Citations

The numbers in the citations below refer to the numbered references in the immediately following Sources Cited section for this chapter.

Page

145   Warlpiri – 9, 60; history – 10; art and artifacts – 25; population in eighteenth century – 30; current population – 25, 40, 41; Central Desert – 25; languages – 7, 22, 48.

146   confrontations with settlers – 56; distinctiveness of Aboriginal groups – 41, 47; multiple groups in settlements – 7, 23; some Aboriginal practices not shared by Warlpiri – 32; government control of settlements – 23, 31, 57.

147   protests – 56; continued conflict with whites – 30, 40, 56; access to ancestral lands – 7, 14, 15, 36; Warlpiri today – 14; residence on Warlpiri land – 23; country camps – 37; Warlpiri in Tanami Desert – 25, 60; gatherings – 25, 41, 58.

148   family units and marriage – 21, 23, 25, 41; subsections – 19; socialization rules – 23, 24, 63.

149   kin groups – 19; personal names – 49; subsection and relational names – 7, 18, 19, 46; personal names – 19; camp layout – 21, 22;

housing today – 22, 46; *Jukurrpa* – 24, 26; Ancestral Beings – 45; communication through dreams – 19, 41, 45, 46; ceremonies – 24.

150   land rights – 19; connection to past through ritual – 17, 29, 46, 59; designs – 17, 19, 20, 24, 46, 59; controversy over art – 2, 20, 43, 44, 55; "two different sets of rules" – 7, p. 84.

151   Old Law – 37; hardships and infant death – 12, 13, 23, 51; borning – 13, 51; Grandmother's Law – 13, 51; country camp – 37.

152   young women rarely live near grandmothers – 23; "We call the country mother" – 36, p. 22; Old Law – 19, 51; "When we lived in the bush" – 7, p. 42; deprived of land and water – 37; children adopted – 7, 57; poverty, etc. – 7, 14.

153   "settle down country" – 37; travel of Ancestral Beings – 19; lack of services – 23, 29, 51; "women's business" – 41, 51, 52; Ancestral Present – 24; Ancestral Times – 46.

153–154   powers "lodged in the country" – 46.

154   ritual and life force – 19; *Jukurrpa* – 19, 24, 42; recent ancestors – 19; ancestral powers – 19; spiritual conception – 1, 7, 24, 34; *kuruwarri* – 19, 46; conception spirit – 19, 41, 46; designs, drawings and stories – 24.

154–155   sex and marriage – 24, 38, 41.

155   men's and women's rituals – 7, 19, 41; increase ceremonies – 19, 41; *yawulyu* rituals – 7, 19, 46; designs – 23, 46; sexual intercourse – 41, 64; sex and conception – 41, 44, 62; substance and spirit – 8, 42; *kurruwalpa* – 19.

156   *kuruwarri* – 19, 42, 46; family size – 7, 16, 41; breastfeeding and conception – 16; nutrition – 7, 23; avoiding pregnancy – 32, 41; abortion – 41; age and childbearing – 7; age of men at marriage – 19, 23, 63; hospitalized babies – 63; modern birth control – 7.

156–157   physical signs of pregnancy – 41.

157   dreams and other signs of pregnancy – 19; where you "found" your child – 19; Ancestral Beings – 17, 42, 46; importance of pregnancy – 22; *paklka jarrimi* – 44; borning – 13, 51; sharing news – 8; determine location of conception – 41; talking with husband about pregnancy – 19; preventing miscarriage – 8.

158   foods to avoid – 23, 41; danger of harming animals – 7; sex while pregnant – 3, 41; working while pregnant – 19, 41; avoid certain areas – 19; relation with co-wives – 6, 11, 24; respect and value of childbirth – 7, 8.

159   ritual for childbirth – 19; borning center – 23, 50, 51; selection of midwife – 7, 22, 41; pain – 63; presence of husband at birth – 19; husband's announcement of birth – 41.

160   birth while traveling – 3, 61; benefits of smoke for mother and baby – 23, 46; midwife's assistance – 41, 52; delivery onto soil – 36; skin

color – 41; smoking over acacia leaves – 22; Grandmother's Law –
13, 51, 63; smoking baby – 7, 22.

160–161 afterbirth – 19, 41, 52.

161 necklace – 19.

162 breastfeeding by co-wife or sister – 41; returning to family – 16, 41;
decorating baby with stripes – 41.

163 *parraja* – 23, 46; *coolamon* – 19, 63; caring for baby – 16; crying and
feeding – 32; rubbing baby with grease – 19; *jungarrayi-jungarrayi* –
63; punishment for poor care – 8; roughness with babies – 8, 35.

164 affection – 7; passing baby to others – 16; reciprocation for child
care – 7; searching for food – 41; hunting and gathering – 22, 23, 25;
wives' provision of food – 8; food distribution – 7, 22; women's
contribution – 7, 8, 19; children in camp – 7, 36; children are
priority – 7, 23.

165 sharing with children – 16, 23; songs and rituals – 19; teaching
daughters – 7, 23, 41; bush medicine – 63; dreaming songs – 7;
ngangkayi – 7, 49; European remedies – 7; prevent illness – 19, 41;
men's and women's responsibilities equally important – 8, 19; "grew
up" – 63.

166 mourning for father – 41, 63; fathers and sons – 23; male rituals –
41; mother – son relationship 23, 41; betrothal – 7, 19, 63; seeing
mother after marriage – 41.

166–167 co-wives – 64.

167 mourning period – 22, 23, 36; avoidance of wife's mother – 33;
European schooling – 37; keeping children out of school – 7, 12;
teasing and talking – 4; few short words – 48; baby talk – 4, 5, 39.

168 exposure to English and learning own language – 4, 28; names as
link to ancestors – 18; simplification of names – 4, 39; naming for
grandparents – 41; name revealed in dream – 18; time of naming –
23, 41; *warungka* – 19; *kumanjayi* – 49.

169 multiple names – 18, 19, 23; sleeping on ground – 36; spirits and
sleeping – 19; sleeping arrangements – 4, 23; visits by Ancestral
Beings – 19; life force of the Dreaming – 23, 24.

170 obligations to children – 63; support from women in kin group – 19;
poem – 55, p. 89.

Sources Cited – Chapter 6

(1) Akerman, K. (1977). Notes on "conception" among Aboriginal
women in the Kimberleys, West Australia. *Oceania, 48,* 59–63.

(2) Anderson, C., & Dussart, F. (1988). Dreamings in acrylic: Western
Desert art. In *The art of Aboriginal Australia.* New York: Braziller.

(3) Bates, D. (1985). *The native tribes of Western Australia.* I. White (Ed.). Canberra: National Library of Australia.

(4) Bavin, E. L. (1992). The acquisition of Warlpiri. In D. I. Slobin (Ed.), *The cross linguistic study of language acquisition* (Vol. 3). Hillsdale, NJ: Erlbaum.

(5) Bavin, E. L. (1995). Language acquisition in crosslinguistic perspective. *Annual Review of Anthropology, 24,* 373–396.

(6) Bell, D. (1980). Desert politics: Choices in the "marriage market." In M. Etienne & E. Leacock (Eds.), *Women and colonization: Anthropological perspectives.* New York: Praeger.

(7) Bell, D. (1993/1983). *Daughters of the dreaming.* (2nd ed.). Melbourne: McPhee Gribble.

(8) Berndt, C. H. (1981). Interpretation and "facts" in Aboriginal Australia. In F. Dahlberg (Ed.). *Woman the gatherer.* New Haven, CT: Yale University Press.

(9) Berndt, R. M., & Berndt, C. H. (1964). *The world of the first Australians.* Chicago: University of Chicago Press.

(10) Bower, B. (1996). Human origins recede in Australia. *Science News, 150,* 196.

(11) Burbank, V. K. (1994). *Fighting women: Anger and aggression in Aboriginal Australia.* Berkeley: University of California Press.

(12) Burns, A., & Goodnow, J. (1979). *Children and families in Australia.* Sydney: George Allen & Unwin.

(13) Carter, B., Hussen, E., Abbott, L., Liddle, M., Wighton, M., McCormack, M., Duncan, P., & Nathan, P. (1987). Borning: Pmere laltyeke anwerne ampe mpwaretyeke. *Australian Aboriginal Studies, 1,* 2–33.

(14) Collmann, J. (1988). *Fringe-dwellers and welfare.* Queensland, Australia: University of Queensland Press.

(15) Coombs, H. C. (1994). *Aboriginal autonomy: Issues and strategies.* Ed. D. Smith. Cambridge: Cambridge University Press.

(16) Cowlishaw, G. (1978). Infanticide in Aboriginal Australia. *Oceania, 48,* 262–283.

(17) Dubinskas, F. A., & Traweek, S. (1984). Closer to the ground: A reinterpretation of Walbiri iconography. *Man, 19,* 15–30.

(18) Dussart, F. (1988). Notes on Warlpiri women's personal names. *Journal de la Société des Océanistes, 86,* 53–60.

(19) Dussart, F. (1988). *Warlpiri women's yawulyu ceremonies: A forum for socialization and innovation.* Unpublished doctoral dissertation, Australian National University.

(20) Dussart, F. (1988). Women's acrylic paintings from Yuendumu. In M.K.C. West (Ed.), *The inspired dream.* Queensland: Queensland Art Gallery.

(21) Dussart, F. (1992). The politics of female identity: Warlpiri widows at Yuendumu. *Ethnology, 31,* 337–350.

(22) Dussart, F. (1998). Personal communication. September 1998.

(23) Dussart, F. (1999). Personal communication. May 1999.

(24) Dussart, F. (In press). *Of the dreaming: Kinship, gender and the currency of knowledge among Central Desert Aborigines.* Washington, DC: Smithsonian Institution Press.

(25) Dussart, F. (In press). The Warlpiri of Australia. In R. Lee & R. Daly (Eds.), *Foraging peoples: An encyclopedia of contemporary hunters and gatherers.* Cambridge: Cambridge University Press.

(26) Eliade, M. (1973). *Australian religions.* Ithaca, NY: Cornell University Press.

(27) Gale, F. (1970). *Woman's role in Aboriginal society.* Canberra: Australian Institute of Aboriginal Studies.

(28) Ginsburg, F. (1994). Embedded aesthetics: Creating a discursive space for indigenous media. *Cultural Anthropology, 9,* 365–382.

(29) Glowczewski, B. (1999). Dynamic cosmologies and Aboriginal heritage. *Anthropology Today, 15,* 3–9.

(30) Gonen, G. (1993). Australian Aborigines. In *The encyclopedia of the peoples of the world.* New York: Henry Holt.

(31) Grolier Society of Australia. (1977). Aborigines. In *The Australian Encyclopedia,* Vol. 1. Sydney: Grolier Society.

(32) Hamilton, A. (1981). *Nature and nurture.* Canberra: Australian Institute of Aboriginal Studies.

(33) Hiatt, L. R. (1978). Classification of the emotions. In L. R. Hiatt (Ed.), *Australian Aboriginal Concepts.* Canberra: Australian Institute of Aboriginal Studies.

(34) Hiatt, L. R. (1996). *Arguments about Aborigines.* Cambridge: Cambridge University Press.

(35) Hippler, A. E. (1978). Culture and personality of the Yolngu of Northeastern Arnhem Land, Part I. *Journal of Psychological Anthropology, 1,* 221–224.

(36) Jackson, M. (1995). *At home in the world.* Durham, NC: Duke University Press.

(37) Japanangka, D. L., & Nathan, P. (1983). *Settle down country.* Malmsbury, Victoria: Kibble Books.

(38) Kaberry, P. M. (1939). *Aboriginal women, sacred and profane.* London: Routledge.

(39) Laughren, M. (1984). Warlpiri baby talk. *Australian Journal of Linguistics, 4,* 73–88.

(40) Levinson, D. (Ed.). (1991). Warlpiri. In *Encyclopedia of world cultures.* Boston: G.K. Hall.

(41) Meggitt, M. J. (1965). *Desert people.* Chicago: University of Chicago Press.

(42) Merlan, F. (1986). Australian Aboriginal conception beliefs revisited. *Man, 21(3),* 474–493.

(43) Michaels, E. (1994). *Bad Aboriginal art: Tradition, media and technological horizons.* Minneapolis: University of Minnesota Press.

(44) Montagu, A. (1974/1937) *Coming into being among the Australian Aborigines.* London: Routledge & Kegan Paul.

(45) Morphy, H. (1991). *Ancestral connections: Art and an Aboriginal system of knowledge.* Chicago: University of Chicago Press.

(46) Munn, N. (1973). *Walbiri iconography: Graphic representations and cultural symbolism in a Central Australian society.* Ithaca, NY: Cornell University Press.

(47) Myers, F. R. (1986). *Pintupi country, Pintupi self.* Washington, DC: Smithsonian Institution Press.

(48) Nash, D. G. (1980). *Topics in Warlpiri grammar.* Unpublished dissertation, Massachusetts Institute of Technology.

(49) Nash, D., & Simpson, J. (1981). "No name" in central Australia. In C. S. Masek, R. A. Hendrick, & M. F. Miller (Eds.), *Papers from the parasession on language and behaviors.* Chicago: Chicago Linguistic Society.

(50) Nathan, P. (1983). Nurses and health business in central Australia. *Australian Nurses Journal, 12,* 38–40.

(51) Nathan, P. (1987). Borning: The congress Alukura by the grandmother's law. *Arena, 79,* 44–48.

(52) Poidevin, L.O.S. (1957). Some childbirth customs among the Ngalia tribe: Central Australia. *The Medical Journal of Australia,* 543–546.

(53) Reece, L. (1971). As Wailbri children learn Wailbri. *Mankind, 8,* 148–150.

(54) Reid, J. (1978). The role of Marrnggitj in contemporary health care. *Oceania, 48,* 96–109.

(55) Rutherford, A. (Ed.). (1988). *Aboriginal culture today.* Sydney: Kunapipi & Dangaroo Press.

(56) Shaw, J. (1984). Aborigines. In *The Collins Australian Encyclopedia.* Sydney: William Collins.

(57) Smith, D. E., & Halstead, B. (1990). *Looking for your mob: A guide to tracing Aboriginal family trees.* Canberra: Aboriginal Studies Press.

(58) Spencer, B., & Gillen, F. (1969/ 1899). *The native tribes of central Australia.* Oosterhout: Anthropological Publications.

(59) Strathern, M. (1979). The self in self-decoration. *Oceania, 49,* 241–257.

(60) Tindale, N. B. (1974). *Aboriginal tribes of Australia.* Berkeley: University of California Press.

(61) Tindale, N. B., & Lindsay, H. A. (1963). *Aboriginal Australians.* Queensland: Jacaranda Press.

(62) Tonkinson, R. (1978). Semen versus spirit-child in Western Desert culture. In L. R. Hiatt (Ed.), *Australian Aboriginal concepts.* Canberra: Australian Institute of Aboriginal Studies.

(63) Vaarzon-Morel, P. (Ed.). (1995). *Warlpiri women's voices: Our lives our history.* Alice Springs: Institute for Aboriginal Development Press.

(64) White, I. (1975). Sexual conquest and submission in the myths of Central Australia. In L. R. Hiatt (Ed.), *Australian Aboriginal mythology.* Australian Aboriginal Studies No. 50. Canberra: Australian Institute of Aboriginal Studies.

Chapter Seven. The View from the *Wuro*

Citations

The numbers in the citations below refer to numbered references in the Sources Cited section that follows these citations.

Page

171 10 million Fulani – 15; Fulfulde language – 9.

172 dairy component of diet – 6; uses and value of cattle – 17; "If the cattle die…" – 10, p. 25; herders' involvement with cattle – 10.

172–173 cattle more important than crops – 15.

173 three-tiered status system 6, 15, 16; women may inherit – 6; bride receives cow – 11; *wuro* vs. *suudu* – 13.

174 components of *pulaaku* (Fulani-ness) – 5, 18.

176 parents become adults – 13.

177 new mother's role – 4; death from childbirth – 15; children sense pregnancy – 15; "making a belly" – 16, p. 150; family should surround first-time pregnant woman – 4.

178 separation from husband during first pregnancy – 4, 6; precautions for woman during pregnancy – 16.

179 husband may suspect later pregnancy – 10; giving birth – 16; newborn's contact with ground – 15.

180 birth of twins – 16; mothering must be learned – 14; care of newborn (umbilical cord, afterbirth, first washing, lighting fire) – 15; washing boys and girls – 16; fire burns until naming ceremony – 15.

181 gifts for new mother and new baby – 2, 10; husband will "know his cattle" – 18, p. 387; new status of mother – girl "who has born one" – 1, p. 39; husband's reaction to infertility – 15; grounds for divorce – 16.

182 dealing with miscarriage – 16; fertility may be due to witchcraft – 3; men may dismiss witchcraft as nonsense – 3; fostering a child – 6.

183 nature of newborn – 13; importance of naming ceremony for newborn – 1, 6; animals at naming ceremony – 1, 6; men's and women's roles at naming ceremony – 13.

184 shaving newborn's head – 3, 6; wash and carry infant after shaving – 15; good and bad days for birth and naming ceremony – 16.

185 care of mother after birth/during rest period – 1; visitors/rest during forty-day confinement – 15.

186 *dyinna* make babies cry – 3; orientation of sleeping mat – 15; dusk as dangerous time for attacks by spirits – 3; dangers to mother and baby during first week – 15; dangers of compliments and how to respond to them – 15; "your mouth points right to your asshole" – 15, p. 175.

187 molding baby's head – 4; protecting baby against spirits and witches: by insults and names, cow dung, necklaces, ear piercing – 15, by amulets, medicinal baths, and Qur'anic washes – 3; private affection, public reserve toward baby – 4; risk from *omre* fever and protecting baby from it – 15.

188 breastfeeding and diet – 4; breastfeed whenever baby cries – 13; meddlesome mother-in-law – 2; power and danger of breast milk – 15; supplementing your own breastmilk – 4.

189 *basi* – 15; *bita* – 15.

190 "One can understand another's personality..." – 2; "The milk that is nursed..." – 14, p. 178; breastmilk transmits personality traits and habits – 15; risks of short breastfeeding period – 2; *marabout* can help wean child – 15; grandmothers and weaning – 2, 15.

192 daily enema – 15; valued Fulani traits (*pulaaku*) – 5, 18.

193 teaching identity of relatives – 15; teaching respect for elders – 13; teaching language early – 16; teaching trust, sense of community, "oneness" of Fulani – 13, 14, 15.

193–194 affection toward children and maternally related kin – 4, 13; shame around in-laws – 13.

194 mother's constant physical contact with/emotional attachment to baby – 13; mothers' relations with/preference for daughters and sons – 4, 10.

194–195 young girls learn domestic and herding skills – 4, 7, 8, 12.

195 father gives son calf – 6; father teaches son herding and farming skills – 6, 10, 13, 15.

195–196   children are like cattle – 10.
196   influence on children by Allah vs. breastmilk vs. parents – 14, 15; young children's nature vs. parents' duty to educate – 14; child's good character inherited from breast milk – 16; disciplinary tactics to avoid – 15; physical discipline/community helps educate child – 15.
197   teaching child emotional control/legitimate reasons for crying – 15; Islam essential to most Fulani – 13; Islamic education now mandatory – 6; literacy in Arabic – 3.
198   fathers should not play much with children – 15; importance of sons to men – 3, 13.

Sources Cited – Chapter 7

(1)   Awogbade, M. O. (1983). *Fulani pastoralism. Jos case study*. Zaria: Ahmadu Bello University Press Limited.
(2)   Barro, M. (1995). Personal communication.
(3)   Derman, W. (1973). *Serfs, peasants, and socialists: A former serf village in the Republic of Guinea*. Berkeley: University of California Press.
(4)   Dupire, M. (1963). The position of women in a pastoral society (the Fulani WoDaaBe, nomads of the Niger). In D. Paulme (Ed.), *Women of tropical Africa*. Berkeley: University of California Press.
(5)   Dupire, M. (1981). Réflexions sur l'ethnicité peule. *Itinérances 2*, 165–181.
(6)   Dupire, M. (1996). Personal communication.
(7)   Ezeomah, C. (1985). *The work roles of nomadic Fulani women. Implications for economic and educational development*. Jos, Nigeria: University of Jos.
(8)   Ezeomah, C. (1987). *The settlement patterns of nomadic Fulbe in Nigeria. Implications for educational development*. Cheshire, England: Deanhouse Ltd.
(9)   Greenberg, J. H. (1966). *The languages of Africa*. Bloomington: Indiana University Press.
(10)   Hopen, C. E. (1958). *The pastoral Fulbe family in Gwandu*. London: Oxford University Press.
(11)   Imoagene, O. (1990). *The Hausa and Fulani of Northern Nigeria*. Agodi: New-Era Educational Company Ltd.
(12)   Maigida, D. N., & Ali, M. A. (1993). *A study of Fulani women in four settlements in Dambatta District (Kano state)*. Zaria: Ahmadu Bello University.
(13)   Riesman, P. (1977). *Freedom in Fulani social life. An introspective ethnography*. Chicago: University of Chicago Press.

(14) Riesman, P. (1990). The formation of personality in Fulani ethnopsychology. In M. Jackson & I. Karp (Eds.), *Personhood and agency. The experience of self and other in African cultures.* Stockholm: Almqvist and Wiksell International.

(15) Riesman, P. (1992). *First find yourself a good mother: The construction of self in two African communities.* Ed. D. Szanton, L. Abu-Lughod, S. Hutchinson, P. Stoller, & C. Trosset. New Brunswick, NJ: Rutgers University Press.

(16) Stenning, D. (1959). *Savannah nomads. A study of the Wodaabe pastoral Fulani of Western Bornu Province Northern Region, Nigeria.* London: Oxford University Press.

(17) Stenning, D. (1960). Transhumance, migratory drift, migration: Patterns of pastoral Fulani nomadism. In S. Ottenberg & P. Ottenberg (Eds.), *Cultures and societies of Africa.* New York: Random House.

(18) Stenning, D. (1965). The pastoral Fulani of Northern Nigeria. In J. L. Gibbs, Jr. (Ed.), *Peoples of Africa.* New York: Holt, Rinehart & Winston.

Chapter Eight. Never Leave Your Little One Alone

Citations

The numbers in the citations below refer to numbered references in the Sources Cited section that follows these citations.

Page

199 accessibility of Falalop and Falachig – 19; Yap – 10; relation to Guam – 6; population of Ifaluk – 19; Woleian language – 1, 6; extent of English spoken – 19; Yap as legendary source of first settlers – 6; Polynesia as historical source of first settlers – 15; colonial history of Caroline Islands – 13, 15.

200 "blackbirding" – 9; Japanese schools – 6, 15; post-World War II status of Micronesia – 15; creation of Federated States of Micronesia – 1, 13; typhoons – 15; fear of island's disappearance in storms – 19, p. 5; U.S. introduced salaried jobs – 15, 19, 20; few jobs held by Ifaluk in contemporary period – 19; gendered division of labor – 6, 15, 19.

201 "A woman who sees a man ... " – 15, p. 35; rank of clans – 19; size and composition of houses, compounds and villages – 19; description of household – 6; gendered outmigration and education pattern – 15; erosion of tendency toward matriarchy – 17; Catholic missionaries – 6, 19.

202   *yalus* – 6; Christian god called *got* – 15; Catholicism changing marriage practices – 17; value sharing, gentleness, cooperation, obedience – 12, 15, 18; socialization of children for valued traits – 11, 12, 15; socialization and discipline practiced by all – 3, 6, 15.

202–203   adoption widespread in Pacific – 5, 7, 8.

203   definitions and estimates of Ifaluk adoption – 2, 6, 15, 16; who can adopt a child – 2; adoptee's relation with both sets of parents – 2, 6, 14; changes from 1940s to 1970s – 4, 6, 9, 13, 15, 16.

206   new baby as king or queen – 6; child later takes care of family – 6, 15.

207   contemporary understanding of pregnancy – 16, 17; earlier ideas concerning cause of pregnancy – 6; fetus looks human at seventh month – 18; when and where soul enters fetus – 6; hair cutting taboo during pregnancy – 6; hair cutting as grief – 17.

207–208   work during pregnancy – 6.

208   determining sex of fetus (male) – 6; men climb coconut trees – 17; determining sex of fetus (female) – 6; reasons to adopt – 2, 6, 15, 18; reasons to refuse to adopt out a child – 6, 15.

209   birth blood taboo – 16; previous childbirth in *Imwelipen* – 6; contemporary childbirth in birth houses – 6, 15, 16, 17; fire in birth house – 6; contemporary midwives – 16, 17; men forbidden from birth house – 6, 15; taboo violation – 6; traditionally, women birthed without help – 6; today, midwives help at birth – 16, 17; avoid crying during childbirth – 6, 16.

210   being *maluwelu* – 6, 15; mothers help in caretaking – 6; who cuts the umbilical cord – 6, 17; cutting the umbilical cord: with sea shell – 6, with surgical instrument – 17; burying the umbilical cord and afterbirth – 6; responses to difficulties in labor – 6, 17; responses to stillbirth – 6, 17.

211   stillborn baby becomes *yalus* – 6, 15; first nursing – 6; value of baby sweating – 6; stomach cloth inhibits startle reflex – 17; necessity of frequent feeding – 6; bathing schedule – 6.

211–212   confinement and rituals in birth house post-childbirth – 6, 15, 17.

212   males glimpsing babies – 6; wood-and-rope cradle – 6; welcome home celebration – 6; sacred fire during confinement – 6, 16.

213   mothers vs. fathers caring for children – 15, 17; duration of postpartum confinement – 6, 17; activities during confinement – 6, 16.

214   adopting out baby – 6, 15; crying – 6, 15; smelling babies – 6; feeding routine – 6; infant formula – 17; falling head – 17; stomach medicine – 6.

215   baby sleeps with parents – 6; earlier postpartum sex taboo – 6; contemporary postpartum sex taboo – 16; naming after three

months – 6; naming after ten days – 18; avoid talking about newborns – 18; infant becomes complete person – 15, 18; ancestor's name taboo – 6; newborn's name may contain parts of ancestor's names – 16.

216   traditionally, fathers didn't approach baby for three months – 6; contemporary fathers approach babies earlier – 16; children as babysitters – 6, 15.

216–217   babies lack intelligence – 6, 15, 18.

217   babies' emotions – 15; neglectful parents punished with sterility – 6, 15; introducing solid foods – 6; duration of breastfeeding – 6, 16; wean older child if baby born – 6.

217–218   optimal times and spaces for sleeping baby – 6.

218   older child's sleeping space – 16; toilet training – 6; acquisition of intelligence *(repiy)* – 6, 15, 18.

218–219   parents and others responsible for children's socialization – 6, 15.

219   punishment vs. praise of children – 6, 15, 18; teaching Ifaluk emotions – 15; teaching *metagu* via the *tarita* – 12, 15.

219–220   teaching proper emotions – 11, 15.

220   adoption – 2, 5, 6, 14.

Sources Cited – Chapter 8

(1) Ashby, G. (Ed). (1985). *Micronesian customs and beliefs.* Eugene, OR: Rainy Day Press.

(2) Betzig, L. L. (1988). Adoption by rank on Ifaluk. *American Anthropologist, 90,* 111–119.

(3) Betzig, L. L., Harrigan, A., & Turke, P. W. (1989). Childcare on Ifaluk. *Zeitschrift für Ethnologie, 114,* 161–177.

(4) Betzig, L. L., & Turke, P. W. (1986). Parental investment by sex on Ifaluk. *Ethology and Sociobiology, 7,* 29–37.

(5) Brady, I. (Ed.). (1976). *Transactions in kinship: Adoption and fosterage in Oceania.* ASAO Monograph No. 4. Honolulu.

(6) Burrows, E. G., & Spiro, M. E. (1957). *An atoll culture.* Westport, CT: Greenwood Press.

(7) Carroll, V. (Ed.). (1970). *Adoption in Eastern Oceania.* ASAO Monograph No. 1. Honolulu.

(8) Flinn, J. (1985). Adoption and migration from Pulap, Caroline Islands. *Ethnology, 24*(2), 95–104.

(9) Hezel, F. X. (1983). *The first taint of civilization: A history of the Caroline and Marshall Islands in pre-colonial days.* Honolulu: University of Hawaii Press.

(10) Labby, D. (1976). *The demystification of Yap: Dialectics of culture on a Micronesian Island.* Chicago: University of Chicago Press.

(11) Lutz, C. A. (1982). The domain of emotion words on Ifaluk. *American Ethnologist, 9,* 113–128.

(12) Lutz, C. A. (1983). Parental goals, ethnopsychology, and the development of emotional meaning. *Ethos, 11,* 246–262.

(13) Lutz, C. A. (1984). *Micronesia as strategic colony: The impact of U.S. policy on Micronesian health and society.* Cambridge, MA: Cultural Survival, Occasional Papers.

(14) Lutz, C. A. (1985). Cultural patterns and individual differences in the child's emotional meaning system. In M. Lewis & C. Saarni (Eds.), *The socialization of emotions.* New York: Plenum.

(15) Lutz, C. A. (1988). *Unnatural emotions: Everyday sentiments on a Micronesian atoll and their challenge to Western theory.* Chicago: University of Chicago Press.

(16) Lutz, C. A. (1996). Personal communication. September 6, 1996.

(17) Lutz, C. A. (1999). Personal communication. May 1999.

(18) Lutz, C. A., & LeVine, R. A. (1983). Culture and intelligence in infancy: An ethnopsychological view. In M. Lewis (Ed.), *Origins of intelligence.* New York: Plenum.

(19) Sosis, R. (1997). The collective action problem of male cooperative labor on Ifaluk Atoll. Unpublished doctoral dissertation, University of New Mexico.

(20) Turke, P. W., & Betzig, L. L. (1985). Those who can do: Wealth, status, and reproductive success on Ifaluk. *Ethology and Sociobiology, 6,* 9–87.

Index

Index

Index

Index

Index

Index

Index

Index

Index

Index

Index